WILD AND OUTSIDE

WILD
and
OUTSIDE

*How a Renegade Minor League
Revived the Spirit of Baseball
in America's Heartland*

STEFAN FATSIS

Walker and Company
New York

First published in the United States of America in 1995 by Walker Publishing
Company, Inc.

Published simultaneously in Canada by Thomas Allen & Son Canada, Limited,
Markham, Ontario

Library of Congress Cataloging-in-Publication Data
Fatsis, Stefan.
Wild and outside : how a renegade minor league revived the spirit
of baseball in America's heartland / Stefan Fatsis.
p. cm.
ISBN 0-8027-1297-5 (hardcover)
1. Northern League of Professional Baseball—History. I. Title.
GV875.N67F38   1995
796.357'64'0977—dc20   95-11847
CIP

Unless otherwise noted, all photographs are copyright © Stefan Fatsis.

Grateful acknowledgment is made to Jon Landau Management for permission to
reproduce lyrics from "These Are Days" by 10,000 Maniacs on page 250.

Printed in the United States of America
2   4   6   8   10   9   7   5   3   1

TO MY MOTHER
AND IN MEMORY OF MARK MADIAS

WILD AND OUTSIDE

INTRODUCTION

The summer of 1994 will be remembered not for the collapse of health care reform in Washington or the fiftieth anniversary of D-Day or an almost-war in Haiti but instead for the death of something dear to millions of Americans: the major league baseball season. During the lost year baseball's most sacred records came under assault: Roger Maris's sixty-one home runs. Ted Williams's .406 average. Lou Gehrig's 2,130 consecutive games. But the chase stopped in August, when the players went on strike, and died a month later, when a car salesman from Milwaukee named Bud Selig, the acting commissioner of a sport that didn't want one, announced that he and his fellow owners had voted to cancel the rest of the regular season, the playoffs, and the World Series. It was the first time in ninety years that the championship would not be played.

Fans mourned, but life went on. It was only the latest slap in the face.

The labor dispute is just a symptom of baseball's troubles, not their cause. The real problems aren't $7 million player salaries or empty rhetoric about imminent financial implosion. Something much more fundamental is ruining baseball: the attitude of its caretakers toward the game. In stadiums dominated by five-story TV screens and deafening rock music, fans pay $17 for a ticket and $5 for a beer. There is nothing pastoral, let alone fun, about major league baseball, where the idea of a promotion is to announce the name of the visiting team's star or hand out plastic fanny packs emblazoned with the logo of a local bank or fast-food emporium. Even retro ballparks like Camden Yards are, at their core, a sham. They are designed as nostalgia, which can't be manufactured, no matter the color of the paint or texture of the bricks. Painting a billboard with the words HIT SIGN, WIN SUIT doesn't make it Ebbets Field.

As they were busy killing their product, the majors barely noticed a minor league with a different set of goals playing just its second season: the Northern League of Professional Baseball. Unlike all but a handful of bush league teams, Northern League clubs are independent of big-league control. The cities—six midwestern towns desperate for professional baseball, four in the United States and two in Canada—have embraced the teams as their own. The players have been liberated from the relentless scrutiny of front offices concerned only with developing major league talent, not with winning baseball games. From minor league rejects to ex–major league stars, Northern League players are glad to have a place to call home.

"I'm in uniform," said Oil Can Boyd, the uniquely cerebral former Boston Red Sox pitcher, now with the Sioux City Explorers, before starting an exhibition game against the all-women Colorado Silver Bullets. "I don't give a shit what it says on it. It could say the Bad News Bears and I'd be playing. I'd be a Bad News Bear. That's true love of the game. 'Cause I don't have to be playing."

The Northern League's appeal isn't new, but it isn't borrowed or mass-produced either. The league involves a loyalty that has vanished from a game in which major leaguers change uniforms and organizations shuffle minor league affiliates annually. An old descriptive applies: "town baseball." Northern League teams—and their players—belong to the cities themselves, not to some far-off parent.

Emotion sets the league apart. Players and managers *need* to win, because winning is the only guaranteed reward. Unlike farm club operators, who are handed a roster a few days before the season, Northern League owners scout, sign, and pay players, selling the contracts of the best ones back to big-league organizations. Striving for a championship, owners have an emotional stake in the performance of their team and its relationship to the community.

Until Branch Rickey's St. Louis Cardinals created the first farm system in the 1920s and '30s by buying minor league clubs— sometimes entire leagues—all teams were independent. As the majors discovered they could save the expense of purchasing players and at the same time control the market, the independents slowly died, and with them the links, as baseball analyst Bill James has written, between player and club, club and town, and player and town that had characterized minor league baseball. In the last three decades, a few independent teams struggled to survive, usually after a major league organization dropped its affiliation. Independent success stories were rare; their owners fought a lonely battle against the game's establishment.

The Northern League changed that. Miles Wolff, one of the minors' most successful owners, gathered many of the rebels in one league. They were dedicated to the notion that the word *baseball* doesn't mean only "major league baseball," which was how the lords of the game defined it. Wolff wanted to restore baseball to its place as an enterprise dedicated to meeting the needs and wants of communities, a business that gives back to fans as much as it takes from them and turns a profit at the same time. If, in the process, the league created an alternative to the currently troubled system, so be it.

In 1990, during a dispute with the minors, the big leagues threatened to develop talent at sterile training camps in Florida and Arizona. Later talk centered on scaling back or eliminating the bottom rungs of the minors; during the strike the Cubs dropped a rookie-level affiliate, citing "financial reasons." Among more extreme executives, there is support—fed by bitterness and jealousy over the minors' renaissance in the 1980s—for turning back the clock to an era when the majors didn't bankroll their development programs.

"It used to be a totally different system," said Eddie Einhorn, the vice chairman of the Chicago White Sox. "You paid for it yourself, you got players to play. If they turned out to be good, we paid for them, fine. Now the thing has become almost a joke—people who are doing this as investments, guys who own six teams—and we're paying all the expenses."

If organized baseball does indeed fracture, and even if it doesn't, splinter leagues could shift power away from the center. If the low minors are axed, talented young players still will need a place to hone their skills. Well-organized independent leagues could sell top talent to the majors for top dollar—a throwback to baseball in the first half of the century.

But that wasn't the Northern League's purpose. Its founders wanted to pump fresh air into an institution suffocated by rulers ever more distant from the game on the field. In the minors you often hear how major league parents have become less friendly and more demanding, how arriviste local owners have taken the fun out of the game by focusing exclusively on the bottom line. But resurrecting the spirit of baseball is no easy task. Citizens have to be willing to sacrifice money, time, and energy. Clubs need to field a credible product. And players have to trust that joining an untested, somewhat outlaw venture will help their careers.

In its first season the Northern League achieved much of its promise. But in 1994 the league divided into large and small markets, just like the majors. The novelty of professional baseball in its cities wore off. The league's only new manager was unfamiliar with independent ball, imperiling a franchise. Players read about the uprising by their big-league idols. So while the league took on the establishment, it was threatened by some of the same issues that were bringing the game down.

This is the story of how a gang of rebels—from the purist Miles Wolff to the chip-off-the-block son of showman Bill Veeck to a happy-go-lucky career minor leaguer named Ed Nottle—battle the big leagues, and sometimes each other. It is about players who, despite being told they aren't good enough, refuse to loosen their grip on a dream born in childhood. It is about communities that rally around something as innocent and traditional as a baseball team. And it is about a place where baseball still can be fun.

"The message to organized baseball is very simple and sweet," said Marv Goldklang, chairman of the league's St. Paul franchise. "You don't own baseball. You don't own it at a professional level. Nobody owns this game."

Mike Veeck in Municipal Stadium, St. Paul (© Kathy Strauss)

ONE

REAL GRASS AND REAL BEER

—Fence sign at Municipal Stadium

Far beyond the 400-foot sign in dead center field—past the warning-track billboard for Slumberland Furniture, past the old electronic scoreboard, past the empty lots backed up against the neighborhood ballpark all dolled up for the night—a train headlight cut a beam through the gray and hazy twilight on a cool June evening in 1993. Like bloodhounds picking up a scent, the fans inside the stadium anticipated the slowly approaching freighter. As a rumble from the rails became palpable, the call began, from somewhere under the grandstands, it seemed, in a whisper.

Train, train, train, train.

It was a hard, one-syllable cry that out of context would have sounded like an angry declaration. But everyone here was smiling and laughing as the Burlington Northern drew nearer. Even the players on the field and in the dugouts, usually oblivious to fan behavior, couldn't help realize what was happening.

Train! Train! Train! Train!

The tracks run parallel to and just twenty feet behind the left-field wall, close enough to tease the strongest batters. Legend has it that Babe Ruth swatted a ball into the open car of a passing freighter during a barnstorming exhibition somewhere in the Mid-west. Chugging away, the train carried its load plus one baseball, which traveled farther than any home run in history, miles and miles to the end of the line.

TRAIN! TRAIN! TRAIN! TRAIN!

It had taken only seconds, but finally, inevitably, the chant reached a frantic, determined crescendo. Four thousand nine hundred and fifty-one happy souls were in attendance—couples and families and retirees who remembered the old days—and most of them were shouting in unison at a passing freight train. As the engine crossed behind left field, coming as close to the stadium as it possibly could, the conductor blasted the horn. He knew he had an audience but didn't realize the significance of the moment, of the game being played inside the ballpark. Then, as the train clacked away, the fans abandoned their rhythmic cry and broke into loud and satisfied cheers, returning their attention to the field.

Baseball was back in St. Paul, Minnesota.

Three hours before game time, two hours before the stadium opened. Foreboding skies on an unusually chill summer evening. A daylong rain hadn't stopped the early arrivals. They paid two dollars to park in an open-air lot adjacent to Municipal Stadium, the aesthetically unappealing ballpark hard by the tracks.

Here in Big Ten football country, those gathering were experienced tailgaters, determined to make a party despite the weather. They popped open trunks and lifted the hatchbacks of American cars to reveal the standard equipment: card tables, grills, folding chairs, tablecloths. The food was standard issue as well: hot dogs, sausages, hamburgers, potato salad, soda and locally brewed beer. Simple equipment, simple foods, simple desires. Midwestern would sound like a cliché, but it was true. These fans were here to enjoy the open air, to support the community, to say they were there on opening night when blue-collar St. Paul finally got back its baseball team and in the process tweaked its big-sister city on the other side of the Mississippi River.

Outdoor baseball, they were saying, the way it was meant to be played. No artificial turf, no Teflon roof, no Hefty bag for a right-field wall like at the Hubert H. Humphrey Metrodome in downtown Minneapolis. Just like the good old days, when St. Paul was a proud minor league town. Duke Snider, Roy Campanella, Lefty Grove, Leo Durocher—they all played for the St. Paul Saints. If anyone had bothered to look it up—or simply bought that night's program—he would have learned that the first professional baseball team in St. Paul took the field in 1884, beating Minneapolis in their first meeting, 4–0, in front of 4,000 fans. Only two out of twelve teams survived that first season of what was known as the Northwestern League: Minneapolis and St. Paul. There was history here.

Pro ball continued in St. Paul, with a few brief interruptions, until 1961, when the Washington Senators moved to Minnesota and became the Twins, making minor league baseball expendable, if not downright unwelcome. Then, twenty years later, the Twins traded their open-air stadium for the climatically correct Metrodome. Until this June night the nearest professional baseball of any kind under the sky was in Waterloo, Iowa. If you wanted to watch major leaguers performing out of doors, you had to travel to Milwaukee, more than 300 miles away.

But now baseball was returning to its roots. For one night, anyway, St. Paul would step out of the shadow of its cosmopolitan "twin." The pride of the long-starved fans would be restored, and they would have fun.

At 5:30 the gates opened and the wet metal grandstands began to fill. It was inexplicable. There was nothing to watch except groundskeepers raking dirt, players warming up leisurely, a technician checking a microphone on the field, roving camera crews from local television stations recording the preparations. The Mindbenders' "Game of Love" played over the public address system as the grounds crew removed blue tarpaulins from the pitcher's mound and around home plate, revealing firmly packed clay the color of rust, blemished only by the whitewashed pitching rubber and pentagonal base.

9

Under the third-base stands, maintenance workers assembled a white picket pen to house Saint, the mascot of the local team. Saint was a pig, part Yorkshire, part Hampshire, and his job was to deliver baseballs to the home plate umpire. For the occasion, the thirty-five-pound heifer wore a Saints T-shirt, white cap, black and white saddlebags, and sky blue sunglasses.

Pots of white and red geraniums decorated the top of the grandstand wall, placed there by Saints president Mike Veeck, inspired by his father, Bill, who'd hung baskets of flowers for four blocks around Comiskey Park during the 1959 World Series. Near the flowers green and white Japanese-style lanterns snapped in the wind like kites desperate for string. Printed on them in bold, black letters was one word: BASEBALL. Nothing else. Not a promo for the home team, not a picture of a millionaire outfielder, not a beer advertisement, not a plug for a radio station. Just BASEBALL.

Like the neighborhood around it, Municipal Stadium has a no-pretense, nothing-flashy appearance. Situated in an industrial park along the railroad line, its cinder blocks are painted brown. Its functionality is void of flourishes; Fenway Park this isn't. Architecturally, in fact, it's just plain dull, all concrete ramps and steel beams and a Plexiglas-enclosed, regulation press box atop the stands behind home plate. Black numbers are painted on its utilitarian benches; no individual seats for fans here. The simple reason, of course, is that benches are cheaper than plastic seats, but the grandstands send another message: People come here for baseball, not to lounge in seventy-two-degree comfort, watching slow-motion replays on a scoreboard, crowd noise bouncing off the white ceiling.

Outside, ticket holders shuffled slowly into the stadium—there were just three turnstiles for the whole place. The Bavarian Musikmeisters oompahed the "Beer Barrel Polka" as the arriving guests without complaint relinquished cans before entering. The tinny PA system played "One Fine Day" by the Chiffons, which everyone seemed to think it was, despite the weather.

Miles Wolff had once written that everything always goes wrong on opening night, and he thought it might be true once more: The first home game of the flagship franchise in a minor league resurrected after twenty-two years. The first independent minor league in more than a decade. The first outdoor professional baseball in the Twin Cities since 1981. The first pro baseball of any kind in St. Paul in thirty-two years, nine months, and three days. A sellout crowd. And rain.

Miles Wolff, the founder of the new Northern League of Professional Baseball, toured the ballpark, inspecting the field and the flowers and the ticket booths and the offices cluttered with boxes of souvenirs. He was asked about the quality of the umpires (suspect) and the scoreboard (needed replacing) and the talent level (fresh-from-college rookies to former big-leaguers). He once again explained the rationale behind the Northern League: independent baseball, free from the control that enslaves minor league clubs to their major league parents but also free from the cushion of financial subsidy from the majors. He patiently answered questions about team goals (to win, not to develop talent, as in the major league farm systems), about the importance of the minors (the majors don't appreciate them), and about innovations planned for his new league (twenty seconds between pitches and ninety seconds between half innings to speed up play).

Wolff tossed a quizzical glance at the squealing pig and walked through a tunnel to the team offices. He climbed a set of metal stairs and opened a door that deposited him just inside the entrance to Municipal Stadium, where fans continued filing in. Tall and professorial in a rumpled brown tweed jacket and blue oxford shirt, Wolff stood with arms folded. He appeared distracted, like a father waiting for his son to return from the nearby bathroom. Long lines formed for souvenirs and food and programs. To the untrained eye the operation looked like a smashing success. Then Wolff said, "They're losing thousands of dollars because they can't serve the people."

The concession stand was almost invisible behind two big columns. Fans couldn't figure out where to stand in order to allow others to pass to get to the first- and third-base ramps up to the grandstands. One person was selling programs. Just one. At the souvenir table a Saints employee and Sheila Goldklang, the owner's wife, tried to control scores of fans clamoring for T-shirts and black caps bearing the team's logo—an interlocked S and P with a small t in Barudan Swiss type. They seemed as powerless as sandbags against the floods that would break through the Mississippi in a few weeks.

Finally, Wolff couldn't bear to watch the chaos, and the crowds, and the lost thousands any longer. He took off his jacket, stepped behind the table, and began selling caps to the masses, $15 for the adjustable model, $20 for fitted. "We should have some seven and a halfs coming up later," he said, absentmindedly shoving $20 bills into his shirt pocket, occasionally dropping one.

Supply and demand were in perpetual excess, and as Wolff searched for caps, he suddenly was as expert in judging hat sizes as a milliner on the Lower East Side of Manhattan in the 1920s. "It looks like it was made on you," he told one woman, grinning like a salesman who had just earned another commission, satisfied a customer's yearning, made another dream come true.

Miles Hoffman Wolff, Jr., is a son of the South in the literary tradition. He is quiet, almost retiring; tall, thin limbed, and a bit awkward; understated in the way he walks, talks, and dresses. Wolff seems like the narrator in a novel by Walker Percy or Robert Penn Warren, observing the action with detachment but ultimately playing a central role. In fact, he had created just such a character in a novel about a murder at a minor league ballpark in a sleepy Carolina League town. A central figure in the story happened to be the general manager of the team, much like the author.

Wolff was born in 1943 and grew up in Greensboro, North Carolina, where his father edited the morning newspaper. As a boy Wolff was among the faithful few who attended minor league baseball games. He caught a ride or walked the mile and a half to the ballpark to cheer the Yankees' farm team. He saw fifty or sixty games a year, sitting in the stands with friends, goading players into giving them the finger, and soaking up the game. Wolff thought to himself, Why don't more people enjoy this? His love of the minors was, well, a little weird. Baseball, especially minor league baseball, wasn't terribly hip. Other leisure activities, namely television, had supplanted the game. More than 300 towns across America lost minor league teams in the 1950s. The broadcast of major league games into minor league markets was killing baseball.

But at fifteen Wolff sought his first job in baseball. (He was turned down.) As a history major at Johns Hopkins University, every spring he asked the Orioles for a summer job. (He never got one.) While in the navy supply corps during the Vietnam War—on flag-waving missions to Africa and India, nowhere near combat—he sent letters to baseball people. (No luck again.) Not that there were lines forming to work in the minors. The bush leagues— run by aging, potbellied, hard-drinking men who had little interest in marketing their product—were dying. Few people wanted to make a career there.

Miles Wolff had other options. He expanded his master's thesis at the University of Virginia into a book about the 1960 Greensboro sit-ins by a group of black students at a Woolworth's lunch counter. His father's connections made journalism an easy choice. But Wolff was set on baseball and showed up at a Carolina League meeting in the fall of 1970. The Atlanta Braves were interested in hiring young people to run their minor league teams, and two days before Christmas Wolff got a call from the organization's farm director. The Braves were moving their Double-A team to Savannah, Georgia. Was Wolff interested in becoming its general manager?

He was paid $600 a month. He learned about groundskeeping, bookkeeping, and promotions. His most forgettable gimmick was Pray for Pitching Day, in which fans presenting church bulletins were admitted for half price. (The manager wasn't pleased, because it showed up his struggling staff.) How badly were the minors slumping? Savannah drew 60,700 fans—about 850 a night—and Wolff *still* was named Double-A executive of the year.

Wolff had simple goals: make enough during the season to write fiction and poetry in the winter in his $100-a-month Savannah beach rental. After three years in the city, he decided it was time to get a real job. But he couldn't decide what that was. So he became a minor league hired gun. A summer in Anderson, South Carolina;

one in Jacksonville, Florida; another in Savannah; one in Richmond, Virginia (where he broadcast play-by-play for the Braves' Triple-A affiliate). Then it hit him: If he was going to stay in baseball, he had to own a team.

Wolff's beloved Carolina League was ailing and needed to expand; in 1978 only four clubs had working agreements with major league organizations. The Braves wanted an affiliate in the league, but only if Wolff owned it. They teamed up, and, for the price of $2,417, Wolff received a franchise in Durham, North Carolina. It was an investment based on love. "The franchises had no value," he said. "You were buying the right to lose money."

The city of Durham spent $25,000 to repair its old stadium, Durham Athletic Park. Wolff hit up his sisters, friends, and baseball contacts for $30,000 in working capital, awarding himself the right to buy 60 percent of the team. By March 1980 the money had run out, and Wolff secretly borrowed $4,000 from the league treasury in a scramble to make it to Opening Day. He asked his general manager—whose grandfather, a minor league pitcher named Buck Weaver, had had his ashes raked into the mound at the stadium—to defer his salary. Two days before the season, the health department told Wolff he needed an ice-making machine, among other things. He had to rent a contraption that sprayed the dry, brown infield green. The night before the opener, someone stole the club's stylish new uniforms. Wolff was ready to call it quits before the first pitch was thrown.

Fortunately for Wolff, Durham, and minor league baseball at large, he didn't. Four thousand, four hundred eighteen fans showed up on that first night. Early in the season the Bulls won twelve games in a row. Duke University law students led cheers and taunted opposing players. Rough-hewn tobacco workers chanted, "Let's go, Bulls!" alongside doctors from the research complexes that had transformed Durham from a tobacco town into the City of Medicine, as the green banners fluttering downtown declared. The beer flowed freely, and, in a city where it was still difficult to get liquor by the drink, Durham Athletic Park became the best bar in town. One night Wolff found himself in the parking lot, turning back fans seeking tickets for a giveaway promotion. That just didn't happen in the minors.

"Durham loves this team," Wolff wrote in a diary he kept that year. "You can go through a minor league career and never see that. The Durham Bulls are an important part of the community. Little kids wear our T-shirts, grown men walk around town with our caps, and girls fall all over our players. I keep saying to myself that this is the minors, that it can't happen like this."

The last game of the 1980 season was too perfect: The Bulls' pitcher tossed a no-hitter, the left fielder stole his 100th base, and the fans demanded curtain calls when it ended. Things only got better. The Bulls had a minority investor named Thom Mount, who happened to be a Hollywood producer. For years he told Wolff he was going to make a movie about life in the bush leagues. Wolff humored him. Then Mount dispatched writer-director Ron Shelton, a former Triple-A player, to scout out Durham. Shelton liked the place and made *Bull Durham*.

The 1987 film turned the Durham Bulls and their outrageously quaint stadium from a local happening into a national phenomenon. T-shirt and souvenir orders poured into a special 800 number. Wolff opened a retail outlet in a mall. The year after the movie, attendance rose 25 percent, breaking minor league records.

By the end of the 1980s, Wolff sat atop a baseball gold mine. After years of indifference from city officials—before the movie a Chamber of Commerce pamphlet didn't even mention the Bulls—even the bureaucrats lined up behind the team. The entire Raleigh–Durham–Chapel Hill "triangle" had adopted the Bulls. The club was poised to draw 300,000 fans. Baseball was thriving.

Part carnival, part comedy act, part sporting event—usually in equal measure—minor league baseball when it's done right knows how to entertain. It has to. Most fans aren't there because of the marquee value of the players, who are just passing through on their way up to major league millions or down and out of the game. They come to watch baseball and to be entertained. And in recent years—thanks in part to the Durham Bulls—they haven't stopped coming. Attendance at minor league baseball games topped 30 million in 1993 for the first time since 1950, when there were three times as many leagues and twice as many clubs, and it rose again in '94. It was the tenth straight increase in minor league attendance.

Minor league team owners learned during the game's renaissance in the 1980s that it is the show that, as George Steinbrenner liked to say, puts fannies in the seats. The ball-carrying pigs, the seat-cushion giveaways, the contests offering fans a chance to hit a homer or break the headlight of a car with a pitched ball—they make minor league baseball worthwhile. And the Northern League was no exception, especially on Opening Night in St. Paul. In the stands behind third base, equipped with scissors, a plastic barber pole, and a chair, Shelby Koebrick offered $10 haircuts. Her opposite number was Sister Rosalind, a nun who performed $5 massages on the first-base side.

As at any big game, the Saints invited dignitaries to toss out the first ball. Don Vogel, a popular Twin Cities talk-show host, was escorted to the mound. Short, round, and jittery, Vogel wore a tight-fitting tan golf shirt and pressed gray slacks. Earlier that week he had practiced for his big moment at the Metrodome and thrown a few perfect strikes on the air—which on the field would be a bit harder since Vogel was blind. The crowd chanted his name, and he waved his arms above his head. Vogel handed over his walking stick, took the ball, and tossed one halfway up the third-base line, sending players and photographers scurrying. The baseball rolled through a gate into the groundskeeper's room. To a roar Vogel marched off triumphantly, fist punching the air.

Next up was comedian Bill Murray, who once played a couple of games for a Class-A team in Grays Harbor, Washington, as a stunt for *Saturday Night Live*. (Murray singled in his first at bat.) A part owner of the Saints, Murray earlier had been selling programs in front of the stadium, mugging for startled fans. Loping to the mound, Murray doffed his Saints cap to the screaming crowd; as with Vogel fans chanted—"Bill! Bill! Bill!" He ripped off his jacket, revealing a Saints T-shirt, replaced the cap, and took a serious, methodical windup. Then he heaved the ball over the backstop ten rows deep into the stands. Murray raced off the hill and dropped to one knee, bowed his head, and crossed himself.

In their previous game, before 889 people at Midway Stadium on September 15, 1960, the St. Paul Saints beat the Louisville Colonels in a playoff game. A month later Calvin Griffith announced that the Twins would play the following season in Metropolitan Stadium in Bloomington. The Saints moved to Omaha, and professional baseball was gone from St. Paul.

There were nearly six times as many people on hand for the Saints' reopener. The announcer, Al Frechtman, was getting excited. He took a ritual dig at the Twins and their indoor bubble: "It's a thrill to have the St. Paul Saints back in action! Outdoor baseball here at Municipal Stadium!" It was how the Saints marketed the game—"wild and outside," with all its meanings: unpredictable like an errant pitch, played under the summer sky, beyond the ranks of organized baseball.

One by one the players were introduced, and they jogged through the drizzle to their respective base lines. The names of most of the Saints and the opposing team, the Thunder Bay Whiskey Jacks, weren't familiar to the crowd. Not that the players cared. They all knew they were rejects, outcasts, cuts, has-beens, not-good-enoughs. For them the Northern League was a second-chance league, an opportunity to prove something to someone in some major league organization—a scout, a coach, a manager, a nameless player personnel director—and a chance to extend a career that otherwise might be over.

The Thunder Bay lineup started with Rodney McCray, a twenty-nine-year-old center fielder who'd briefly made it to the big leagues with the Mets. Todd Rosenthal, the first baseman, had played the previous season for the Salt Lake Trappers, one of only three independent teams in all organized baseball. Ty Griffin, the second baseman, was a 1988 Olympian who had been released after four years in the Reds organization, perhaps more for his attitude than for his abilities. The right fielder, Jason Felice, at twenty-nine a minor league old-timer, had extended his career in Mexico the previous season. Dan Gray was the catcher, released by the Dodgers. In left field was Dennis Hood, who hadn't played in 1992. At third Brad Kantor, cut by the Indians after having spent the previous year in Class-A. Ken Arnold was the shortstop, a Class-A reject of the Cubs.

For the Saints, Rick Hirtensteiner was in center field, banished from the Expos farm system. Greg D'Alexander, the third baseman, was starting his third season of independent baseball. A thirty-three-year-old player-coach, Jim Eppard, was the designated hitter; he'd played eighty-two games in the majors for the Angels and the Blue Jays, his statistics forever recorded in *The Baseball Encyclopedia*. Eddie Ortega at second base, released by the Phillies, was a former Salt Lake Trapper. Shortstop Jerry DeFabbia, a rookie from Fairleigh Dickinson University, had been ignored in the major league draft. The left fielder was Kent Blasingame, a Texas Tech grad whose impressive lineage—his father, Don, played twelve years in the majors and his grandfather Walker Cooper, eighteen years for seven National League teams—hadn't helped him on draft day. Right fielder Scott Meadows had reached Triple-A in the Orioles system before getting his walking papers. Behind the plate was Frank Charles, a Giants reject. Pitching was Jim Manfred, cut by the Mets after three seasons in the low minors.

As Challenger Post 521 played the national anthem, the only familiar name on the Saints stood with one gloved hand behind his back and his cap over his heart. Leon "Bull" Durham, nearly thirty-six years old, wanted to make a comeback. He wore black Nike high-tops and the number 30 on his jersey. During ten major league seasons, Durham had hit 147 homers, appeared in an All-Star game, and played on a division winner, but now he was just another reject, seeking redemption a few years removed from a drug problem. He joined the fans in singing "The Star-Spangled Banner." When it was done, Durham pivoted 180 degrees, trotted back toward the Saints' dugout, and clapped his hands once. "Let's go, babe," he said.

Miles Wolff took his position behind a fence separating the field from the storage room beneath the grandstands. With him were other league officials, shuffling around waiting for the game finally to begin and the nervousness that accompanied any opening night to end.

No longer a salesman, Wolff wore his brown tweed jacket again. He stared through the chain-link fence onto the field and didn't talk much. He had been through many openers before, but this one was special. This was his league, his idea come to life.

As if the clouds knew this opener had to be different, the drizzle stopped and a halo of light enveloped the stadium, moist and white and misty. Manfred took his warm-up tosses as the fidgety infielders swept the dirt in arcs around their feet, scooping up practice grounders and throwing effortlessly to first base. The fans were happy after the frivolous pregame ceremonies, and the crowd chatter was animated and boisterous. McCray, the onetime New York Met, stepped into the batter's box to lead off for Thunder Bay. The

Municipal Stadium

first pitch was a ball but drew cheers anyway, simply because it was the first pitch thrown in competition by a professional baseball player in St. Paul in a long, long time. McCray struck out.

A half inning later the Burlington Northern freighter announced its passage.

Opening Day was but an introduction. Trains kept blaring past Municipal Stadium in the summer of 1993, and the Northern League rumbled into the consciousness of baseball fans in the upper regions of the great Midwest.

As in Miles Wolff's Durham of 1980, almost nothing went wrong in St. Paul. The Saints won the home opener in the bottom of the ninth and three months later celebrated the league championship by winning three of four games from the Rochester Aces, a franchise that wouldn't enjoy a Cinderella ending. Leon Durham smacked a home run in the finale, on top of eleven during the regular season, which tied for the league lead, proving to himself he could still play the game. Over the seventy-two-game schedule, the Northern League averaged 3,209 fans—exceeding Wolff's expectations—and St. Paul led the way with 4,940. Five out of six franchises made money. Former major league star Pedro Guerrero joined the Sioux Falls Canaries in midseason, boosting the league's credibility. Players were thrilled to have joined.

"I'm sorry it's taken me so long to write back," one of the Saints, a pitcher named Don Heinkel, wrote to the front office after receiving a gold, diamond, and onyx championship ring, "but the gratitude surely has been in my heart for the ring, letter, and personal note, but especially for allowing me to be a part of such a great experience last year. We had been promised rings from winter ball which never materialized, had one from Birmingham that got stolen, but now have the best one to help me remember all of those good years and especially the last one—where my World Series dream died but all of the good and fun things of baseball were still there in St. Paul."

But Miles Wolff knew that it was only the maiden voyage. A love of baseball had propelled the Northern League in 1993, as well as the thrill of participating in a fledgling venture. Commitment to baseball was essential in 1994. While the league had demonstrated that it was possible to field competitive, quality teams independent of oppressive major league farm systems—and that fans would still reward you—success wouldn't come without stability. The Northern League still was in its infancy. The second year would be crucial.

Wolff wasn't willing to rest on one perfect night, or one terrific season even. There was too much at stake: the money and reputation of the baseball men who had formed the Northern League, the pride of communities that had spent taxpayer dollars on baseball, the desire of players struggling to fulfill a fantasy. They were all sending a message to the baseball elite, but it would be an empty one if the league didn't survive.

Miles Wolff had come too far and risked too much to let that happen.

Miles Wolff in Wade Stadium, Duluth

TWO

Out where the handclasp's a little stronger,
Out where the smile dwells a little longer,
That's where the West begins.

—Arthur Chapman

T o a lifelong southerner, a place like Duluth, Minnesota, seems cold almost any time of year, the mythical sort of town where temperatures routinely plunge below zero, known only through television commercials for reliable car batteries. In such parts of the world, the seasons are so acute and the climate so inhospitable as to appear utterly uninhabitable. It was that way in April 1991, when Miles Wolff made a pilgrimage to Duluth to look at a baseball stadium. It was cold. Chunks of ice floated on Lake Superior. In the rest of the country, including Wolff's hometown of Durham, the baseball season was beginning. In Duluth it looked as if it might snow.

The previous summer a baseball booster from Minnesota had sent Wolff a photograph of a ballpark called Wade Stadium. Wolff hadn't heard of it. Built in the early 1940s as a Works Progress Administration project, the brick stadium looked like a classic, as baseball architecture went. Wolff decided he had to see it for himself. His idea of forming a new minor league was still embryonic. He had received a few calls from interested parties and had begun scouting around for a region where professional baseball was dormant. He hadn't had much luck in places like Burlington, Vermont, and Trois-Rivières, Quebec, which had ballparks but little public interest. And he didn't expect much on his trip to Duluth. Many towns boasted about facilities that turned out to be completely inadequate for professional baseball.

Wolff learned that a few dedicated souls in Duluth—old-timers, coaches, stadium lovers—a few years back had formed a committee known as Save the Wade, so he figured there was some interest in baseball in the city. But the group hadn't raised much money, so he also concluded that devotion went only so far. Locals could get sentimental about old buildings. Wade Stadium might not have been worth saving.

Then he approached it. From the outside Wolff saw a fully enclosed brick behemoth, a structure full of mass and power, a ballpark stuck in a time capsule he had accidentally unearthed. Inside Wolff surveyed a giant concrete outfield wall, a planked wooden roof, a wire-mesh net protecting the grandstands. All around was disrepair—the concrete flooring buckled, wiring was exposed, the roof leaked, holes dotted the backstop, the stands were covered with pigeon dung. "If we tried to light the field up now," the groundskeeper said, "I'm not sure what would happen."

Wolff didn't care. "You could just feel baseball in it," he recounted. On the spot he made a decision: Wade Stadium had to have a professional baseball team, and that team had to be part of his new independent league.

To Miles Wolff, Wade Stadium was Durham Athletic Park all over again. When he first saw the DAP in the winter of 1979, the seats were rotting, rats roamed freely, and the infield was chewed up from a rodeo. But Wolff was undeterred. He saw in Durham what he would see years later in Duluth: a place to revive baseball and stir a few dreams. He painted Durham Athletic Park blue and orange—Bulls colors—kept ticket prices low, and sponsored promotions nearly every night. The movie people left behind some souvenirs that added to the show, notably a giant bull in right field that snorted steam after home runs.

In the early years in Durham, Wolff patrolled the main concourse when the gates opened at six o'clock, greeting fans by name. When a vendor called in sick, Wolff jumped behind the counter to pour beer or roll hot dogs. When reporters needed an interview, he sat in the ground-level press box directly behind home plate. After the last pitch was thrown, Wolff opened the taps and let the beer flow while he analyzed the game with his manager, players, and staff. He made his office in a rocket-shaped ticket tower in front of the stadium that was adorned with the club's logo, a bull charging through a capital *D*. The days lasted sixteen hours, but damn if it wasn't fun.

But *Bull Durham* changed everything. Despite its success the movie was a sour experience. Wolff hated the filming, which flouted his tightfisted ethics. When a scene called for Tim Robbins to play a guitar, the crew bought a $2,000 model. When Wolff rounded up 3,000 fans from his mailing list for an afternoon ballpark scene, it was rescheduled for that night, inconveniencing his ticket holders. The net effect of the film was more and more Bulls fans, which improved profits but strained the old DAP, which truth be told was collapsing.

The stadium had taken on a modifier—*historic* Durham Athletic Park, which was another way of saying run-down. The cost of repairing it was pegged at $3 million to $4 million. For that you could build a new park. Wolff figured the city fathers would agree. "There was no love for Durham Athletic Park in this town," he said. "It was a symbol of old tobacco Durham. They wanted to get rid of it."

Wolff already had spent three years fighting to block Raleigh from building a stadium for a competing franchise. Now he proposed bringing a Triple-A team to Durham—the major leagues were mulling expansion that would add farm clubs. But the debate over building a new ballpark dragged on for months. In 1989, with a chance to allocate $17 million for a development project, the city and county cautiously tabled the matter. Opposition quickly surfaced, killing the plan.

To Wolff the bottom line was that he had saved the Bulls from a Raleigh challenger and the team needed a new home. He wasn't threatening to skip town—not yet, anyway—but he was clear about what the Bulls had given Durham and what Durham owed the

Bulls. From the politicians' perspective, he was naive. Deciding whether to spend millions of dollars of public money took time. They scheduled a countywide referendum on the stadium project.

Wolff, in the meantime, was frustrated. He was involved in politics, where he'd never wanted or intended to be. The debate over the stadium concerned baseball, but it had nothing to do with the game. Wolff hated that, and the public spotlight that came with it. He was in baseball to run a good operation, to foster community spirit, to show local officials that the game could do some good. Baseball was making him wealthy—Wolff didn't deny that. But there were times he was willing to trade the money for the anonymity of running a small-town operation. Like in the old days.

God only knew how long it had been since he'd put on a pair of shorts and his Johns Hopkins T-shirt, climbed on the back of a tractor, and cut the DAP's infield grass. (When Durham hosted an All-Star game, Wolff mowed while his baseball executive guests were off playing golf.) He couldn't remember the last time he'd stood behind the concessions counter pouring beer or shot the breeze with his staff. It was all attorneys and politicians and public hearings. When he showed up at the park, Wolff was preoccupied, complaining how he had to meet with this lawyer or attend that council meeting.

As delays mounted Wolff announced he was considering moving to a new sports and recreation park outside the city—but still within the county—envisioned by a local television executive, James Goodmon. Durham felt betrayed, but the city-county project was still on the table, and the design was stunning: a ballpark facing an abandoned American Tobacco Company warehouse, a majestic outfield backdrop similar to one in Baltimore being planned by the same architectural firm, Hellmuth Obata Kassabaum. Duke would occupy part of the warehouse. Pharmaceutical giant Glaxo would build new headquarters across the street. The private investment amounted to nearly $100 million.

But political realities intervened. Relying largely on the Chamber of Commerce and local VIPs, Wolff didn't mine the grass roots for support of the $11 million referendum on the ballpark. The Bulls didn't tell a skeptical public that the DAP turned a profit, that the team attracted fans from outside the county, that the stadium development project would add tens of millions of dollars to the tax base and a couple hundred thousand a year in sales tax revenues. Political action groups opposed the stadium. Letters to the editor called Wolff a carpetbagger. In March 1990, by a vote of 12,984 to 9,051, Durham County residents rejected the stadium project.

Wolff was beaten. He faced a choice: fight anew for a downtown stadium or move the team outside city lines. Both options struck him as invitations to more political wrangling. Owning the Durham Bulls wasn't about baseball anymore. It was a headache.

Two weeks after the vote, Wolff met with Jim Goodmon. "Jim," he said, "I don't want to move to your site. I want to sell it to you."

Goodmon didn't hesitate. "I'll buy it."

The price was never disclosed publicly, but Miles Wolff's money-down-the-drain investment of $2,417 turned out to be worth about $4 million.

As the publisher of *Baseball America*, the bible of the minors, and the owner of the most successful and best-known team in the game, Miles Wolff constantly fielded queries from would-be investors who wanted to jump on the minor league bandwagon. He usually answered a few questions and hung up the phone, never to hear from the caller again.

But within a couple of months in 1990, shortly after deciding to sell the Bulls, Wolff received calls from baseball boosters in Duluth, Minnesota; Sioux Falls, South Dakota; and Thunder Bay, Ontario, of all places. They all asked how to attract a minor league team. The timing was uncanny. Ten successful, exhilarating years with the Bulls were coming to an end. Wolff had turned a labor of love into a pile of money. He wasn't ready to leave the game, but he needed a new project.

Wolff had operated ball clubs, and he had owned the Bulls. He was never interested in working for a major league organization; fostering the game in small towns was his true calling. He also was a historian who knew that the minors once had been stocked with independent clubs and leagues that operated free from major league control. After selling the Bulls he had plenty of two things: time and cash. Forming an independent league would satisfy his urge to bring baseball to the people while escaping the politics of the game.

Wolff pulled out an atlas. After locating Thunder Bay he determined that minor league baseball was absent for hundreds and hundreds of miles around the upper Midwest—the biggest chunk of real estate on the continent without professional ball. Wolff knew the region once had been a proud and vital home for minor league teams. To avoid racial conflict in the South, many black stars were sent north for their apprenticeships. The old Northern League boasted a long list of stars: Hank Aaron, Lou Brock, Roger Maris, Jim Palmer, Willie Stargell, and Gaylord Perry, to name just a few. Earl Weaver had managed a season in the Northern. Wolff also knew that the Northern League had been the last established minor circuit to go under, in 1971.

The idea of resurrecting a minor league was appealing: You could draw on history, and the Northern League had plenty. It dated to 1903. Twenty-nine different cities had hosted teams. During the Depression clubs were permitted just one new ball per game to save money. Until 1963 the Northern was one among the dozens of leagues at the lowest classification levels: Class-D and later Class-C. Two years later, at a time when the minors appeared doomed, the league nearly collapsed; its major league parents saved it by creating the first Class-A short-season operation, with games beginning in June to avoid the awful spring weather. Even that couldn't prevent the inevitable. Teams and working agreements shifted yearly, and attendance spiraled downward. In its last season the Northern League, down to four teams, attracted a *total* of 65,000 fans.

But minor league baseball, of course, had changed since then. Like the pioneers who had settled the region, Wolff smelled opportunity in the upper Midwest to resurrect not only baseball but the maverick independent baseball that he had admired for many years. So he began visiting. Duluth had Wade Stadium, love at first sight. Sioux Falls, with an influx of high-tech business, reminded Wolff of a resurgent Durham a decade earlier. Everywhere he went people said they wanted baseball.

Wolff snapped pictures of ballparks. Fargo, North Dakota, and its sister city, Moorhead, Minnesota. Aberdeen, South Dakota, where Wolff drove in a blizzard, had hosted an Orioles farm club in the old Northern League; Wolff photographed the snow-encased stadium. In Thunder Bay, Wolff discovered an old ball yard with a view of grain towers astride Lake Superior. A local backer said 4,000 fans had turned out for semipro baseball not long ago.

One by one cities emerged. St. Paul was an ideal location— taking on the big-league Twins would be risky, but a fun-filled challenge for sure—and the recreation department was eager for a stadium tenant. St. Cloud, Minnesota, was a longtime Northern League town, but it relied on the Twin Cities for television, and local publicity was essential. Sioux City, Iowa, was large enough but had no stadium; when Wolff visited, a local development official showed him the site of an old ballpark—amid piles of manure in the city's meatpacking district. In its favor, Sioux City had a mayor who swore to build a stadium.

By early 1992 Wolff had the makings of a league. Representatives from nine cities assembled at the Radisson Hotel in St. Paul in March to learn about independent baseball. Mike Veeck, who was certain to be part of the league, spoke about the minors and his iconoclastic father. Van Schley, a longtime independent club operator, offered direct testimony about his Salt Lake Trappers, the most successful independent of the 1980s. Wolff wanted to show the cities that independent baseball could work.

It was a legitimate concern. "Franchise hustlers" a year earlier had accepted $30,000 apiece from several cities on the promise of starting a league in the region. Wolff knew that someone without baseball experience couldn't waltz in and form a league. But cities didn't understand. Wolff had to make his league squeaky clean.

Wolff's advantage was his background, his extensive baseball contacts, and his honest approach. By bringing the cities together in St. Paul, he demonstrated he was for real, not some field-of-dreamer out to make a quick buck. "Check on my credentials," he told the officials. "This isn't a money thing. We think baseball should be in your community. Nobody is going to get rich on this. I'm not going to be able to come in and sell this franchise and walk out."

If the league succeeded, of course, the owners could sell their clubs for the going minor league rate—well over a million dollars in the right market. But Wolff wouldn't charge an up-front franchise fee to join the league. Clubs supplied their own operating capital, and after two years an owner who wanted to keep his franchise would pay Wolff $50,000. The cities were impressed. Wolff decided that he needed a minimum of six towns to begin play, and Sioux Falls, Thunder Bay, St. Paul, and Duluth, which would share the franchise with its neighbor, Superior, Wisconsin, were a lock. Ownership groups began falling into place.

Marv Goldklang, who owned three minor league clubs plus a piece of the New York Yankees, was penciled in for Duluth but took St. Paul because he didn't want to have to change planes to get to town. Instead, indy stalwart Mal Fichman recommended as owner in Duluth an Oregon businessman named Bruce Engel, who had helped run an independent team in Erie, Pennsylvania. On Wolff's word alone, Harry Stavrenos, who ran the California League club in San Jose, immediately said yes to Sioux Falls. For Thunder Bay, Wolff needed a plant—no one was willing to take a club in Thunder Bay, wherever that was. Ricky May, a sporting goods retailer who had been general manager of the Bulls for two years, had told Wolff he was looking for new challenges. He'd get one.

At a meeting at the Minneapolis airport in July 1992, Wolff officially awarded franchises to the four cities plus Fargo-Moorhead, which was to vote on ballpark renovations. City officials strutted like peacocks with civic pride. St. Paul's mayor delivered a rousing speech about how a minor league team—playing outdoors—would boost the city's image. Sioux City's mayor didn't have a team but pledged to get that stadium built—and then outdraw natural rival Sioux Falls, whose representative was having none of it.

These spiritual descendants of the great explorers and pioneers who'd settled the nation's frontier cared more about baseball than people in any other towns Wolff had passed through in his minor league career. Without that enthusiasm you couldn't build baseball.

It reminded Wolff of *The Music Man*. Cities needed a bit of Professor Harold Hill, who wasn't really a musician but led the band anyway. "You can't force it down their throats," Wolff said. "But if they believe, it happens."

Sioux Falls took the first step. Before Wolff had even awarded franchises, the city approved $233,000 for ballpark renovations. Stavrenos hired a general manager who worked out of a tiny, run-down office beneath the stands at Sioux Falls Stadium. On June 15 Stavrenos signed a three-year lease at around $5,000 a year. The city in turn would bank 5 percent of all ticket sales above $400,000. It was a far cry from the old Northern League, when the Sioux Falls Packers had generated gate receipts of $10,285.20—for the entire 1970 season.

Stavrenos had sold the city by touting the virtues of independent baseball. Despite complaints from amateur baseball boosters about the intrusion of a minor league team, the city realized the advantage of a club that would attract two or three thousand—rather than hundred—fans per night. Smartly, Stavrenos also asked for the stars (the stadium needed $2 million to reach major league–approved standards, he told the local Sports Club) but was willing to settle for the moon ($1 million would be fine). He never expected that much.

But Sioux Falls, named for red-rock cascades along the Big Sioux River, is a modern American success story, befitting its boom-and-bust history. Its founders had paid $3.15 per city block and expected to sell lots for up to $200, but the Panic of 1857 halted settlement. By the Civil War only a couple dozen families remained. But statehood and the Dakota Boom attracted thousands of homesteaders, and growth was aided by the railroad and factories powered by the nearby falls. Sioux Falls would be a "second Chicago," promoters claimed, as they did throughout the Midwest.

At the turn of the century, Buffalo Bill rehearsed his Wild West Show on the eastern edge of town, but Sioux Falls was struggling again, its impressive brick factories closing one after another. The Great Depression was followed by the important siting of an army training facility. The agriculture decline of the 1980s was followed by the current economic revival. Sioux Falls survived.

As the Northern League came to town, the city boasted one of the nation's lowest unemployment rates. Citibank's huge credit card–processing operation was hiring furiously. The John Morrell & Company meatpacking plant was a stalwart after more than eighty years. The livestock market was the nation's biggest. With no corporate or personal income tax, Sioux Falls was attracting new business, blue- and white-collar alike. Jobs were plentiful, and people from depressed small farm towns were flocking to a city unhurt by the recent recession.

Sioux Falls's reputation was cemented in 1992 when *Money* magazine named it the best place to live in America. The city had to spend to live up to its notices. Baseball was worth it, and part of the town's lore. An early club, in 1889, that wore bright yellow uniforms had been dubbed the Yellow Kids after a popular comic strip. A sportswriter began referring to the team as the Canaries, and the name stuck. Those Sioux Falls teams were considered mavericks, because they paid players a full-time wage and hired talent away from other clubs. Over the years the city fielded teams in various circuits, some of which included black players; in a classic contest the early Negro Leagues pitcher John Wesley Donaldson struck out thirty batters but lost 1–0 in eighteen innings in a game played in Sioux Falls.

In the 1930s FDR's Works Progress Administration built a baseball stadium in Sioux Falls. In that decade too Branch Rickey signed on Sioux Falls as part of the extensive St. Louis Cardinals farm system. The club's uniforms resembled those of the parent, with a canary instead of a cardinal perched on both ends of a bat. Sioux Falls joined the Northern League in 1942, but eleven years later the club was sold and moved to Winnipeg, and the city was without minor league baseball. While the link with the league was restored in 1966, the Sioux Falls Packers fared no better than any other struggling bush-league team. When the league folded, so did professional baseball in Sioux Falls.

But Harry Stavrenos quickly detected a desire in this new boomtown. Every time he met with Sioux Falls officials, Stavrenos left with improvements that he hadn't requested. He recommended building a new concession stand. He got the facility of his dreams. A walk-in freezer for ice cream. An eight-burner stove. Hot dog warmers for ten concession booths. Beer pumped directly from a back-room refrigerator to taps at the counter. To a minor league baseball owner, it was heaven.

The $233,000 investment became $1 million. Sioux Falls would unveil an impressive little ballpark, with new plastic seating, metal bleachers down the lines, a modern scoreboard with a computerized message line, and a fresh coat of gray and blue paint.

Four cities were solidly committed. But Moorhead's city council unexpectedly rejected stadium renovations. Wolff scrambled for a replacement. Wausau, Wisconsin, was deemed too small, and the stadium in St. Cloud wasn't available. Winnipeg's prospective owner dawdled, hoping for a Triple-A franchise. In Sioux City, Wolff had lined up an owner with experience building a ballpark, but the mayor wouldn't push for construction funding until a fifth team had signed on.

Wolff considered Rochester, Minnesota, a strong candidate for expansion a year or two after the league got going. The city has the world-renowned Mayo Clinic and, with its trim suburbs bursting with doctors, a wealthy and educated population that would take to baseball. The stadium met minor league standards, but city officials had ruled out a 1993 lease.

Rochester was suggested as a possible site by Richard Jacobson, an amateur baseball promoter who had owned strip bars and a mobile-home business. In July, Jacobson picked Wolff up at the Minneapolis airport and drove him to the ballpark. On the return trip he mentioned that he wanted to own the club. Wolff was noncommittal but later invited him to a Northern League tryout camp and even asked him to bring along three dozen baseballs.

Because Rochester wasn't a likely 1993 candidate, Wolff filed away the possibility. But other cities were dropping out, and in September Jacobson called to say the city had changed its mind. Wolff traveled to Rochester for a park board meeting late that month. The stadium was available.

All along Jacobson expected to own the club. Wolff in one conversation indicated that might be possible—but only along with experienced baseball people to give the franchise credibility. Then he had second thoughts. Standing in the parking lot after the park board meeting, Jacobson said he wanted to name the team the Black Sox. Wolff demurred. Links with the 1919 Chicago White Sox team accused of throwing the World Series weren't what a new league stressing fun and independence, not to mention credibility, needed. Jacobson persisted anyway. He also focused on what players he would sign—another red flag to Wolff, because that job would have to fall to an experienced baseball operator. After Wolff recommended a baseball veteran to be involved in the team, Jacobson never called him, and never tried to find local partners either.

Wolff needed Rochester, but he needed reliable ownership even more, and Jacobson was too risky. In bolstering his case Jacobson alluded to mysterious cash holdings not listed on his financial statement. He told a newspaper he was the planned owner of the team. Wolff heard rumors about shady dealings at the strip joints. A cop in Jacobson's hometown, Cannon Falls, wouldn't "confirm or deny" even knowing him. A Minnesota contact told Wolff to "watch out." He received unsolicited phone calls warning against Jacobson. "The league had to be very, very clean because baseball would be looking for ways to knock us down as an independent league," Wolff later said. "They didn't like this idea. So our ownership had to be really strong."

Jacobson didn't fit in. Wolff called him to say he couldn't have the franchise. The bar owner was devastated, but Wolff pushed ahead. By the end of October, he had signed a lease with the city and recruited an old Atlanta Braves colleague, Charles Sanders, to own 20 percent of the team. Jacobson asked for, and agreed to accept, 10 percent. It was an unpleasant experience that left him unsure about the ball club's prospects, but Wolff had his fifth team.

About a month later, though, Jacobson reneged, suing Wolff for total ownership. With a pending lawsuit, during the season the club became untouchable. The case was dismissed, but Wolff wound up spending $200,000 of his own money on the Rochester franchise. The city, meanwhile, didn't support the Aces, who posted the league's lowest attendance despite advancing to the playoffs. The franchise folded after the season and a new one was awarded to Winnipeg for 1994.

W ith Rochester aboard Wolff set his sights on Sioux City, where baseball surely would be a tonic. Sitting at the junction of Iowa, Nebraska, and South Dakota, in the 1980s Sioux City looked as if it might slip into the Missouri River and disappear. It was the culmination of a long and slow decline.

In the early twentieth century, Sioux City was bigger than Denver and Omaha. It was a beloved cattle and corn market, where the cows that jumped from ferryboats crossing to Nebraska were said to swim back to the Iowa shore. The railroad powered the early prosperity. "SAVED AT LAST. IT HAS COME" was the headline in the *Sioux City Journal* of March 14, 1868.

The settlers at what was the last outpost on the American frontier were as proud and fierce as the native Sioux Indians who predated them. In Sioux City a preacher named George Haddock was shot for advocating temperance. Residents built the world's first Corn Palace, an 18,000-square-foot fairyland marvel with windows, minarets, and buttresses covered with corn, sorghum, cattails, and other grains and plants, illuminated by electricity and gas jets. "This must be a very rich country," remarked one visitor, President Grover Cleveland. A local set his love of Sioux City to verse:

This land o' our'n, I tell ye's got to be
A better country than man ever see.
I feel my spirit swellin' with a cray
That seems to say, "Break forth and prophesy."

Disaster, however, was one sure prophecy. Sioux City endured droughts, locusts, Indians, floods, financial panics, a polio epidemic, and the Depression. Stockyards closed, and agriculture fell on hard times. People fled Sioux City like it was Dodge City; population declined by about 15 percent from 1970 to 1990. "I would drive five hours to go to Kansas City to do something," said Jim Wharton, who was both mayor and a city councilman in the early 1990s. "We had no malls. We had nothing. People couldn't get out of here fast enough."

Wharton had a dream for improving his town: minor league baseball. The last team had folded in 1960, but Sioux City had a storied heritage. Unfortunately, the biggest story occurred in 1891, when the Sioux City Cornhuskers captured the Western Association title and took on the Chicago Colts of the more established National League in a postseason series. The teams played six games in Sioux City during Corn Palace Week. Tickets to the Evans Park grounds cost fifty cents, and spectators were lured by the promise of brass bands and a balloon ascension. "Come early and avoid the rush," the local newspaper advertised. "Today's game will be one of the greatest ever witnessed on a diamond."

The Huskers did the impossible: They won the first contest, 8–1, and proceeded to take four of six from the Colts, who were led by Iowa native Cap Anson—"the great and only Anson." For an encore Sioux City beat the American League champion St. Louis Browns five straight games. "Kings of the Ball Field," declared the *Sioux City Tribune*.

Barnstorming big-leaguers came to Sioux City. In the same year that he hit sixty home runs, Babe Ruth swatted one out of Stock Yards Park before 5,000 fans in a game between the "Bustin' Babes" and Lou Gehrig's "Larrupin' Lous." But in later years baseball struggled in Sioux City. One game in 1940 generated a total gate of $29. In the 1950s, the team, known as the Soos, sold $10 shares to 2,000 citizens to raise operating capital. But that couldn't save it. The club switched leagues and major league affiliations, and finally shut down.

Jim Wharton and his political partner, Bob Scott, who alternated as mayor, were unconcerned with the history. They just wanted minor league baseball. In 1992, when they heard that Miles Wolff would be in Sioux Falls on a visit, they invited themselves for a meeting. Wharton promised to build a ballpark that would be ready for the 1993 season. At the preliminary league gathering in

St. Paul, Scott told the other towns, "In Sioux City we have a saying: Millions for baseball, not a nickel for the arts center." Cute, Wolff thought, but impossible. Not everyone in town supported the prospect of a multimillion-dollar boondoggle for a sport that had flopped before. It was a political risk for Wharton and Scott, but the roly-poly local pols figured it was worth it.

After its long decline Sioux City's economy was beginning to come alive by 1992. Malls sprang up. The meatpacking industry hung on. New industries arrived, helping push down unemployment. At Gateway 2000, a growing personal computer company that located its headquarters just outside Sioux City, the workforce averaged twenty-eight years of age. Young people needed something to do. Sioux City was building a $14 million riverfront park system. Mötley Crüe was playing downtown. Baseball fit right in.

Screw the local naysayers, Wharton and Scott thought. While we're at it, screw the economists who counseled against spending taxpayer money on baseball stadiums and the Class-A Midwest League, which dismissed Sioux City's interest. Wharton and Scott commissioned architects. They interviewed prospective owners. They devised ways to allocate money without a public vote. Once Wolff secured Rochester as his fifth franchise, Sioux City was ready to commit to the league and bought land for a ballpark five miles from downtown. It was a cornfield.

By a 4–1 vote the city council approved the necessary revenue bonds. In September, Sioux City tendered bids from three local contractors. Ground was broken in October. It was a herculean task: build a state-of-the-art baseball facility in eight months, three of which were the harsh Iowa winter. Wolff scheduled Sioux City's first seven games on the road.

The city spent $4 million on a baseball league that hadn't yet played an inning. It was a political performance worthy of a place in the chutzpah hall of fame. But when the stadium opened on time and on budget, and fans filled Lewis and Clark Park, Wharton and Scott had an answer for critics who said they should have been filling potholes, not building monuments to a children's game. "What good are nice streets if you've got no place to drive to on a Saturday night?" Wharton said. "We gave 'em a place to drive to."

Wade Stadium

THREE

If it wasn't for the minors, where would the majors be?

—*The Baseball Magazine*, 1913

I n 1990, while Miles Wolff was battling the politicians in Durham, he was also fighting the bureaucrats who run major league baseball. What transpired was enough to send even the most devout baseball operator—and Wolff, who over the years had owned a piece of teams in Durham, Asheville, and Burlington, North Carolina; Utica, New York; Pulaski, Virginia; and Butte, Montana, was as strong a candidate for the honor as any—running madly from the sport.

Major league baseball in the 1980s had watched the minors grow fat using their raw materials—players whom the big-league organizations scouted, signed, and assigned to one of their farm teams. The envy was understandable. The big-league barons were losing battle after battle with the powerful Major League Baseball Players Association; they most recently had been found guilty of colluding not to sign free agents. Salaries had escalated to previously unthinkable heights, and despite record television contracts and fan attendance, the majors cried poverty. Meanwhile, the minor leagues thrived. Attendance, profits, and franchise values all were at record levels.

The main piece of evidence used by the majors against their

supposed brethren was the resale price of minor league clubs, which indeed had risen beyond anyone's wildest imagination. In 1986 Joe Buzas sold the Double-A Reading Phillies, which he had bought from the Philadelphia organization for one dollar, for a million dollars plus one (so Buzas could say he made a million). By 1990 Single-A clubs fetched $2 million or more. Double-A clubs went for $4 million. The Triple-A Vancouver Canadians sold for $5.5 million. In subsequent years sale prices rocketed even higher.

Bush-league franchises became a trendy investment, with everyone from Warren Buffett to Jimmy Buffett grabbing a piece of the action. No one argued that the business principles applied by the entertainers, lawyers, and investment bankers who bought teams didn't improve the quality of the product. Year after year fans responded by flocking to minor league parks—many newly built or renovated—in record numbers. It was a heady time, and the success of the minors made the majors seethe.

Major league organizations spent $6 million every year supplying and supporting minor league affiliates. Triple-A salary costs averaged $785,000 per team, according to the commissioner's office, and the parent club paid all but $21,000. The majors estimated that they paid about 85 percent of the nearly $1 million spent by a top farm club on bats, balls, uniforms, hotels, travel, and meals. Factor in travel to and from spring training; player signing bonuses; the salaries of minor league instructors, managers, coaches, trainers, and umpires; and generous television rights payments, and it added up.

"We train them in spring training, then drop them off on their doorstep," Bill Murray, the major leagues' director of baseball operations, told a reporter. "All we're looking for is a fairer shake in setting the structure, seeing to it that it is able to meet the needs of our clubs." In other words, the majors wanted to cut a better deal with the nouveau riche minor leagues to reduce their own expenses.

At issue was a fat document governing the relationship between the major and minor leagues known as the Professional Baseball Agreement. The PBA periodically came up for renegotiation, and in years past the two sides would sit down over lunch, scratch out a few changes in pencil, and that was that. But in the spring of 1990, rumors swirled that the majors were going to come down hard. Minor league officials could scarcely believe it. "We're in the same family together," said Joe Gagliardi, president of the Class-A California League.

It sounds naive, but that's how baseball had been for decades, before owning a minor league franchise was a lucrative proposition. There was winsome, heartfelt talk about a warm, fuzzy, all-inclusive "baseball family" that didn't discriminate on the basis of rank. The majors didn't look down on the minors as ungrateful charity cases. The minors didn't consider the majors incompetent powermongers.

Minor league executives generally reserve their ire for those who own the twenty-eight big-league clubs. They are careful not to denigrate the "baseball people" who understand the importance of a strong farm system. The minors are basic R & D, the laboratories where the products are tested. Farm directors, scouts, minor league coaches and managers, player development officials—they know the minors are indispensable, for training players as well as generating fan interest nationwide. "A necessity in baseball," said David Dombrowski, general manager of the Florida Marlins.

The major league owners are the villains—the shipping executives and media conglomerates, beer salesmen and television moguls, pizza makers and widows of car dealers who didn't grow up in the game and don't have any historical affection or appreciation for the minor leagues. "*They're* the ones," Harry Stavrenos said.

In the old days the men who ran baseball had, like their players, apprenticed in the minors. Bill Veeck made his start hustling in Milwaukee. Calvin Griffith, the tightfisted Senators and Twins owner, managed a team in Charlotte, North Carolina, where he met his wife. Walter O'Malley, the omnipotent Dodgers owner, sent his sons to the farm system to learn the business. When the Pioneer League in big sky country was on the verge of failure, as it was several times in the 1960s and 1970s, the Dodgers and Giants rescued the rookie circuit. The Braves and Pirates kept the Western Carolinas League from folding after it shrank to four teams.

The bond between baseball people and the minor league communities in which they cut their teeth is personal and lasting. Miles

Wolff talks about Savannah as "my town"—meaning his first baseball town. Everyone in baseball has a town. Riding in an elevator
at the winter meetings one year, Wolff bumped into Buzzie Bavasi,
the former Angels and Padres general manager, whom he had never
met. Bavasi glanced at the Bulls owner's badge and immediately
began reminiscing about running Durham decades before. "It was
like I was a long-lost friend," Wolff said.

By the 1980s the camaraderie was dying. The old-time major
league owners were "dinosaurs," as Bill Veeck said when he sold
the Chicago White Sox out of fiscal desperation to a lawyer who
peddled real estate partnerships (Jerry Reinsdorf) and a television
syndicator (Eddie Einhorn). The dinosaurs had been supplanted by
free-spending businessmen who didn't understand the economics
of baseball, let alone its competitive nuances. The new owners had
no loyalty to farm clubs in Memphis or Durham or Pawtucket. The
minors were just another balance sheet item—one that could be
cut. Compared with the major league players union, the minors
were an easy mark.

The first get-together between the two sides, in July 1990, offered
a glimpse of the new reality.

The leaders of the National Association of Professional Baseball
Leagues, the minors' governing body, sat on one side of a long conference room table at the Marriott Marquis Hotel in Atlanta. Facing them were representatives of major league baseball's owners,
including Charles Brumback, the austere, combative chairman of
the Tribune Company, which owned the Chicago Cubs, and his
union-busting lawyer, Dennis Homerin, both fresh from an ugly
battle with striking workers at the Tribune-owned New York *Daily
News*. "They were sending us a message that this was important to
people who were powerful," recalled George Yund, a lawyer for the
minor leagues.

At that meeting the major leaguers projected computerized out-
lines of their demands onto a large screen. Brumback, with help
from Frank Casey, a Washington lawyer retained by the commissioner's office, curtly ran down the list. The rumors had been true,

and the proposals were drastic—the most complete overhaul of the relationship between the two tiers of professional baseball since the majors had at once saved and subjugated the dying minors in 1963.

Baseball's barons flexed their muscles in every possible arena. They wanted to eliminate "special consideration" payments created to compensate the minors for major league television broadcasts into their territories. They wanted to give the commissioner veto power over minor league franchise sales and relocations. They wanted control over player contracts, which until then were owned by the minor league clubs. They wanted to impose a set of facility standards that would require massive expenditures by clubs and communities. They wanted to eliminate transaction fee payments that organizations made to farm teams for player moves, an important revenue source.

To top it off, the commissioner's office wanted the minor league clubs to make lump-sum payments of up to $150,000 each to their major league parents. It was baseball through the looking glass: The majors had become the impoverished do-gooders, supplying the talent with which minor league club owners made millions. Finally waking up to the minor league renaissance, the majors wanted a piece of the action.

From the National Association's perspective, it was about control. The majors wanted total domination. They viewed the minors as mere subjects in the fiefdom of baseball who were taking advantage of the throne. Some of it was understandable—the majors, after all, had a right to ensure that their future stars played in safe and professional surroundings. But to Miles Wolff and other owners, many demands were petty. One urinal for every 125 seats? An extra three inches of walking space in box seats? What business did the majors have mandating that?

After months of bitter sessions in New York, Cincinnati, and Chicago, and lopsided proposals from the majors, Wolff was ready to urge his fellow owners to take a stand and break away from the big leagues. First, he thought, the 150 National Association clubs had the best available ballparks locked up. When the majors threatened to lease other facilities, what did they have in mind? Little League fields? Second, under the existing PBA, the farm clubs technically owned minor league player contracts, so whom did the majors think they were going to use as their talent? Control over the players was a lawsuit waiting to happen. Third, no one who knew anything about developing professional baseball players wanted them to play at spring training sites in Florida and Arizona, as the majors were threatening. Such an arrangement meant no stadiums, fans, media, or competitive pressure—what players need before they can play in The Show.

After a day of frustrating conferences in December 1990 in Los Angeles, where the minors gathered for baseball's winter meetings—the majors dropped out because of the rift—Wolff drove to Malibu with his minor league colleagues Mike Veeck, who was running the independent Miami Miracle, and Van Schley of the Salt Lake Trappers. Schley took the group to an Italian restaurant called La Scala. Charles Bronson sat at a nearby table.

Over pasta, Veeck agitated Wolff. "We don't have to take this, Miles. Let's walk," said Veeck, who had inherited his father's disdain for the ruling classes. "The minors have got to take a stand. The big leagues can't operate without us."

Wolff was dissatisfied with the entire process, tired of acceding to the majors' every demand. He took mental notes for a rabble-rousing speech to the troops. "They say they're going to start their own minor leagues. Let's see them do it. Prepare to go independent. You still have control of the players who are under contract. We can sign some bonus babies who will be your property. We can do this."

After dinner Wolff stopped by a late-night party. Dozens of somber minor leaguers filled a hotel suite. Charles Sanders was the only major league representative in the room. The Atlanta Braves' vice president of minor league administration was a longtime friend of Wolff who also viewed himself as a friend of the minors. Nursing beers, Wolff and Sanders disappeared into a corner and for ninety minutes discussed the state of the game. The relationship between the majors and minors was falling apart, and neither man was pleased.

But when Wolff said he wanted to lead a revolt, Sanders became blunt: "Don't do it, Miles. The major leagues are dead serious. They have to win this. It doesn't make sense, it won't work, but they will do it. They will destroy the minor leagues. You may be able to pull this off, Miles, and you'll win the battle, but you'll lose the war."

Wolff was surprised. He had been convinced the majors wouldn't dissolve a ninety-year relationship and form their own farm system. But he respected Sanders. As they talked Wolff gradually changed his mind. He started thinking about the Butte, Montanas, and Lynchburg, Virginias, of the world, the little towns that surely couldn't afford to operate independently, paying player salaries and other operating costs. If we fight, Wolff thought, fifty or seventy-five communities will lose baseball. If we give in, it will be embarrassing, but at least the game will survive. That was always Wolff's primary concern: preserving baseball.

So when the minor league representatives gathered in the ballroom of the Westin Bonaventure Hotel two days later, Miles Wolff didn't say a word. By just one vote, the minors agreed to a deal. In exchange for continued backing from the majors, they relinquished control over player contracts. They agreed to pay the majors a flat annual fee based on ticket revenues and to spend millions upgrading stadiums. Wolff understood that the economics of minor league baseball had changed, and he could live with the new deal. But he was sickened by how it had been produced—the confrontations, brinkmanship, threats, challenges, and capitulations. "Why do I want to be in business with these people?" he asked himself. "They aren't nice people."

Wolff wasn't alone. People like Mike Veeck and Van Schley, Harry Stavrenos and Mal Fichman, even Marv Goldklang, a Wall Street lawyer who owned a share of the Yankees, considered themselves philosophical outcasts from the baseball establishment. Over the years they had managed to find one another in baseball, but they'd never had a chance to break ranks and work together as a group. Miles Wolff's Northern League gave them the opportunity.

Throughout history baseball has had its share of rebels. At the turn of the century, Ban Johnson broke the National League's monopoly, luring players frustrated by a cap on salaries and recruiting knowledgeable baseball men such as Charles Comiskey, Connie Mack, John McGraw, and Clark Griffith. His American League invaded the National League cities of Washington, Boston, Philadelphia, and Baltimore. "If we had waited for the National League to do something for us," Johnson said, "we would have remained a minor league forever."

In the 1910s and '20s, Jack Dunn's Baltimore Orioles of the International League dominated the minors. Dunn despised the majors' restrictive reserve and draft policies, hoarded top talent, and balked at selling it for less than top dollar. Strapped financially, he sold Babe Ruth and two other players in 1914 for about $25,000. A decade later his star pitcher Lefty Grove fetched $100,600. With talent and energy he constructed some of the best minor league teams of all time outside the system.

Miles Wolff never saw himself as a latter-day Ban Johnson or Jack Dunn, but he always loved the idea of independent baseball. His mentor was a man named Bob Freitas, a rumpled minor league baseball salesman who for $11,000 a year inspected the health of clubs from the Mississippi River to Honolulu as a field representative for the National Association. During the dog days of the 1970s, Freitas did anything he could to help minor league teams stay alive. He saved the Pioneer and Northwest leagues when clubs were dropping like characters in an Agatha Christie novel, often by convincing someone to start an independent, like the ones he had operated in the golden age of the minors.

In the postwar euphoria of the 1940s, minor league baseball grew furiously. Other than movies and radio, Americans had few entertainment options. During the war President Franklin D. Roosevelt had encouraged the minors to keep operating as a morale builder, and ten leagues with sixty-six teams began the 1943 season. Four years later the number of leagues rose to fifty-two; twenty-three minor league clubs outdrew the sad-sack St. Louis Browns that season.

In 1949 the minors peaked: 448 teams in fifty-nine leagues. Their names conveyed the romance and vitality of a rich and varied nation—the Piedmont League, the Three-I League (Indiana, Iowa, Illinois), the Big State League (Texas and only Texas), the Cotton

States League, the Evangeline League, the Sunset League, the Kitty League, the Longhorn League, the Colonial League, the Border League, the Tobacco State League. The Northern League, too, where Aberdeen, South Dakota, behind a future major league pitcher named Bob Turley who won eleven straight decisions, defeated Eau Claire, Wisconsin, four games to one for the league championship.

In those days profit and loss was unimportant, because most clubs were owned by either major league teams or civic leaders. "You know, we had a great year last year. We only lost four thousand dollars," the president of a Class-D team said one winter. "However, when we sat around the table and made [the loss] up . . . we decided that there wasn't anything that had happened in our community that had brought as much happiness to as many people as did the baseball club."

But America's habits changed. Television gave people a reason to stay home on summer nights; they could watch a host of new programs, including some major league baseball. Air-conditioning made them comfortable, so no longer did one need escape outdoors to the ballpark. As families moved to the suburbs from the cities, simply getting to downtown stadiums became a hassle. During the 1950s minor league income dropped and stadiums fell apart, as towns had little money for repairs. The majors, for their part, refused for years to compensate any minor league clubs for broadcasting games into their territories. The fact was that the minors had overexpanded. As the farm system spread, the number of unaffiliated minor league teams—independents—fell from 169 in 1951 to just 13 six years later. The cumulative effect was a staggering drop in minor league attendance; from a record of nearly 42 million fans in 1949, the gate plummeted to less than 20 million in 1954 and less than 10 million in 1963.

Major league relocation and expansion only encouraged the decline. When big-league clubs struggled, they invaded the biggest minor league markets: The Boston Braves left for Milwaukee, the St. Louis Browns moved to Baltimore, the Philadelphia Athletics took Kansas City, and, the coup de grâce, the Dodgers and Giants snatched Los Angeles and San Francisco—all in the 1950s.

As the decade ended the majors committed half a million dollars to help failing teams in the low minors. But money couldn't stem the tide. When it looked as if the entire system would collapse, the minors were rescued in 1963 by a document called the Player Development Contract. The majors abolished the Class-B, -C, and -D leagues but provided subsidies to guarantee operation of at least 100 clubs. The plan worked, but in the process the minors sacrificed their last trace of independence.

The minors were still foundering when Miles Wolff met Bob Freitas at baseball's winter meetings in 1973. Freitas was serving double duty as National Association field rep and Northwest League president. On the verge of extinction, the league had had just two healthy teams when Freitas arrived, so he placed an independent team in Portland, Oregon. The club was owned by Bing Russell, a onetime minor leaguer better known as the deputy sheriff on *Bonanza*. It was the only independent baseball club since the 1964 Quincy Gems had had the double distinction of finishing last and drawing the fewest fans in the Midwest League.

Portland played in an absurdly large, 30,000-seat stadium but quickly proved successful—attracting twice as many fans as any other Northwest League club in its first season and more than 100,000 the next—impressive numbers for a low minor league team. The team was true to its nickname: Mavericks. Its president once threw a chair at an umpire, and players shouted obscenities from bus windows as they drove down the Main Streets of opposing towns. They loved their independence. Buoyed by Portland's success, by 1976 the league's north division was all independent: Portland, Seattle, and Grays Harbor.

But the indies weren't a panacea, just triage. Minor league team owners still quit in the middle of the night, bills went unpaid, fans didn't care. "The industry was in a shambles," said Bob Richmond, who succeeded Freitas as the Northwest League's president. "Every year the big problem I had was trying to keep the damn thing going till next year."

Teams in the low minors were averaging a few hundred fans a game. The institution of baseball for a time seemed out of fashion, somehow insignificant in the turbulent era of Vietnam and Watergate. Freitas worked quietly in hopes the game would recover. His indies helped the minors survive. "It's inspiring, when you think about it," Freitas said in a long profile of him in *The New Yorker*. "These independent clubs, these little shoestring operations, are taking on the big-league organizations that spend millions on player development. I really hope they succeed and stay in business."

Humble and unprepossessing, Freitas touched dozens of people, including Wolff, who listened to him praise independent baseball—teams that belong to the towns, not to some faraway major league organization, and whose purpose is to have fun and win games. "Freitas believed," Wolff said. "He's not selling, he's believing." When Freitas suggested placing an independent club in Victoria, British Columbia, in 1974, Wolff raised $9,000 and drove cross-country. He had two competitors for the franchise, and both had a lot more in the bank than nine grand. He didn't get the team, but he was sold on independent baseball.

Three years later, a time when minor league clubs still were being sold for the cost of their bills outstanding, Bing Russell raised

Sioux Falls Stadium

a few eyebrows when he was paid $206,000 for the territorial rights to Portland, which went Triple-A. The same year, Columbus, Ohio, spent an unprecedented $5 million refurbishing an old stadium. In 1982 the Louisville Redbirds drew a minor league record 868,000 fans. Buffalo, New York, built a $45 million stadium and soon attracted more than a million fans a year, outdrawing some major league clubs. Overall minor league attendance ballooned from 10 million in 1969 to 16 million ten years later and 23 million a decade after that.

But independent baseball didn't benefit from the minor league renaissance. The Gulf Coast/Lone Star League in Texas managed two fitful seasons. The Inter-American League, an unusual Triple-A independent with teams from Miami to Maracaibo, Venezuela, folded before the end of its only campaign. A few independent teams took the field in the 1980s. Miles Wolff, along with Van Schley and Marv Goldklang, owned part of the Utica Blue Sox, but the club played in one of the worst stadiums in baseball and had scant fan support. Mal Fichman steered the Rocky Mount Pines to a 24–114 Carolina League mark, earning him the sobriquet Malfunction. Harry Stavrenos recruited ex-big-leaguers with drug problems to play for the San Jose Bees. Goldklang bought the Miami Miracle, a perennially lousy club and lousy draw in the competitive Class-A Florida State League.

Only Van Schley's Salt Lake Trappers succeeded as an independent. The club set an all-time record for consecutive wins with twenty-nine, drew more fans than any Rookie-level team ever, and routinely captured the Pioneer League title. Their egos bruised, major league organizations began stocking their Pioneer League clubs with better talent to try to bring down the Trappers.

For Miles Wolff, though, the independent dream remained unfulfilled. In the mid-1970s, Wolff was halfway to Texas to take a franchise in the Lone Star League when the circuit folded. A decade later Wolff and Schley drove around Louisiana scouting cities for a possible independent league that never materialized. Throughout the boom years in Durham, as his own frustration grew, Wolff never forgot how Bob Freitas had championed independent baseball.

"From '73 on, if you had asked me the one thing I want to do in baseball it would be to run an independent team," Wolff recalled after reviving the Northern League. "I know enough about the finances of minor league baseball to know that it's a tough go to be independent. But I also know that in the right city at the right time in the right place this thing is going to work. And I want to be able to do it."

He dreamed of running one independent team someday. With the Northern League, he had six.

Van Schley *(left)* and Stephen Bishop

FOUR

I love young talent. Give me some scratchers and fighters,
give me some guys who make $15,000 who want to make
$30,000. You keep the $100,000 players. Give me the
ones who want to win.

—Leo Durocher

Minor league baseball players break down into two categories: prospects and everyone else. Prospects are the top draft choices who sign fat contracts paying six- and even seven-figure bonuses. They are investments. In the world of big business baseball, they can relax in the knowledge their major league organization will take care of them. Prospects bat in their regular spot in the lineup regardless of slumps. They throw their maximum allotted pitches every game no matter the score. They are coddled by coaches, who take extra time for instruction, and by front-office executives, who inquire after their progress.

The less heralded players, the lower draft picks and the free agents, ride the bench, wondering when or if they'll play and worrying about their performance every time they do get into a game. Even in practice they weigh each comment from a coach or manager to determine where it fits in the grand scheme of their careers. "You're just hanging on every word people are saying," said Joe Brownholtz, a crafty left-handed pitcher who was shocked when the Texas Rangers let him go in the spring of 1994 after he compiled a 20–9 record and 2.53 earned run average in three seasons at the Rookie and Class-A levels. "You're thinking, 'Hey, I did this, so where am I going to go, and who thinks that?' "

But in baseball, politics, not talent, often determines the fates of players. "Baseball is not a meritocracy when it comes to advancement in personnel," Marv Goldklang observed. "When a kid is battling to win the starting second-base position against two or three other people, that's the kind of judgment that should be made straight up. The better player wins the job." But some scouts have more influence than others, and influential ones make sure their players survive. High draft picks have an advantage because of the role played by their scouts, or because an organization puts itself on the line with a selection, or because spending big money on a player dictates that you protect a larger investment before a smaller one. "Whatever the reason or motivation," Goldklang said, "there's something that strikes you as unfair."

So when the New York Yankees' $1.55 million farmhand Brien Taylor blew out his shoulder in an off-season fistfight, the New York front office restrained its collective anger and paid for a year of physical therapy. Taylor would get his second chance. But when an undrafted, $850-a-month outfielder in the Atlanta Braves organization named Stephen Bishop batted .382 in the Pioneer League, he was cut. Second chance? Hell, Bishop thought, I didn't even get a first chance.

The Braves, naturally, viewed it otherwise. They saw in Stephen Bishop a kid who was getting old for his experience level—twenty-three finishing Rookie ball—and who tore up his knee during his first spring training. Age and injury: two negatives right there. Bishop had hit well for average, but in a limited number of at bats and with unimpressive home run power—not what the Braves had expected when they signed the tall, muscular free agent. And Bishop wasn't tailored to any single spot on the field, playing a little first base, a little outfield, even some third base.

Atlanta's farm system consisted of 200 players distributed on eight teams, one of the biggest in the majors. Bishop wasn't a prospect, and the Braves didn't have the time to make him one. "It becomes a business decision," said Rod Gilbreath, a Braves minor league player development executive. "A lot of times you'll have your twenty-five-man roster but only four prospects. So what you have often is twenty-one players who are basically there to help the four prospects develop. Sometimes in those twenty-one players you find a diamond in the rough." Bishop wasn't one of the gems.

"We're basically a young organization," Gilbreath said. "He had a little bit of age going against him, a lack of a position. When you sign an older player, you look for results right away. We're not running a YMCA. You have to make a move. You can call him a victim of numbers." Or you can call him a reject.

From his home in the Southern California beach town of Malibu, in the first months of 1994, Van Schley made call after call—twenty or more in a day—in an endless search for baseball players. As a rule Schley wants players whom the major leagues have deemed unworthy or simply overlooked. He wants the guy released by an organization after a couple of productive seasons when a judgment is made that he can't play in The Show. He wants the shortstop having a terrific college season who won't get drafted because he lacks one or two "tools" that separate him from his can't-miss peers. He searches for minor league journeymen who have given up on making it to the majors and fled to Mexico. He wants the kid who—*pssssst*—somehow slipped through the cracks.

But signing players to an independent team is like buying a used car. No matter how far you take a test drive, no matter how hard you kick the tires, no matter how reliable the mechanic who checks under the hood, it's impossible to feel secure about your purchase. Performance is the only yardstick, but performance comes after the fact—after you sign a player and give him a chance to put on the uniform and play the game. Even in major league farm systems, there are few guarantees. Independent ball takes the risks further. It is the ultimate game of chance. You pore over statistics, analyze batting practice swings, talk to coaches and managers and scouts, but ultimately the decision to sign a kid comes down to one inexact criterion: a hunch. If you have a feeling about a player, you sign him. If you like what you see in a tryout camp, you sign him. If you get a good recommendation from a reliable source, you sign him. It isn't brain surgery, Schley likes to say. It's just baseball.

Mathematics confirms how hard it is to get paid to play baseball professionally. Countless thousands of boys (and girls) play in Little League and high school. About 22,000 are skilled enough to make a National Collegiate Athletic Association team, 9,000 at Division I schools. The odds against making it increase rapidly from there. About 1,500 of the best schoolboy and college players are selected in the majors' free agent draft every June. Even then not all are hired. In 1994 the 200 minor league baseball teams in the United States and Canada employed about 4,700 players, nearly all affiliated with the majors. The big leagues provide another 700 jobs, twenty-five on each of the twenty-eight teams.

Major league organizations have but one goal: to develop major league talent. Every year they cast off players they determine don't have a chance. For players, getting cut is like a criminal conviction: always on your record. Most organizations are loath to sign someone released by another club. If Team X gave up on him, the reasoning goes, why should we take a chance? They must know something we don't. He had his shot. He failed. *Next.*

During spring training some clubs release fifty minor leaguers, others fewer than ten. It depends on the philosophy. The majors collectively spend more than $200 million a year on salaries, bonuses, and related expenses of their farm systems, and they can be pretty defensive about the investment. Some are reluctant to cut players once considered top prospects but whose skills have plateaued, because doing so might reflect badly on their drafting abilities or hurt a scout's feelings. And because the majors are looking for what Schley calls "stone-ass prospects," why replace one middling talent with another when neither has the right stuff?

But for Schley nothing is sweeter than finding a kid whom the major leagues, with their multimillion-dollar budgets and transcontinental network of scouts—not to mention their infinite wisdom—decided didn't have the skills to play professional baseball. A reject. A kid like Steve Bishop.

Stephen Charles Bishop turned twenty-three years old in September 1993. He stood six feet four inches tall and weighed 205 pounds.

Bishop's slim, strong frame first screamed *athlete* and then, upon closer inspection, *baseball player*. Everyone said Bishop looked like another Braves star, David Justice; his friends even called him Baby Justice. Bishop thought he had a good work ethic, took instruction well, and was eager to improve. After the Braves called on January 8, 1994, to tell him he was released, however, the reality was much simpler: Stephen Bishop was jobless.

Adversity was nothing new to Bishop. Sure, he had been a Little League star growing up in the affluent San Francisco suburb of Moraga, but that wasn't unusual for a kid who was bigger than his peers and showed athletic promise in football as well as baseball. He batted over .350 as a freshman and sophomore at tiny Campolindo High School but didn't make the varsity. Bishop never learned why, but he wondered whether it was because he was one of the only blacks at the nearly all-white school. As a senior he received the Mr. Clutch award, but no collegiate interest. Still growing into his body, he began playing well in the fall of his second year at a junior college. Major schools called. Oklahoma. Arizona. Tennessee. Nebraska. Arkansas. It was heady. And fleeting. When Bishop batted only .255 in the spring, the recruiters vanished. He accepted a scholarship to the University of California at Riverside.

Bishop took it as a slight and took out his frustrations on the baseball. In his first season at Riverside, he led the team in hitting and was named first-team all-conference and all-region. But he wasn't drafted that June. In a summer college league in Ohio that used wooden bats—unlike the aluminum sticks that help inflate college batting statistics—Bishop hit .342. Finally, an organization noticed. He worked out for the Braves, who offered him a contract with a bonus of about $3,000. But Bishop knew that many players who turn pro after their junior year never finish college. The Braves refused to give him enough money to complete his degree, saying that was a perk reserved for draft choices. So it was back to Riverside, where Bishop again led the club in batting, including a .440 average against nonconference opponents, mostly Division I schools, which Bishop took as a point of pride. Baby Justice reeled off a twenty-two-game hitting streak wearing batting gloves given to him by his look-alike idol, whom he tracked down at Candlestick Park in San Francisco.

Bishop's performance improved as the chip on his shoulder grew. In a regional tournament he had six hits in eleven at bats, drove in five runs, stole two bases, and scored five times—the same numbers as the tournament MVP. When the announcer read off the statistics of the winner, Bishop stood up in the dugout. Hearing the name of an opposing player, he quickly detoured to the water cooler.

A major league scout told Bishop not to worry. But after the previous season Bishop had learned to be wary, and he was right: Again, the phone didn't ring. Then the Braves called expressing interest. Each day in the summer of 1992, Bishop checked for a message. Finally, in the middle of September—after the minor league season had ended—the Braves offered a contract. Bishop signed, dreaming of playing alongside his idol, David Justice, and his friend Tony Tarasco, one of the club's top prospects, who was living with Bishop in Atlanta.

"I want to be one of the guys," he said, "who when they come to the plate, the crowd goes '*AAAAAAAAHHHHHHHHH.*' "

Shielded from the rain by the dugout roof, Van Schley leafed through a stack of player registration forms. It was shortly after nine on a chilly February morning in 1994 in Melbourne, Florida, on a practice field at the spring training home of the Florida Marlins. Schley was looking for some rejects.

As an independent baseball operator, Schley would be persona non grata at most spring training sites. Outsiders like him are regarded with suspicion usually accorded door-to-door salesmen, and Schley's Salt Lake Trappers had shown up the major leagues' purportedly infallible talent machine. But Schley has friends in the big leagues, many of them with the Marlins. He's stopped banging his head against the wall trying to deal with uncooperative major league executives. When he finds a legitimate prospect—in eight years Schley sent more than sixty Trappers into organizations, including major league pitcher Tom Candiotti—he tries to push the player into the hands of his favored major league contacts, often Gary Hughes, now the Marlins' scouting director.

Take Tim Clark. Schley signed the former eighth-round Milwaukee Brewers draft choice when he was released after two not-unrespectable seasons. In Salt Lake, Clark flourished, leading the Pioneer League with a .357 average. Schley could have started a bidding war for Clark's services, but instead he called Hughes. The following season, at Class-A High Desert of the California League, Clark led the minor leagues with a .363 average, 185 hits, and 126 runs batted in, and was invited to the Marlins' major league camp. It was a symbiotic relationship. Schley knew Clark would get a fair shake with the Marlins; Hughes knew Schley wouldn't peddle him a stiff. So when the Marlins held an open tryout camp, Schley was welcome.

Flipping through the player bios, Schley had a system. Players lacking college experience were out. He wrote down the names of those previously released by major league organizations, as well as undrafted college graduates. He cross-referenced them in the *1994 Baseball America Almanac*, which detailed top minor league and big college performers. He also checked the *1993 Minor League Digest*, which contained the previous year's statistics of every minor leaguer.

Schley looked up Michael Collins: a five-foot-eight, 150-pound second baseman who batted .172 in nineteen games with Billings of the Pioneer League in 1992. "A guy like that almost has no chance," he said.

Schley wanted players not good enough for the Marlins, because their chances of advancing to the majors were slim, but talented enough to play in the Northern League, which had an eclectic mix of playing skills.

In a small tablet of lined yellow paper, Schley noted the vital signs of his potentials, beginning with the number assigned by the Marlins for the tryout.

777 HENRY BURROUGH (MIN) DOB 71
    NO-HIT APPY—92

Burrough, born in 1971, played in the Minnesota Twins organization but didn't hit well in the Rookie-level Appalachian League in 1992, making him less than desirable.

778 MIKE LITTLE (CUBS) DOB 71 LS-4

The "LS" stands for limited service, baseball jargon for the level of a player's experience. The 4 represents the number of years completed.

To qualify for a year of service, a player has to accumulate either seventy-five at bats or thirty innings pitched. Baseball people can be heard saying about a player, "He's an LS-1. Worth taking a look at," or "LS-4. He had his chance."

102 R CLINTON BROWN 69 HOU
107 R MORRILL BUTTE—BAD STATS
108 R TODD RIZZO—FREE AGENT LA
109 L RESPONDEK MON

Schley circled the L—left-handed pitchers are always in demand— and placed a star next to the name. Mark Respondek had pitched admirably before in the Montreal Expos organization. He also was an Australian who flew in for spring training. That merited some attention for the effort (and expense) alone.

710 BISHOP—1B-OF
735 WILLIE ROMAY 7/5/70
217 BRAD DANDRIDGE—SD OF

Schley had invited Stephen Bishop to the camp. Bishop had played for the Idaho Falls Braves in the Pioneer League, Schley's old territory, and he was recommended by a friend and former Salt Lake Trappers manager now with the San Diego Padres organization, who met Bishop auditioning for bit parts in a baseball commercial. Strapped for cash, Bishop had flown in from his mother's house in Atlanta. That merited some brownie points. "He's a definite maybe. At this stage definite maybe is the highest you can go. I'd say his chances are between 20 percent and 60 percent," Schley said. Romay merited a star. A fifth-round draft choice of the Seattle Mariners, Romay had signed "too young," Schley said, playing two years in the Seattle and Los Angeles organizations before getting released. Tall and lean at age twenty-three, he sported trendy long sideburns and angular good looks.

After running, fielding, and throwing drills, the 170 players who had appeared at the tryout were unceremoniously cut to a couple of dozen who performed in a scrimmage. After that the Marlins decided to sign two players: a pitcher and Willie Romay. Schley wasn't surprised. Romay was a no-lose proposition. If he made the organization's new Double-A team in Portland, Maine, Florida had landed a prospect for free. They didn't have to sacrifice someone in a trade. They didn't have to pay a bonus or a fee to select him from another organization in the annual Rule 5 draft of minor leaguers.

While the speedy outfielder would have been well matched for the Northern League's talent level, he also had a bit too much minor league experience to be attractive. To prevent teams from stocking up on veterans and to promote balance, Miles Wolff had established strict roster requirements. Six of each team's twenty-two players had to be rookies—which meant no prior experience in a National Association league, or fewer than seventy-five at bats for position players or thirty innings pitched in a season. Four veterans, who had five or more years of professional experience, were allowed. Clubs could sign two LS-4s but then had to sign an equal number of LS-1s. Rosters were filled out with LS-2s and LS-3s, up to eight of each. Because there was an abundance of quality older players, it was important to be careful about whom you signed. To prevent clubs from hoarding and then discarding personnel, players who were signed before the season had to stay on the active roster at least two weeks after Opening Day.

Northern League teams also were limited in what they could spend on players. Wolff established a salary cap of $72,000 per team—for the entire season. That worked out to about $1,000 a month per player. A few top players earned as much as $2,500 monthly, and rookies were paid a rock-bottom wage of $700.

Putting together a Northern League roster was a balancing act. Rookies were Van Schley's specialty, and that was why he was attracted to Stephen Bishop: With just sixty-eight at bats in Idaho Falls, he qualified as a rookie. Bishop, however, didn't necessarily want to play in the Northern League. For the moment he was upset the Marlins hadn't signed him.

After the tryout Gary Hughes encouraged Bishop to keep playing, to sign with the Northern League. "You've got some ability, and it'd be crazy not to pursue what you're doing," the veteran scout said. "You've got to get someplace where you can play. Here, if anything, you'd be like a fifth outfielder on one of our clubs. It's just the way it is right now. Everybody's got a lot of outfielders. That's why you're here now, because you just ran out of opportunities. I'd urge you to figure out some way to stay alive at this thing. Hey, at the end of the summer, we may add another team and we may be looking for a guy. We stay closely in touch with what they're doing. That's all I can tell you. OK? Good luck to you."

Bishop shook his head. Baseball was one raw deal after another. The Braves had released him so late it was difficult to hook on with another organization, despite a recommendation from Willie Stargell, the Hall of Fame first baseman, who had tutored Bishop the previous summer.

"I can't explain why they released me. I have no idea," Bishop said. "They say it's a numbers game. Obviously, a lot of it has to do with something other than playing ability, because you saw the guy they're about to sign out of here. I mean he didn't really do anything today. But they knew his name. I didn't have a chance to sign with anybody. I don't know what I can do about that now. I have some pretty influential people behind me. [Stargell] didn't understand why I got released, but he said he was going to help me do what I had to do to sign. It's frustrating.

"I just need a chance to play a season to put up some numbers. I just want to play every day and show that I can hit and I can play the field, that I deserve to be playing baseball for a living. I've been playing this game since I was four years old. I don't want to stop now."

Bishop was the perfect Northern League candidate. He was angry over his release. He was frustrated by his rejection by the Marlins. He couldn't afford more airplane tickets and motel rooms and rental cars to attend spring training camps. He had something to prove.

Van Schley liked what he saw. One week after the tryout he mailed a contract to Stephen Bishop.

The Northern League owners and managers had found one another not because they had fantasized innocently about a baseball life, or because they needed a job, or because it looked like an easy path to riches. They were like-minded baseball visionaries who understood what the modern game lacks, organizationally as well as spiritually. In 1993 they had proven to the baseball world that there is a place for a serious, top-flight independent league. In 1994 they wanted to stake a claim to permanence. But there were more temporal goals as well. The six Northern League teams wanted to win the championship. They each had a style.

At the ballpark the owner of the Sioux Falls Canaries wore high-top basketball sneakers, hooded sweatshirts, and John Lennon sunglasses, parking himself in a corner of the grandstands with his Walkman tuned to the game on the field. Harry Stavrenos looked like a kid hanging out in the schoolyard, a gym rat looking for a pickup game. But he is a veteran baseball man, and an independent one at that. In assembling a team he relied more than others in the Northern League on major league sources—particularly the San Francisco Giants, parent of his team in San Jose—but he knew how to evaluate talent. He also liked signing veterans. Pedro Guerrero, the onetime World Series MVP for the St. Louis Cardinals, and Carl Nichols, a backup catcher for Baltimore and Houston, played for the Canaries. Stavrenos thought ex-big-leaguers helped the Northern League, and there were plenty to be had. *"Frank Tanana,"* Stavrenos leaned over to whisper one day, as if leaking inside information. *"Steve Balboni."*

Sioux City's owner, Bill Pereira, was still learning about player personnel; he had been in baseball only since the late 1980s, when he bought and turned around a team in Boise, Idaho. For field expertise Pereira relied on his manager, Ed Nottle, a thirty-five-year minor league veteran and piano bar crooner. Pereira grew up in California during the heyday of the defiantly independent Pacific Coast League, which retained major league–caliber players year after year. It wasn't surprising he believed every Northern League team should have at least one name star—the Explorers signed Oil Can Boyd for 1994—and favored retaining players from one year to the next to cultivate relationships with their adopted town. It could help a player's post-baseball career—a Sioux City outfielder worked in a car dealership in the off-season—and the name recognition didn't hurt ticket sales.

The owners of the two Canadian clubs—concert promoter Sam Katz in Winnipeg and sporting goods retailer Ricky May in Thunder Bay—relied exclusively on their managers. Doug Simunic, an ex-Triple-A catcher with an overhanging gut, had led the Rochester Aces to the Northern League playoffs in 1993. He was an inveterate complainer with a combative attitude, but he knew how to manage a baseball team. With the help of personal contacts, he would assemble a good club in Winnipeg. Amiable and soft-spoken, Dan Shwam was back for a second year in Thunder Bay. A high school teacher and coach in Utah, Shwam came to the Northern League via Salt Lake, where he coached first base for Van Schley's Trappers. The Whiskey Jacks were his team to create.

Duluth was the question mark for 1994. After the first season owner Bruce Engel had sold the club to start his own independent circuit in California. The buyer was a St. Paul Saints season-ticket holder named Ted Cushmore. An articulate and intelligent top General Mills executive who had longed for baseball since his college playing days, Cushmore wasn't involved to turn a fast buck—a last-place franchise in a year-old independent league is hardly a can't-miss proposition. To handle the baseball end, he replaced Mal Fichman with Howie Bedell, a former major league player, coach, and farm system director. But independent baseball is a different species from the majors. Bedell hadn't seen any Northern League games in 1993 and didn't know the talent level. Around the league there was some anxiety about his ability to adapt to independent baseball.

Marv Goldklang of St. Paul was a hands-on owner. He studied player lists, attended tryout camps, conferred with his colleagues and manager, and ultimately decided whom to sign. Upon arriving at a Northern League spring tryout camp in Fort Myers, Florida, Goldklang made it his first piece of business to unfold a sheet of yellow legal paper from his back pocket—on it were the names of potential players to discuss with co-owners Van Schley, whose card described him as director of player procurement, and Mike Veeck, who ran the Saints on a daily basis, as well as manager Tim Blackwell, a former catcher for the Red Sox and Cubs who had managed in the Mets organization before getting fired.

The Saints' four majority partners—Goldklang, Schley, Veeck, and Bill Murray—each owned 23 percent, but Goldklang was chairman of the board. While Schley scouted most of the players, Goldklang also savored locating, signing, nurturing, and selling the young athletes, and then following the team's fortunes with religious devotion. During the season Goldklang listened to radio broadcasts via telephone.

When he had owned the independent Miami Miracle, his manager would call to replay that night's game—never mind that it was one o'clock in the morning and Goldklang's wife was asleep beside him. The players were his kids, and he cared about the final score in a way he never had with the farm teams he'd owned over the years.

"It's real," Goldklang said, "and winning and losing helps make it real. The game is baseball. The game isn't selling popcorn and soda. When you're involved in putting together the team and making significant decisions relating to the team, you're involved in baseball."

In the Northern League winning is everything. Nobody cares about "developing" talent in the major league sense—keeping only players with the potential to make The Show someday—though everyone wants the best to get a chance with an organization. By the first week of April in 1994, when big-league organizations were cutting down their minor league rosters, St. Paul's began filling up.

Three pitchers were quickly signed—all LS-3s, all sight unseen—from a list of released players sent to the six teams by Nick Belmonte, the league's one-man central scouting bureau, a job Schley had held in 1993. By spring Belmonte's list included more than 400 names. The league held a series of tryout camps around the country, including two in Florida. Schley attended them all, as well as college tournaments, always toting around statistical biographies of released players faxed from an outfit called Howe SportsData at a cost of $5 apiece. Goldklang took in a few tryouts, too. Both men chased leads on promising players. Schley handled younger talent, which he believed is hungrier than veteran minor leaguers. Goldklang dealt with older players and their agents.

Schley opposed re-signing players for a second season, figuring they would lose the drive to play well and return to an organization, and he liked shuffling in new players to strike a little fear in the clubhouse. That's baseball's "tight asshole" theory, holding that when an owner patrols the ballpark the players should be nervous. Goldklang felt that approach works fine with rookies just out of college, who will play hard out of fear for their futures, but that older players need to be treated with more respect. The differences set the stage for conflict in the summer of 1994.

Some minor league players leaped at the offer to join the Saints. Any baseball was better than no baseball. Others, like Vince Castaldo, were more cautious. During dinner one night in Miami, Goldklang disappeared to make a phone call. On the other end was Castaldo, a tough-as-nails third baseman who had been released in spring training by the Expos. At Triple-A in 1993 Castaldo had batted a career-low .241 in just seventy-seven games before quitting in frustration late in the season. He was a competitor: quiet and pensive, angry that his career had been derailed. He was suspicious of the talent level in an independent league, but he craved redemption. After speaking with Goldklang, two weeks passed before he signed with St. Paul.

Leon Durham was returning for a second year in St. Paul, adding coach to his player duties in preparation for his next baseball career. None of the other Saints had big-league experience. The middle infield had played for the team in 1993, returning over Schley's objections. The outfield would include two players with Double-A experience. Castaldo was a bona fide Triple-A player. The rest of the club? Rookies and Class-A rejects.

With no veterans the pitching staff was the youngest in the league. Its only LS-4 hadn't pitched since 1992, although he had reached Triple-A. The potential second starter also had missed a year. The projected closer was a former twelfth-round pick who had pitched just four games in 1993 after returning from elbow surgery.

They were question marks, but independent baseball is filled with them. After all, if they were stone-ass prospects, they wouldn't be there. Analyzing his pitching staff with lawyerly thoroughness, Goldklang thought it represented the best available talent—meaning it had potential, some demonstrated previously, some waiting to be unleashed.

"Last year the major weakness of the league was pitching, which is one of the reasons I decided to take a little different approach," he said. "The talent just wasn't there—you had junkers, guys who had below-average everything. You just hoped they went out there and threw strikes with sufficient consistency so it gave you an opportunity to stay in the ball game.

"This time we went for pitchers who would impress major league player development–type people, who are looking at prospects. I just hope the kids step up and are able. I think we have the potential to have four quality starters and a quality reliever. But I can't say that with any confidence, because they haven't pitched effectively at anything above the A-ball level. Every other team will have more experienced pitchers than we have. No question about it."

Stephen Bishop ran out of options. He scraped together the money to return to Florida for tryouts with the St. Louis Cardinals and Baltimore Orioles, to no avail. A friend paid his way to Arizona, where the Chicago Cubs said Bishop might be welcome at extended spring training—a repository for injury rehabs and potential filler players. That could be a wasted season, and at his age Bishop couldn't afford a year without competition. The Milwaukee Brewers gave him a private audition: ten swings, ten grounders, glad you could make it.

Even St. Paul's contract offer had a catch: If he didn't make the team Bishop would play for the Ogden Raptors of the Pioneer League, an independent club to which Van Schley had arranged to send a few players. Even in an indy league, Bishop thought, I can't catch a break. Playing for an independent was bad enough, but a *farm team* of an independent? "I'm going to have to go out there and bust my ass," Bishop said. "Which is cool. I need to sign on with another [major league organization] team. Adversity is nothing new to me. I actually thrive on it. If I didn't have it, I might not do as well. I might take things for granted.

"I really want to play in St. Paul. You play in front of a lot of people. I don't want to go back to the Pioneer League. I need to be challenged. I don't think it would do me any good to go back. I could see if I had struggled and I needed to establish myself, I would go back. But I didn't. I want to move up and see if I can play at the next level. I want to be in an atmosphere where it's exciting, where people support the team, where there's community involvement."

Bishop had questions about the team, the city, the fans, even the uniforms—he wanted to know what colors the Saints wore. He was itching to play baseball. He was setting goals, first to make the team, then to win a starting job, help the Saints win another championship, and—he was a little embarrassed even to say it—receive player of the year honors. "My plan," he said, "is to go up there and do some damage."

Bishop arrived in St. Paul for preseason workouts, young, handsome, and hip. He packed his assortment of chic baseball caps that he often wore turned backwards—a new all-navy St. Louis Cardinals model, a white one with a black brim from the minor league Greensboro Bats—and wore a gold hoop in each ear. To avoid a trip to Ogden, he needed to make the team.

In the ritual ten- and twelve-inning intrasquad games that determined the final roster spots and helped the Saints get into playing condition, Bishop was pleased with his performance. Like most baseball players he could quickly rehash every at bat, playing up the successes and glossing over the bad days.

Bishop *thought* he was playing well, but how could he be sure? He was staying late after practice to field bucket after bucket of ground balls at third base as a potential backup for Castaldo. He carried a baseball in his hip pocket to throw against a wall at Municipal Stadium, drumming in the mechanics of fielding and throwing until they became second nature. Bishop did it partly because he was willing to work hard but also because he wanted to make a good impression. He wasn't intimidated by the more experienced players, and he didn't let their better skills make him doubt his own.

Other players told Bishop he didn't have anything to worry about. But manager Tim Blackwell wasn't offering any clues. "Steve is marginal," Goldklang said a couple of days before final cuts. "He has probably not played well enough to make the team, but because of the fact that he's a rookie and appears to have greater potential than some of the others, right now it appears he will make the team."

He didn't have a single position. He didn't hit for much power. He wasn't quick out of the batter's box after hitting the ball. But he knew enough to wait for a pitch he could hit, a discipline many young players lack. The question was this: Which was better for Bishop—playing every day in Ogden or staying in St. Paul and getting instruction? Manager Tim Blackwell never had a doubt. He knew Bishop should stay with the Saints from the moment he laid eyes on him.

"I said, 'Look at this! He's a statue! What is he doing? Why did they release him?' And then just watching his actions and stuff, I said, 'This is just a young kid that for whatever reason they just didn't give a chance.' This guy looked a long way from just catching up to his body. He's got a long way to go. I just wonder why they would give up so quickly on a kid that's got a body like that and shows that kind of potential, just physical strength. He can generate some bat speed. I just see raw, raw physical ability."

Miles Wolff had structured the Northern League to give rookies a chance. But if they sat on the bench and didn't receive the sort of instruction they would in, say, the South Atlantic League, where organizations send *potential* prospects, was it counterproductive? It was a question kids like Steve Bishop would help answer.

Blackwell saw a project, an eager young player with a good attitude, good build, and good looks who was determined to improve. Blackwell had just the mentor: Leon Durham. "I think a league like this can do something. If we can just get him enough at bats, I just think he's going to be a kid who can respond and improve right away," Blackwell said. "I saw him and said, 'He's going to have to play his way off the team.' And then I said to Bull, 'He's yours.' "

So while Goldklang worried about what Bishop the untested rookie without a position could contribute to the team, and Bishop suffered the psychological torture of not knowing his fate, the on-field directors were of one mind. At the end of spring training, when final cuts were to be made, Blackwell and his two coaches, Durham and Rob Swain, drew up their individual rosters. Bishop was on all three.

So happy about making the Saints, Bishop momentarily stopped obsessing about how baseball was unfair because he wasn't in a major league organization. He had a job. Life was suddenly simpler. Now he wanted to win a starting job and a championship ring—the first of five, he imagined, one at every level of baseball. "I called my mom and told her," he said. "She's treating it like I made The Show. I've got to treat every season like that. Step one of the mission has been completed."

Nick Belmonte *(left)* and Marv Goldklang

FIVE

St. Paul! Are you crazy? St. Paul is a graveyard!

—Cincinnati owner John T. Brush
to Charles Comiskey, 1894

On a sunny afternoon one day before the start of the season, the 1994 St. Paul Saints gathered for a final practice at Municipal Stadium. Artists busily finished painting outfield fence signs while construction workers installed rows of benches in two new grandstand sections. The players were feeling one another out, but by all appearances they were a loose bunch.

Leon Durham, the veteran player-coach, challenged center fielder Darius Gash, a onetime Padres prospect who had been cut after playing at Double-A in 1993, to a batting-practice hitting contest. Durham went four for four. Gash went oh for four. "Get outta there!" Durham yelled as Gash whiffed at the last pitch. Loose.

Then there was Vince Castaldo, the intense Triple-A third baseman, who treated every b.p. swing as if it were the bottom of the ninth with the winning run dancing off third. After five unsatisfying swings, he whacked his bat against the backstop. A few minutes later, after four more, he barked at Durham, "That's not enough cuts, man."

"Then get a machine," Durham said. "We're not a fucking machine." After Castaldo walked away Durham continued. "Shit, that boy's bitching about everything. Not enough swings. Shit, get a tee."

Tim Blackwell gathered the players in a circle along the third-base line to go over the signals. There were four: take, bunt, hit and run, and steal. When Blackwell covered his walrus mustache with his hand, the next sign was operative. Touching the right side of his chest meant steal, the left side hit and run. The right thigh was the sign to take a pitch, the left to bunt. Of course, the players would forget them constantly.

"If I'm messin' with my mustache, you've got the green light," Blackwell said. "Squeeze, I'll take off my hat and scratch my head when I'm talking to the guy. You guys all have the green light until I decide you can't steal."

Blackwell is a quiet motivator who doesn't offer Knute Rockne locker-room speeches. He had been let go by the Mets organization despite winning three minor league titles in four years, and some wondered whether it was because he isn't a strict disciplinarian. But Blackwell isn't a player's buddy either and doesn't tolerate nonsense. He is a devoted Christian involved in baseball prayer groups whose wife, four children, and dog followed him to St. Paul for the summer. But he doesn't proselytize, on matters religious or otherwise. That day his only requests were that his players be aggressive on the bases and not throw their helmets. He left the rah-rah stuff to Durham.

"We start tomorrow," Bull told his teammates. "Ain't no pressure on nobody. If you don't get any hits, don't worry about it. Do something defensively. At least try to do something to try to help the team win. It's going to take us all to go out and win the championship again. If you make an error, we know you didn't mean to do it. We're all going in this together. It's a great game. I'm thirty-seven, and I'm still out here having fun, learning something. Let's all stay together, back each other up. Let's stay together throughout the whole summer. On the field, off the field. Let's have some fun."

Blackwell closed out the meeting. "Six A.M. The bus is leaving. Be on it or be under it."

Vince Castaldo stuck around for extra batting practice.

The response to the St. Paul Saints in 1993 had been as unexpected as it had been intoxicating. The challenge in the second season was not to be lulled into security because of the success of the first. Mike Veeck already had given that speech to his staff. Although there were more seats in the stadium and more signs on the outfield walls—including one for a local bagel shop in which the tops of three cutout bagels poked above the fence and were in play—there had to be more substance. People would be looking for flaws, ready to say the Saints' first season was a fluke. But the club certainly had made an impact—even on the big-league Twins, who were offering a "season ticket" package for $175, which coincidentally was the price of a 1993 season ticket to Municipal Stadium.

"I told everybody, last year was special, magical. We're not even going to build on last year, that's how dangerous last year is—even as a philosophy or an intangible," Veeck said one early summer afternoon. "I want this year to be different, I want it to be tangibly different. I want there to be increased services. I don't want anybody to have any ideas that what happened last year can happen again. In short, stay humble."

The Saints president had learned about humility and much else from his late father, Bill, the populist owner of the Cleveland Indians, St. Louis Browns, and Chicago White Sox who delighted in ripping the stuffing out of the shirts of the high and mighty who ran major league baseball. Whether it was sending the midget Eddie Gaedel up to bat or sticking S & H green stamps under stadium seats, Veeck's promotions rankled baseball's millionaire barons.

Bill Veeck believed the game should be fun for all patrons, not just baseball lovers. So he gave away flowers on Ladies Day (a tradition begun by Mike Veeck's straitlaced grandfather, William, who ran the Chicago Cubs), devised scoreboards that erupted with home-run fireworks, let a group of St. Louis Browns fans call the plays on Grandstand Managers Day, and offered special nights for every ethnic group imaginable. He installed full-length mirrors in women's rest rooms and nurseries for children. He wanted to integrate baseball before Branch Rickey signed Jackie Robinson but was stopped by the American League. During games Veeck roamed the park talking with fans. Afterward he held court at local bars with reporters.

"He would go through the stands, and people would just fall over for the right for him to sit down for an inning," Mike Veeck said. "He talked about the game, he talked about what they did, he talked about what they liked about what he did and what he was doing wrong. He was, in short, everyman. He was a blue-collar, beer-drinking guy who loved to laugh and who hated authority. He couldn't resist tweaking their nose."

When the economics of the game intruded on his fun, Veeck fought back. Always a clever financier, he cobbled together enough money to buy the White Sox in 1975. The only problem was that player salaries were exploding like one of Comiskey Park's scoreboards. With his son Mike devising gimmicks, Veeck in 1977 combated free agency with his "rent-a-player" strategy—acquire players with one season left before free agency and then let them go. It worked, for one year anyway. By 1980 the White Sox were in deep financial trouble, and Bill Veeck's health was failing as well. He hated the thought of caving in to the barons, but Veeck had no choice but to sell. One of the new owners, Eddie Einhorn, quickly, and cruelly, promised to "bring some class" to the South Side of Chicago. Bill Veeck never again set foot in Comiskey Park.

"Dad could not be buried. We had to cremate him," Mike Veeck said. "Because if we buried him, every time those bums made a bad move he'd've rolled over, and he wouldn't have had a moment's rest."

Mike Veeck only belatedly followed his father into baseball. In the early 1970s, Veeck *fils* had mostly drunk beer and played guitar, in a rock band called Chattanooga Glass. Over a drink one night that lasted hours, Bill Veeck suggested that his son come to Chicago and work for the White Sox. While Mike's ideas generally were credited to Dad—such as fan picnic areas and luxury boxes—he took the heat for Disco Demolition Night. Fans bearing a disco record were admitted for a dollar; between games of a doubleheader, the White Sox blew up the stack of LPs with dynamite. A near-riot ensued. Chicago forfeited the second game. The barons wagged their collective finger yet again at those lowbrow, trouble-making Veecks.

Baseball would exact its revenge. After his father sold the club, Mike Veeck didn't get a single job offer in baseball. Veeck maintains he was blacklisted. He went to Florida, hung drywall, worked in a jai alai fronton, and joined an advertising agency, eventually forming his own. Baseball—where Veeck still desperately wanted to be—didn't seem a possibility again until a minor league owner named Marv Goldklang called in the fall of 1989.

"I think there ought to be a Veeck in baseball," Goldklang said.

"You ought to get another line," Veeck replied.

Two months later Veeck was sitting in a trailer crawling with palmetto bugs, operating one of the worst teams in professional baseball, the Miami Miracle. If history repeats, then Veeck was re-living his father's beginnings, though at a later age. Miami was Mike Veeck's Milwaukee, the independent team where his father's baseball career began. It was a testing ground for ideas. Jericho the Miracle Dog delivered baseballs to the umpire. A blind man broad-cast the games on radio. The Phantom of the Ball Yard handed out roses to female patrons. On Field of Screams Night, fans lounged on water beds while watching horror movies on a screen in center field after the game. Another evening they stayed for a séance.

When Goldklang was invited to join the Northern League, Veeck wanted in badly—but as an owner. He borrowed money for a piece of St. Paul. When he first saw the ballpark in November 1992, trains clacked by, the state fairgrounds dominated the back-drop. The neighborhood was industrial and the stadium utilitarian, but any improvements would be praised. To get a feeling for the city, he walked from downtown to the ballpark, eight miles in all. The atmosphere appealed to Veeck. Plus, Charles Comiskey had moved his St. Paul team to Chicago in 1900 to form the White Sox, and Veeck's father always had liked St. Paul.

Like his father, Veeck is a relentless promoter willing to speak to groups ranging in size from two to two thousand. Like his father, he stresses the notion that baseball is more than runs, hits, and errors. Veeck believes you can achieve fun at any level of the game—independent, affiliated minors, or majors—but not if you take yourself and the business too seriously. Why isn't there room in the major leagues for levity? Like his father, Veeck can't understand. Not that he's complaining. The Saints were the perfect antidote to the mayonnaise-on-white-bread Twins, who play in a giant indoor tennis bubble.

The Saints had nothing to lose by creating a "rivalry." The Twins, on the other hand, would have done just as well to have ignored the St. Paul club. Instead, they took the bait. Before the 1993 season had begun, Andy MacPhail, the Twins' general manager, who like Veeck is a baseball scion, deemed the Northern League a bush league.

"I suppose you could consider it professional baseball in that they're paying players," MacPhail said. If that wasn't enough to get the city of St. Paul behind the new club, he said, "It is a deception to suggest these kids are pursuing a dream of major league baseball." MacPhail went on to encourage fans to take in a University of Minnesota baseball game, implying the quality would be better. Later in the season, as the Saints were selling out game after game—compiling one of the top attendance rates per capacity in all of professional baseball—MacPhail declined a challenge for a charity game between St. Paul and the Twins' Triple-A club. "It wasn't practical," he said.

Practical is anathema to Mike Veeck. The goofier the gimmick the better. Hence Saint the Pig. Hence Irish Night, in which the Saints wore green caps and ran around green bases. Kitchen Appliance Night. Man on the Moon Night. Mary Tyler Moore Appreciation Night. They brought fans to the ballpark and gave the ballpark over to fans. The experience in St. Paul was participatory, from the grandstand barber—a gimmick begun by Bill Veeck in Comiskey Park—to the barrage of witty commentary from Brooklyn-born public address announcer Al Frechtman and his wittingly hip musical tastes. (The team's unlikely rally song was the Sammy Davis, Jr., rendition of Isaac Hayes's achingly dated theme from the movie *Shaft*.)

Veeck helped create an atmosphere that teetered on the edge of anarchy—but was always purposeful. The scene could appear spontaneous, but in fact much was carefully organized, on time schedules prepared before each game. St. Paul proved receptive to the lunacy—some of which had flopped in Fort Myers—because the fans usually got the jokes. But it took effort, a fact other Northern League teams recognized grudgingly if at all when discussing the league's moneybags, prima-donna, Hollywood-connected, flagship franchise. To outsiders commenting after the first season, St. Paul's success seemed natural. A huge market, good stadium, wealthy owners, knowledgeable fans. One general manager of a team drawing under 3,000 fans bragged how he didn't use scripts, like St. Paul. An opposing field manager wanted to win to show the "know-it-alls" in the big city.

You could believe Mike Veeck or not—and that was the conundrum with the admitted showman, a champion of the underdog dressed in overdog's clothing. He swore that St. Paul wasn't an automatic moneymaker but the league's most difficult sales job. Receptive, maybe, but not if you didn't hustle. Hustling was how Bill Veeck had assembled financial deals that perplexed and angered the rest of the baseball fraternity, and it was how Mike Veeck made baseball fun again in the home of the Twins. "Nobody was standing in line to take the St. Paul franchise, seven miles from the Metrodome," Veeck said. "They may say now, oh, it's a cakewalk. But they didn't want any part of operating seven miles down, and I was frightened, too."

To understand St. Paul it is important to understand what motivates many of its resident fans: a distaste for Minneapolis. From the time of its earliest settlers—who included a French-Canadian named Pierre "Pig's Eye" Parrant, so nicknamed for a crooked, marble-hued blind eye that made him look, well, piggish—St. Paul has had a pioneering spirit that initially attracted more migrants than Minneapolis. The rivalry was almost immediate. The Great Census War of 1890 broke out when Minneapolis's population exceeded St. Paul's for the first time. St. Paul cried fraud. "It Means War!" the *Minneapolis Journal* thundered back. Fittingly, a federal probe revealed that *both* cities had inflated their numbers.

St. Paul was the tough town, a home for railroad yards and Prohibition thugs. The famed gangs of John Dillinger and Kate "Ma" Barker sought refuge there. At the same time St. Paul was the capital, a province of arts and letters, where F. Scott Fitzgerald danced down stately Summit Avenue after a publisher accepted his first novel, *This Side of Paradise*.

With tall buildings that literally look down on its more understated sister across the river, Minneapolis became the well-heeled business center. Out-of-towners would say they were going to Minneapolis, even if they meant St. Paul. They may be called the Twin Cities, but they aren't twins at all. Minneapolis is the straight-A older sister; St. Paul labors in her shadow and feels silly for trying.

Baseball was the perfect outlet for the rivalry. So great was fan interest in the first match between amateur clubs from the towns in 1867 that there weren't enough buses or livery teams to transport everyone to the park. After the game, won by St. Paul, 47–29, the sides gave each other three cheers and repaired to a hotel for a sumptuous dinner. But the clubs didn't remain cordial for long. Just a few years later, in an early professional league, the Minneapolis team boasted having "real ballplayers," compared with the local talent on the St. Paul club, which was known as the Apostles and then, maintaining the religious theme, the Saints.

In 1894 Charles Comiskey bought the Sioux City club of the renegade Western Association and moved it to St. Paul. Before the season opener the Saints paraded through town in an open streetcar led by a brass band. More than 3,000 fans turned out. The Twin City Mandolin Club performed before the game, shades of a Veeckian promotion. Comiskey's win-at-all-costs tactics rankled the Minneapolitan gentility. The *Minneapolis Tribune* even whined that its team wouldn't play unless Comiskey promised that the Saints would refrain from spiking the Minneapolis players and throwing dust and dirt into their eyes.

As members of the American Association, the Saints would face the Minneapolis Millers for nearly sixty years. St. Paul played in cigar box–shaped Lexington Park—361 feet to right field, 472 feet to dead center, and 315 feet to the left-field wall, which it shared with a dance hall. Minneapolis had cozy Nicollet Park, just 279 feet to the right-field wall, over which Joe Hauser deposited sixty-nine home runs one season. The teams would play spirited holiday doubleheaders, a morning game in one city, an afternoon contest across the river; fans waited at either end of the Lake Street Bridge and booed the rivals when they crossed city limits. Even the clubs' major league affiliations heightened the rivalry—the Saints became the Brooklyn Dodgers' top farm team, while the Millers belonged to the New York Giants.

The demise of minor league baseball in St. Paul only fed the city's inferiority complex. After the Saints abandoned Lexington Park, the city built 15,000-seat Midway Stadium, designed to expand to major league proportions. But the Millers built a colossus—Metropolitan Stadium. When Calvin Griffith decided to move his Washington Senators to Minnesota in 1960, the delegation that received the news at an American League owners meeting in New York didn't include a single representative from St. Paul. Complaints abounded that St. Paul had gotten the shaft. A *Pioneer Press* columnist wrote that the two cities had buried the hatchet and worked as partners to land the Twins and, that same year, the football Vikings. "Well," he wrote, "it seems the partnership is a one-way street—all Minneapolis."

Thirty-three summers later St. Paul finally had its own ball club again, and it continued to feed off the urban rivalry. Veeck understood the paradigm right away. In mocking reference he hung an old Twins sign in the concourse of Municipal Stadium: a map of the state of Minnesota with two smiling baseball-headed characters shaking hands.

In *Baseball America's 1994 Directory*, under the heading "Scouting," the following are recorded for the Toronto Blue Jays: one director of scouting, one scouting administrator, one administrative assistant for scouting, four special assignment scouts, one western states supervisor, one advance scout, a director of Canadian scouting, nineteen scouting supervisors (from Merrick, New York, to Elk Grove, California), three scouts, a director of international scouting, a Latin America coordinator, and thirteen international scouts (five in the Dominican Republic, five in Australia, two in Venezuela, and one in Aruba). And that's seven fewer people than in 1993.

While the Blue Jays had their forty-seven-member scouting department, Northern League teams had but a handful of talent finders. Nick Belmonte, the league's director of baseball operations—whose résumé includes the following: minor league player, Salt Lake Trappers manager, stand-up comic, office copier salesman, baseball camp operator, and SportsChannel baseball broadcaster—helped all six clubs. The St. Paul Saints, however, were better stocked than the other five. The manager, Tim Blackwell, was paid a year-round salary above $30,000 and played a big role in the club's makeup. Mike Veeck knew a thing or two about ballplayers. And then there was the independent baseball brain trust: Marv Goldklang and Van Schley.

Marvin Stanley Goldklang ran the Saints from a glass office building in Jersey City, New Jersey, not far from his boyhood home of Bayonne, where his father owned an appliance store. He grew up in an Orthodox Jewish family and loved baseball, although he couldn't play Little League because his faith meant no Saturday activities. But Goldklang threw a baseball hard enough to pitch in high school and at the University of Pennsylvania. The wild right-hander whom the school paper once compared with Ryne Duren wisely decided his prospects were better in the field of law than on a baseball field.

Goldklang flourished at the New York firm of Cahill, Gordon, handling arcane tax and corporate securities issues. He loved the megabuck takeovers, international financing, and venture capital deals involving big investment banking firms and corporate titans. Goldklang made partner in just seven years and was earning half a million dollars annually by the age of forty. But he wasn't satisfied. In 1979 he had lucked into a minority ownership stake in the New York Yankees—an investment born when he overheard some Yankees brass during spring training, around a hotel pool where Goldklang was vacationing with his father. The investment was lucrative, but owning a piece of the Yankees was dull. "After the excitement of attending some owner meetings and after the first couple of times you sit in the owners' box at Yankee Stadium, that's basically it as a limited partner," he said.

Goldklang figured he knew more baseball than his fellow partners, but he had no outlet for ideas. At Cahill, though, he had inherited a client named Van Schley, who a senior partner said was involved in frivolous pursuits such as filmmaking and some "baseball stuff." Goldklang's job was to handle the legal details for some of Schley's ventures. So he listened as Schley detailed his wanderings in independent minor league baseball.

Evander Schley, the son of a wealthy New York stockbroker, had dropped out of college, served in Vietnam, worked on a film crew at Woodstock, dabbled in photography, formed a television documentary film company, and hung out with a New York–Hollywood arts crowd. Baseball was a lark. Sitting in a hamburger joint in 1977, Schley read an item in *Sports Illustrated* about an independent circuit known as the Gulf States League. He always had liked baseball and thought the league sounded quirky—the item was about a team whose players slept on the beach because the owner was too cheap to pay for hotel rooms—so he made a few calls and went to a league meeting, at which Schley raised his hand and was awarded a franchise in Texas City, Texas. When the league folded Schley lost $50,000, but he was smitten. He headed to the Northwest League, which had a history of independent teams, signing players for the Grays Harbor Loggers. Schley had found a niche: scouting rejects.

Goldklang didn't know a thing about the minors, but in Schley he saw someone with money who was involved in the game he loved. Goldklang was on the fast track, but was he happy? Happy the way Van Schley was happy? When Schley called his lawyer asking how to finance concessions equipment for his latest team, the Utica Blue Sox, Goldklang asked how much he needed. Six thousand dollars. Goldklang wrote a check. He was deeper into baseball but still unsatisfied. He had the suburban dream house, three young children, a successful career, and a midlife crisis. So he quit his job.

In 1986 Goldklang bought a chunk of the Pittsfield Cubs, a Double-A team owned by Miles Wolff and Stuart Revo. Goldklang soon after became a pigeon in Revo's baseball deals, buying minority shares of clubs in Charleston, South Carolina, and an independent team in Miami. In 1989, when Revo decided to sell his investments, Goldklang bought them for around $3 million. By 1994 he owned farm teams in Charleston; Fort Myers, Florida; and Fishkill, New York.

Schley, meanwhile, landed in Salt Lake City in 1985, taking over a new franchise in the Rookie-level Pioneer League, which had clubs in places like Medicine Hat, Alberta, and Butte, Montana, where the deliciously named Copper Kings played. In his first season in Salt Lake, the Trappers won the league title. The next year fan interest started booming, the Trappers prevailed again, and attendance topped 100,000. Salt Lake three-peated in 1987, drawing 170,000 fans.

That season, with a lineup featuring a potter from Pago Pago, a Japanese pitcher, and a part-time model, the Trappers won their first home game, beating the Pocatello Giants, 12–6. They won again the next night, and the night after that, and kept on winning until they tied the all-time record of twenty-seven consecutive victories held by the long-forgotten 1902 Corsicana Oilers of the Texas League and the 1921 Baltimore Orioles of the International League. The following evening network camera crews camped out in the parking lot of Derks Field in Salt Lake. Scalpers fetched $10 for $4 tickets. Ten thousand fans showed up, and the spillover crowd climbed trees and took to rooftops. The Schley-assembled collection of castoffs broke the record as they had started the streak, with an easy win over Pocatello. When it ended they celebrated in the locker room with rank cigars and cheap champagne and a whooping war cry, a mantra for independent players everywhere: "Re-jects! Re-jects! Re-jects!"

Goldklang had his independent experience, too, though less uplifting. The Miami Miracle played in the Class-A Florida State League, a prospects' circuit. But the Miracle had no prospects. Independent since 1985, the team obtained players the way all independent teams did: by scrounging. In Rookie or short-season Class-A leagues, independents can compete. There are enough undrafted collegians and released one- and two-year pros to fill a respectable roster, à la Salt Lake. But the Florida State League plays a 140-

game schedule, with strict rules about player ages and experience. Miami was a perennial doormat.

Major League Rule 4 of the Professional Baseball Agreement details the procedures for the annual amateur draft. In 1990 major league clubs made the first-round selections. Triple-A teams handled the second round, Double-A the third, and Class-A the fourth and remaining rounds. Typically, the minor league affiliates assigned drafting rights to the parent. But doing so wasn't required, and Goldklang concluded that the Miracle could participate in the draft. The majors were shocked, but they relented, and the Miracle selected sixteen players in 1990, the one and only time an independent club joined in the draft. Miami still finished dead last, and when the city was awarded a major league expansion franchise the following year, Goldklang found himself without players, a town, or a stadium. He moved across the Everglades to Fort Myers and eventually signed a player development contract with the Twins.

Although the Miracle Experiment was nothing to brag about, for Goldklang the experience was liberating. He had learned how to stock a minor league baseball team, seen that the players were treated fairly, and by elbowing his way into the draft sent a message to the big leagues. *This* was why he wanted to be in the game—to analyze players' strengths and weaknesses, to assess a club's chemistry, to improve the product on the field, and to give players a chance to move up the baseball food chain. "Professional baseball has built itself into such a humongous bureaucracy that there very often isn't enough air to breathe," Goldklang said. "This was free. You did what you wanted to do."

Goldklang and Schley wanted to do it well, and the St. Paul Saints set high standards. The club had its storybook championship in 1993. Preseason ticket sales in 1994 were audacious: 23,000 on the first day alone, when fans lined up for a mile down Energy Park Drive. The Saints knew that 6,305—Municipal Stadium's new capacity—would be the standard attendance. As a reward to fans, nothing less than a championship would do. The fun began on Opening Day, after the Saints had lost two of three on the road in Thunder Bay. When Mike Veeck implored his staff not to be fooled by the previous year, he could have been talking about Opening Day. If they tried to top the 1993 show, the Saints would fail on the field and at the gate. The karma, not to mention the planning, had to be good.

Rain staged a repeat performance. Gray and drizzly at two o'clock, an eleven-minute deluge at 4:30. In between, the first tailgaters arrived, just like a year before, roller-skating and tossing Frisbees in the parking lot.

The stadium resembled a construction site, as workers assembled the last of the new grandstand benches and laid mortar and cinder blocks for support walls. While the players took batting practice, Alan Mortensen, Terry Verdick, and Patti Boekhoff finished painting the fence signs, for the law firm of Milavetz, Gallop & Milavetz, Don's Appliance and TV, and one that read, "BACK, BACK, BACK . . . . Nothing Goes Down Smoother Than Mother's Root Beer Schnapps." Veeck aesthetically arranged pots of geraniums, begonias, petunias, asparagus ferns, and other assorted houseplants around the park. Saint the Pig—"The prince of pork, the sultan of swine, the buddha of bacon himself!" Al Frechtman said—was back, weighing in at more than 700 pounds and prompting inquiries on whether the team would stage BLT Night. (Saint would be spared a trip to hog heaven.)

As the rain this time cleared for good, the knowledge that baseball would be played here caused goose bumps. Frechtman played a tape of great baseball moments, including radio play-by-play man Russ Hodges's call of Bobby Thomson's 1951 pennant-winning homer. Players shagged fungoes. Fan noise amplified every minute. The new Saints stared into the stands, amazed at the palpable energy that seemed to charge the air. Many had never played before so big a crowd. "God, there's a lot of people here," Stephen Bishop said.

After a little Bill Murray shtick and the presentation of rings to members of the 1993 championship team, the nine starting Saints took the field to the theme from *The Magnificent Seven*. It had all the makings of another magic night in St. Paul. Clearing skies, a packed house, carnival lights glittering in the state fairgrounds beyond left field. Leon Durham looked woeful striking out in his first two at bats, and the Saints trailed the Sioux City Explorers 3–0 in the seventh inning, but it was as if victory were foreordained.

From the top row of the right-field bleachers, the scene was like a watercolor landscape. The clouds were low in the horizon, gray, blue, and orange in a cotton sky, a Rorschach test of cirrus and nimbus. Ferris wheel lights flickered red then yellow then green from the fairgrounds, and when a train passed the conductor waved a flashlight to the crowd's delight.

Fans stomped on the metal bleachers and joked with Sioux City's right fielder. Children sat atop the fence, feet dangling in play. The *Shaft* theme played. Left-handed-hitting Vince Castaldo homered over the freshly painted Slumberland sign in left center field to make the score 3–1. Behind right field kids played king of the hill on a knot of dirt left by the construction crews. An inkblot of clouds crept toward the stadium.

In the bottom of the eighth, three straight singles cut Sioux City's lead to 3–2. A muffed bunt loaded the bases. Up came Castaldo. In came a left-handed pitcher, Kevin Kobetitsch, to face him. Castaldo mashed the first pitch off the top of the left-center-field fence for a three-run triple that put St. Paul ahead 5–3. A half inning later the new closer, Jason Bullard, retired the side to preserve a 6–3 win.

Goldklang pumped his fist in the air. "Winning is such a sweet feeling," he said. "This is *real* winning and losing." Schley beamed and applauded. The players gathered in the infield, knocking fists together in the current jock salute.

Before the celebration had ended, the stadium lights dimmed and "Burning Down the House" by Talking Heads blared from the loudspeakers. Beyond the fence in right field, flames and explosions burst from a six-story-tall cement tower where the fire department conducted training sessions. Sirens blew, engines raced to the scene. For a second no one was sure whether the fire was, well, *real*. Then *fireworks* exploded from the building's roof.

Mike Veeck had been wearing a St. Paul Fire Department helmet around Municipal Stadium all day. Now everyone knew why. He had staged a minor league classic: a towering inferno. "Cheap theatrics," he crowed. "Ain't nothin' like 'em." Somewhere, Bill Veeck smiled.

Ted Cushmore

SIX

*I wanted to get into baseball in the worst way, and
that's exactly what I did.*

—Charles O. Finley

Early on a Saturday afternoon, the day after the Duluth-Superior Dukes' home opener, Ted Cushmore slouched at a restaurant table in Duluth's charmingly renovated waterfront district, wondering what he had gotten himself into. "This is bad," he said.

To emphasize the obvious, or maybe to remind himself of the reality, he repeated it. Not once, but twice. "This is bad. This is bad."

What the new owner of the Duluth-Superior Dukes meant was that he had a bad team. The Dukes didn't just lose their first three games of the season on the road in Winnipeg. They were outplayed, outclassed, outmanned. Certifiably crushed, by scores of 9–1, 7–2, and 4–0. A Winnipeg outfielder named Ted Williams (no relation to the .400 hitter) stole bases at will. Duluth couldn't hit, and its pitchers were easy prey. It quickly became clear which of the six Northern League teams was the patsy.

The Dukes returned from an eight-hour overnight bus ride and somehow managed to win their first game at Wade Stadium, beating Sioux Falls, 10–6. But Duluth fans, who had faithfully streamed into the ballpark even at the end of a last-place 1993 season, knew they had a losing club on their hands: They booed during a five-run rally by the opposition. *During the first game of the season.* Imagine, Cushmore thought, what'll happen if we keep on losing.

After the game the Canaries' manager, a sixty-eight-year-old minor leaguer named Frank Verdi, who had seen more than a few teams in his time, blared into a reporter's tape recorder: "We lost to a fucking college team. It was a fucking disgrace. They're a fucking college team."

While St. Paul had Van Schley and Marv Goldklang's combined twenty-plus years in independent baseball, Duluth had as an owner a businessman who hadn't been involved in organized baseball since his last game as captain of the Colgate varsity more than thirty years earlier. For a field manager, whose job it is to assemble the team, Cushmore had hired Howie Bedell, who had a long and impressive baseball résumé—former major league player, farm director of the Philadelphia Phillies and Cincinnati Reds, bench coach for the Kansas City Royals, first-base coach for the Seattle Mariners.

There was one job, though, Bedell had never had—running an independent club—and he grossly underestimated the Northern League's talent level despite receiving ample advice from Cushmore, who had watched the St. Paul Saints in 1993, and from Nick Belmonte and others in the league. Bedell signed what appeared to be some of the worst players released by major league organizations—including his thirty-year-old son, Jeff, who hadn't played in a minor league game since he was cut by the Royals eight years earlier after two undistinguished seasons at Class-A, where he hit a combined .231.

But Cushmore's definition of *bad* transcended the quality—if you could call it that—of the Duluth-Superior Dukes. *Bad* meant that a total of 1,788 fans showed up at Wade Stadium on opening night. *One thousand seven hundred and eighty-eight.* Cushmore was shocked. That was more than a thousand less than the team had *averaged* in 1993. At the home opener a year earlier, 4,528 fans had turned out—including 336 who paid to watch the game standing up. Granted, it was the first professional baseball game in Duluth after a twenty-two-year absence, but the fans had kept coming after that, even though the Dukes had languished in last place nearly all season.

Over the winter season-ticket sales fell to 850 from 950, but Cushmore wasn't alarmed, because many fans with whom he had spoken said they loved the Dukes (despite their record) but just couldn't get to enough games to justify season tickets. Seemed reasonable enough. But when Cushmore was advised by his staff a few days before the home opener that the club had sold just 500 additional tickets for the game, alarm bells went off. Even a novice owner knows you shouldn't have to rely on walk-up sales for Opening Day. The place should have been sold out long in advance.

The bad news kept coming. The local paper, the *News-Tribune*, had covered the team in depth in 1993 but didn't write a pregame story about the Dukes on Opening Day, which could have helped the gate. The stadium program for Game Two trumpeted in bold capital letters PIZZA HUT SCHEDULE MAGNET NIGHT, but the freebie hadn't arrived in time from the manufacturer, and fans were going to get rain checks. Not only that but the shipment of the season's second promotional item—Pepsi-sponsored batting gloves—had been held up at the Canadian border.

The weather had been awful on Opening Day—the threat of rain prominent all day long—but weather wasn't a good excuse because tickets should have been unavailable anyway. It was Duluth, too, where a typical early-summer day features heavy morning fog off Lake Superior, a gray tarpaulin of clouds, and the seemingly ever-present possibility of rain. As Cushmore put it, "Every day in Duluth at a quarter to five it rains." In other words, people were used to it.

On Saturday, about three hours before game time, Ted Cushmore stared fatalistically out the window of the Lake Avenue Cafe. He ordered a hot fudge sundae to cheer himself up. The sky was dark and brooding. Rain dripped from the eaves. "There goes seven thousand dollars," he said. "We're going to have two hundred fifty people there tonight. We're going to set an all-time Northern League attendance low. This is a fun business, isn't it?"

Nick Belmonte sped up Interstate 35 to Duluth on the two-and-a-half-hour drive from St. Paul, where he had watched the Saints' dramatic season-opening, come-from-behind win over the Sioux City Explorers. It had been everything Duluth wasn't on Opening Night. Municipal Stadium had been packed, the atmosphere was festive, the team was talented, the weather was terrific, the baseball was exciting. Belmonte, though, had the last-place Dukes on his mind.

He was in the middle of a quickly developing rift between Ted Cushmore and Howie Bedell over the state of the Dukes. Not in the middle, actually, but way over on Ted Cushmore's side. Cushmore had called Belmonte and requested a meeting—sans Bedell—to figure out how to overhaul the team.

As director of baseball operations, Belmonte was the league's central scouting bureau. He compiled lists of released and college players, inspected their statistics, called up scouts, coaches, and development personnel to check on backgrounds, and recorded his personal comments. Then Belmonte faxed the lists to all six teams at the same time. If a team needed a player with a particular experience level for a particular position, Belmonte offered a name or began a search. If a team was interested in a player, he passed on a telephone number. If more than one team set its sights on the same person, Belmonte played it straight: "You're not the only team that's interested in this guy," he would say. "You better move fast."

It was a tricky job. Belmonte was open to criticism largely because of his prior relationship with Van Schley. Not only had Schley done Belmonte's job for the Northern League's inaugural season, but Belmonte had managed the Salt Lake Trappers—to Pioneer League championships—in 1990, 1991, and 1992. Schley and Belmonte were close friends, and everyone in the league knew it—and suspected that Belmonte passed on his best tips to St. Paul. Belmonte denied it. They all had access to the same information, and they all had his telephone number and could call as often as they liked. If Schley chose to telephone more than others in the league, that was his prerogative. Howie Bedell chose not to call Belmonte at all.

Ted Cushmore may have been a baseball novice, but early in the year, well before the season, he detected a problem. Of the more than 400 released minor league players whose names Belmonte had faxed to each Northern League club by mid-April, the Duluth-Superior Dukes had signed exactly two: Dave Maize and Rob Mitchell. Belmonte had written nothing next to Maize's name on his list. There was a reason. The catcher had batted .185 in his only season above Rookie ball and had had just thirty-five at bats in 1993. Mitchell was 7–20 with a 5.30 earned run average in three seasons in the Phillies organization. Bedell told Cushmore that he signed the pitcher because he was a nice kid and Bedell knew his parents.

The names of players Bedell was signing began trickling into the league office. Jamie Arendt, an LS-1 infielder with a .227 career average in parts of three seasons who hadn't played at all in '93. Greg Wiseman, an LS-3 first baseman with a .225 career average who was mystified by the curveball and who also had sat out the previous season. Scott Englehart, who had pitched just twelve innings in the minors—all in 1992—and had been cut by the Dukes in 1993. Bedell hadn't seen Englehart play, signing him on the basis of a videotape and a telephone conversation. Mike Hubel, a backup catcher who'd batted .219 in 114 at bats for the Dukes. Hubel was even rewarded by Bedell with an extra month's pay to play for the Northern League All-Stars against the all-women Colorado Silver Bullets, a perk other teams saved for their best players.

The clincher was Eric Parkinson, who was classified as a veteran but had pitched just two innings above Class-A. In five seasons of Rookie and Class-A ball, Parkinson had compiled a 22–45 record and a 5.06 earned run average. In the Northern League you simply didn't waste a veteran slot on a Class-A pitcher; veterans were your studs, aces, go-to guys, producers. With numbers like Parkinson's, veteran or not, you shouldn't waste any spot at all.

When he heard about the Parkinson signing, Cushmore began to panic. Not only was Bedell hiring marginal players but he was offering them contracts well before tryout camps and spring training, when better players might emerge. An unwritten rule in the Northern League was that you snagged a few veterans early—competition for them was keenest—and filled out the roster shortly before the season.

Bedell, however, simply didn't want any input. Cushmore was insistent. He called Nick Belmonte and said, "I'm paying one-sixth of your salary, and I want Howie to use your service." Belmonte as a matter of course sent Bedell the materials everyone else in the league was receiving, but he also followed up with telephone calls a couple of times. "I've got it covered," Bedell would say from his Pottstown, Pennsylvania, home. "Everything's fine. Thanks for calling."

But it wasn't fine. Belmonte told Miles Wolff he was worried. The numbers didn't lie. In 1993 Eric Parkinson had been 2–8 with a 5.85 earned run average at Salem of the Carolina League. Wolff knew the Carolina League, knew its talent level, and knew the quality of players the Northern League wanted. It was a leaguewide issue. Signing mediocre players dragged down the overall talent level, weakening the league's credibility.

"I called Howie and said there was some concern," Wolff recalled. "Howie said, 'My sources said the kid can pitch. He's got a great arm. He'll be fine.' You have to express some concern. But Howie knows more baseball than I'll ever know."

The league president also spoke with Cushmore, who in turn called Belmonte for an appraisal. Cushmore didn't need thirty years in baseball to be able to compare the experience and statistics of the Dukes with those of other Northern League club rosters. One day in the spring, Cushmore called Belmonte. "What do you think of this horseshit club I've got?" he asked. "Are we going to win a game? I don't think we're going to win a game."

Howie Bedell was being second-guessed before the season had even begun, and he didn't like it. Bedell was a major league guy. In large part that means you don't tolerate know-nothing owners telling you how to do your job. Let the baseball guys run the baseball operation—the owners should handle the business side only. Plus, Bedell didn't like centralized scouting bureaus, even one-man operations. Central scouting means pooled information. How can you trust that the information you're receiving is good, or that a scout isn't playing favorites, or that he isn't passing on your confidential information to someone else? The only way to build ball clubs is to rely on your own people, and Nick Belmonte wasn't Howie Bedell's guy or even the Duluth-Superior Dukes' guy.

And how much did Nick Belmonte know about baseball anyway? Bedell's contacts were men with thirty or more years in the game. Belmonte had played minor league ball for a few years and managed an independent Rookie team. Bedell thought Belmonte had gone behind his back and told the owner that he was assembling a lousy team. That broke the code. (When Cushmore said that *he* had called Belmonte for an appraisal of the Dukes, Bedell didn't buy it. Anyway, Cushmore said, he's just trying to help.)

The organizational world in which Howie Bedell had lived doesn't have or want the all-for-one-and-one-for-all mentality necessary for success in the Northern League. Bedell didn't understand the league, or even independent baseball, where owners more often than not play a large role in player personnel. Bedell's contacts may have been baseball maestros, but they hadn't seen the Northern League either and couldn't assess the new manager's needs.

"Howie was looking for prospects," Miles Wolff said, "kids with good arms who had some talent that could be developed. He was looking at it as a farm director. The Northern League is not about development. It's about winning in the next forty-five days," the length of each half of the season. (The Northern League divides its schedule into halves, with the winners meeting in the championship series.) Major league guys hate judging a player's talent based solely on past performance. They believe they can take a kid who has the right "tools" and turn him into a ballplayer. In independent baseball you want numbers and desire—performance now—not tools.

It was a philosophical standoff, but it was too late. The Dukes were undeniably bad. Duluth had signed twenty-four players before the season, which meant two had to be placed on the disabled list. Everyone was guaranteed two weeks on the roster—two weeks of losses, Cushmore figured.

The new owner already was kicking himself. He had paid too little attention to the player personnel and placed too much trust in his front office. Off the field the club had failed to remind the people of Duluth and Superior that they had loved their Dukes in

1993, that the club needed continued backing. Cushmore and his staff had taken too much for granted. Consequently, the team was stinking it up and fans weren't buying tickets. Cushmore had to solve both problems, fast. The morning after Opening Day, he met with the president of a local public relations firm, who agreed to work with the Dukes pro bono. He held a staff meeting and, for the first time, was angry. We have to market the team better, he told his employees, and we have to do it immediately.

Michael Edward Cushmore was born in 1940 and raised in Germantown, a middle-class neighborhood of single-family homes on the north side of the sprawling city of Philadelphia. Baseball had always been a part of his life. Cushmore remembered his first major league game clearly. A hot Sunday after the war in Shibe Park, home of the Athletics. Doubleheader. Bleacher seats with his insurance-salesman father, who doffed his shirt and baked in the sun with his oldest boy from one o'clock until the last pitch was thrown around seven. On other days Cushmore would listen to his uncle broadcast color commentary for the Athletics; the Cushmores always were fans of Connie Mack's hardscrabble Athletics, never the Phillies.

Cushmore could play a little, too. In high school he led a Penn Charter team that won seventeen straight championships and regularly sent kids to the professional ranks. (Cushmore's brother spent a few years in the Tigers organization.) In summers during college Cushmore played in a semipro league, where he was scouted by Tommy Lasorda. A low minor league offer came, but Cushmore knew he wasn't a genuine prospect—and he had a nagging nerve injury in his throwing arm—so he passed up baseball for business.

The early 1960s were a time of big corporations, the rise of the MBA and organization men, and Cushmore was smart and ambitious. In business he *was* a prospect. After getting a master's degree from the University of Pennsylvania's Wharton School, Cushmore left Philadelphia for a job in brand management marketing with General Mills in Minnesota. By 1979 he was a vice president, and he kept rising. Cushmore became president of a frozen pizza division, the Betty Crocker division, and, finally, the Gold Medal flour division. By the time he looked up, Cushmore's business card labeled him a senior vice president, one of the top seventeen executives in an $8 billion company. But as with Goldklang the Wall Street lawyer, something was missing. "I've never been totally comfortable in corporate life—and it's kind of embarrassing after spending twenty-eight years to say that," he said. "I've always wanted to have my own business."

But Cushmore also had two children from his first marriage and another in a second marriage, so risk taking was never entirely feasible. Corporate life was a golden handshake, if at times it seemed like a set of golden handcuffs. But one of the perks was retirement at age fifty-five. Cushmore wanted to leave General Mills, but he didn't want to play golf all day. A new venture would have to grab him, arouse some passion. When his brother sent him a copy of *Stolen Season* by David Lamb, a book about the romance of minor league baseball, he found the answer.

Problem was, Cushmore didn't know anything about the business. He did know that investors had made a killing in the minors. But that had been in the 1980s, the bull market for franchise values. Getting into the game as an owner in the '90s seemed foolhardy. But Cushmore was eager to learn. When his youngest son's school held a silent auction in 1993, Cushmore paid $150 to lunch with Andy MacPhail, the general manager of the Minnesota Twins. MacPhail wasn't much help on the business of the minors, but he did offer an introduction to Mike Veeck, president of the new independent team that was coming to St. Paul. MacPhail was dubious of the venture, though. A glorified beer league, he told Cushmore. The majors don't miss any players. The Northern League won't finish the season.

MacPhail's predictions notwithstanding, Cushmore bought season tickets to the Saints. One Saturday he went to Municipal Stadium to arrange a twenty-seat package for his son's Little League team. Veeck wasn't around, the sales staff was helping with a clinic on the field, the office was chaos. When Cushmore asked who could get his tickets, someone said, "He might help you." It was Marv Goldklang.

The two men hit it off. They had a mutual friend, Craig Stein, the owner of the Reading Phillies, and both had attended Penn. Goldklang got feelers from people who said they wanted to buy minor league teams all the time, but Cushmore seemed serious, not interested in making a quick buck. Goldklang also knew that the league was having trouble in Rochester, and that Duluth might be up for sale.

A week later Cushmore found himself in Rochester talking with Miles Wolff about the ball club there. For two months he studied the situation, but it wasn't positive. The lawsuit over the team's ownership was unresolved, attendance was the lowest in the league, and the club was losing fistfuls of money. Rochester was going nowhere. Still, Wolff wanted to find a way to get Cushmore involved in the league. As with Goldklang, Wolff felt the General Mills executive brought more to the table than money. "He cares a lot about the game," Wolff said. "He's had this dream—that a lot of people who call me do and I tend to dismiss them. They tend to back off. Ted never backed off. He was deadly serious the whole time."

During the playoffs between Rochester and St. Paul, Wolff told Cushmore that Rochester was dead and the club would be moved. But would he be interested in another franchise? During a game in Municipal Stadium, Wolff visited Cushmore at his seats behind home plate. Duluth's owner wants to sell, he said. That night Cushmore struck a deal on the telephone with Bruce Engel. They even agreed on a tentative price: $500,000.

"My expectations were that we would draw 100,000 people, that we would play .500 or better ball, and I would make a decent but not spectacular return on my investment on an annual operating basis. And that eventually I would see some appreciation in the franchise value," Cushmore said. "I wasn't trying to make a killing. Anybody who buys a baseball team, a minor league team, in the nineteen nineties expecting to make a killing is probably overreaching a little. I did this because I love the game. I wanted to participate."

Ted Cushmore has sandy hair and a gracefully weathered face that inspires quick friendship. Away from the office, he dresses smartly and casually in chinos, golf shirts, comfortable sweaters, and deck shoes, much as one would expect from a wealthy suburbanite. He is soft-spoken and reserved, which no doubt contributed to his ascent through General Mills. He figured it would work with the Dukes, too, because operating a second-year minor league baseball team isn't supposed to require delivering motivational lectures to the staff or seizing control of the players from a baseball veteran.

But Cushmore was using all of his vacation days from General Mills—he had a year to a possible retirement—tending to the Dukes. He was working nights from home, spending weekends in Duluth, and sometimes driving five hours round-trip for a week-night game. He knew he had made mistakes with his manager and front office—he just hoped they didn't add up to a half-million-dollar mistake.

"I need a catcher," Cushmore told Nick Belmonte. Catching was a problem. Neither Dave Maize nor Mike Hubel hit well. What did Belmonte think? Was anyone available? Belmonte had a "catch-and-throw guy," a good defensive player who wasn't much of a hitter. Better to wait. (Adding insult to the catching problem, the first issue of the team's fan newsletter featured a color photo and story about the soon-to-be-released Mike Hubel: "Hubel exploded from bullpen to start at catcher," the headline read.)

What about pitching? Belmonte relayed a trade offer from Doug Simunic in Winnipeg: starter Scott Freeman, who had shut out the Dukes in the opening series, plus a middle infielder for center fielder Steve Dailey, who'd hit .281 in Rochester in 1993 (where Simunic had managed) but who was struggling now. It was worth considering, but the infielder was marginal, a bid by Simunic to free a roster spot for a better player.

Cushmore ate his hot fudge sundae. That morning he had helped the grounds crew roll the tarpaulin on the infield before the inevitable rains. Life in the minors.

Belmonte studied the Dukes roster. The team had not one veteran player in the field—a crucial mistake. "We're a young and hungry team," Cushmore joked, forcing a smile. Jeff Bedell's name came up, and both men cringed. Cushmore wanted so badly to do well—not only to attract enough fans to at least break even (about 2,500 a game would do it, he figured) but because this was baseball, and he cared about baseball. He wanted the on-field part of his investment to succeed as much as the stadium operation itself. In other words, Cushmore wanted to win.

Belmonte recommended some possible rookie signings. Cushmore scratched out names and wrote down substitutes. Revamping the roster would be not only time consuming and risky—and involve releasing players just two weeks into the season, never a pleasant task—but expensive, too. Every signing cost at least $1,000 for travel and hotels. Cushmore cared about the money—while he may have been idealistic about baseball, he wasn't going to flush his life savings away—but at the same time he was prepared to do what it took to field a competitive team.

"Can we win this thing?" he finally asked Belmonte. "With these changes, can we win this thing?" The question was rhetorical. Cushmore knew it would take more than a new pitcher and a new catcher, but he needed to find a way to get motivated.

"We're gonna kick their ass."

Wade Stadium is a stirring setting for a ball game, a classic of Depression-era architecture and that long-gone innocence of outdoor baseball. Situated in West Duluth, the Wade, as the ballpark is called, lies in a flat stretch of the city amid small, one-family homes and the old DM & IR ore docks. Parking is free, and a bowling alley sits across the way.

The Wade opened in 1941. Seventy-five men on each of two shifts built it in just over a year. The stadium was financed with $75,000 in city funds plus another $250,000 in state and federal money—a Works Progress Administration project conceived in the spirit of the times as an asset to public life.

So many paving stones from a Duluth street were used to build the Wade that, unlike other minor league parks, the brick facing extends fully down both lines. The outfield wall stands twelve feet

Wade Stadium

high and is made of concrete. When the wind blows off Lake Superior, it is cold and foggy, but a wooden roof covers the grandstands. A metal net drops perpendicularly from the roof to the playing field to stop foul balls. One expects to see men in black ties and fedoras cheering politely as athletes in baggy gray flannels leave their gloves on the field between innings.

On July 16, 1941, against the rival Superior Blues across the water in Wisconsin, the Duluth Dukes lost their first game in what was then called Duluth Municipal All-Sports Stadium. (It was renamed Wade Municipal Stadium in 1954 after the death of Frank Wade, who helped reestablish the Northern League in 1933 and later owned the Dukes.) The Dukes—who inherited the nickname of one of the team's managers, Darby "Dook" O'Brien—thrived along with the rest of minor league baseball in the 1940s, averaging about a thousand fans a game in the Class-C Northern League.

But on July 24, 1948, the *Duluth News-Tribune* carried a page-one Associated Press dispatch that forever scarred baseball in the city:

4 DULUTH DUKES KILLED
AS BUS, TRUCK COLLIDE

One Other Killed, 14 Hurt
In Fiery St. Paul Mishap

ST. PAUL (AP)—Five men were killed and 14 injured shortly before noon today when a bus carrying the Duluth Dukes baseball club and a heavy truck collided head-on on highway 36 between Western and Dale streets here.

Four of the dead were reported to be members of the Duluth Dukes. The fifth was the driver of the truck.

The wreckage burst into flames and cremated some of the victims before passersby could pull them out.

Screams could be heard from inside the bus, described by one witness as "a mass of flames." Red and gray uniforms of the Dukes—who were traveling from Eau Claire, Wisconsin, for a series in St. Cloud, Minnesota—were scattered across the roadway, one lying next to the body of a player covered with a white sheet.

The manager, George Treadwell, who had been driving the bus, and three of his players were dead; a fourth player died a few days later. Treadwell was a baseball teacher who loved the minors. In selfless words that nearly five decades years later seem hopelessly quaint, he once said: "It's like prospecting, I guess. You're always on the lookout for a nugget, only it isn't gold, it's baseball talent. And in this kind of job, when you think you've found one, you guard it jealously and polish it and you get more of a kick out of making it shine than if you were it yourself." A fan composed a poem to the fallen Dukes:

They needed a ball team in heaven,
A good one was wanted, you know;
God sent down an Angel to choose one,
About four or five needed to go.

The diamond was ribboned in satin,
The bases were made of pure gold;

The boys saw the field all a-glisten,
And all the tickets were sold.

The Dukes vowed to play on. The parent club, the St. Louis Cardinals, and other Northern League teams loaned players, and the Dukes returned to All-Sports Stadium one week after the crash for memorial games against Superior. Frank Wade, unable to cope with the tragedy, sold the club two years later.

Baseball in Duluth was as resilient as the French explorer and trader Daniel de Greysolon, Sieur du Lhut, who landed on the western edge of Lake Superior in 1679 on his way to find the Dakota Indians. (Du Lhut was on a mission of peace: He sought harmony among all tribes.) The first professional baseball team in Duluth was formed around the time that "gangs of immigrants" began arriving to begin construction of the northern end of the Lake Superior and Mississippi Railroad in the late 1880s. Duluth was to be a center of commerce rivaling Chicago—but, as one writer promised, without the "sickening heat and annoyances and tricks of sharpers on more southerly routes." The historian Thaddeus Stevens went so far as to compare the potential of Duluth with the great inland European cities—Paris, Berlin, Vienna.

If Duluth's importance was never fully realized, the predominantly Scandinavian, Irish, German, and Canadian population brimmed with optimism. Duluth was a city on a hill with scores of brick factories making leather and canvas, cigars, brooms, looms, refrigerators, and beer. U.S. Steel built Morgan Park, a company town, to take advantage of Minnesota's rich iron ore deposits. The city boasted monumental public buildings and a vibrant cultural life; opera, a symphony, vaudeville shows, and feature films all played at Duluth's theaters.

Even as industry declined in the 1970s and '80s, the city retained its heritage. Factories were converted into restaurants, stores, and offices. In the waterfront district original signage on the old brick revealed the homes of "Zenith Machine Co.—Manufacturer of Ze-

nith Home Laundry Equipment" and "Paper Products Co.—
Wholesale Tested Papers."

Sports always were popular. Duluth had a National Football
League franchise in the 1920s, the Duluth Eskimos, featuring the
Hall of Fame runner Ernie Nevers. (The club played most of its
games on the road because other teams didn't want to travel to
Duluth.) A Duluth club played in baseball's historic Western Asso-
ciation for one season, in 1891, and was part of the Northern
League upon its inception in 1903.

As the minors struggled Duluth and Superior could support only
one Northern League team, which played in the Wade, drawing
just a few hundred fans a game. Even pennant winners in 1969 and
1970 didn't draw well. The Dukes lost their operating agreement
with the Chicago White Sox in 1970, one year before the Northern
League itself folded. It would be two decades before professional
baseball returned to one of America's aging ballpark jewels.

Not everyone shared Wolff's vision for resurrecting Wade Stadium and baseball in the Twin Ports of Duluth and Superior. The
leading naysayers were the sportswriters. "Nostalgia can't pay for
the Wade" was the headline over a column in the *News-Tribune*
two weeks after the city received its Northern League franchise.

"Not many fans want to pay money to get splinters, especially
while watching games of an unaffiliated league whose players bear
little resemblance to stars like Kirby Puckett or Paul Molitor," the
columnist wrote. There were too many other recreation and entertainment options in Duluth. Movies. Malls. Concerts. Jogging. Bik-
ing. Minor league baseball was all nostalgia. It'll never work, the
writer said.

Another sportswriter, Bruce Bennett, wrote soon after: "They
say fix up the ballpark, build a team, create a league, and we'll have
our own field of dreams. Sounds more like a pipe dream to me."

Baseball was dying in Duluth in the 1960s, when Bennett arrived
in town, so how could it possibly work now? "Heck, if they couldn't
do it with the support of the major leagues, which supplied the

players, the payroll, the transportation costs, and just about everything else, how can this venture survive with none of that input?"

"Face it: Duluth is a hockey town. In the summer it's boats and cabins and golf and travel and the Twins. Is there room for more?"

It sounded as if the sportswriters of Duluth didn't want *their* summer evenings interrupted by professional baseball. But the people of the city had other ideas. They flooded the *News-Tribune* with letters favoring the Dukes' revival and bashing the opponents.

"Minor-league baseball is alive and well," Frank H. Giesen wrote. "Two years ago, I moved back to your area. The only feature lacking in our area was baseball. Now, with a team, UTOPIA has arrived. Please give it a break and a chance to survive."

"I love to watch baseball played on real grass, instead of at the Metrodome," said Ernest Walli of Tamarack.

"I live fifty miles from Wade Stadium and would attend as many games as possible," Joe Zauhar of Floodwood wrote.

"Kirby Puckett is a great player, but you never get close enough to see him. I'll take a Lancelot Nobody who can hit farther than I can and will shake my kids' hands," said Patrick McKinnon of Duluth.

Duluth was a community ready to embrace tradition, not dwell on old failures that had little to do with the present. It wasn't the 1960s anymore. People were realizing that, along with the old factories that deserved a better fate than a wrecking ball, baseball in an era of domed stadiums, artificial turf, and $6 million men could be restored to a more natural state. Attending a baseball game in a historic but renovated setting could lift an entire community's spirits.

On one of his trips north, Miles Wolff had estimated the Wade needed up to $300,000 in work, and he gently prodded the city by praising its ballpark: "My mouth waters when I look at it." Duluth's politicians—and citizens—understood what the sportswriters couldn't. The city council allocated $250,000 to $300,000 for a new roof, asbestos removal, new lights, and new seats. The optimism and cash kept flowing—just as in Sioux Falls—and the city wound up spending $527,000 to fix the Wade. The public responded. By Christmas 1992 the Dukes had sold 450 season tickets,

500 caps, and two-thirds of the outfield fence signs. Two weeks before the opener, fans lined up to purchase tickets at the Dukes' office in a downtown shopping mall.

In the end, after the Wade was lovingly restored, after the Dukes were assembled and the sounds of professional baseball echoed under the WPA project's new wooden roof, the sportswriters jumped on the bandwagon:

"I like what I see these days at Wade Stadium," the same Bruce Bennett who had scoffed at the revival of minor league baseball wrote during the first season.

> In fact, I love it. Sure, the Duluth-Superior Dukes are in the Northern League's cellar, but the ballpark is bustling. It's good to see professional baseball flourishing in town again, it is good to see the stadium fixed up, and it is great to see the support the team has received.
>
> Cynics say the Northern is a league populated by has-beens, guys who couldn't make it to the big leagues and are just hanging on. I prefer to see the other side, a bunch which loves to play baseball, experienced players who, yes, may be a tad short of the talent required to be big-leaguers but who can still play very good baseball.

Hindsight is a beautiful thing.

Spectators saw a baseball game in Wade Stadium on Saturday, June 11, 1994. Ted Cushmore saw a horror show. The rain had stopped by game time, and the evening turned out to be quite pleasant: cool temperatures, a few white and gray clouds in a low, azure sky. It was a fine night for a baseball game. Trouble was, the people of Duluth, so enthusiastic in their support a year earlier, didn't agree. When the turnstiles stopped spinning—spinning very slowly, that is—the attendance totaled 1,479 for the game between the Dukes and the Sioux Falls Canaries. Cushmore's dire prediction of 250 fans was wrong. On the other hand, 1,479 fans also meant big losses.

If you had entered Wade Stadium's grandstands through the first-base ramp shortly before game time that night, the first thing you would have seen would have been a man lying on his back in the aisle against the backstop. Paramedics rushed to attend to the gentleman, who a half inning into the game was seated in the front row, apparently recovered from his fall. The paramedics should have stuck around to help the Dukes.

The game's first batter, Sioux Falls's Rex De La Nuez, hit a routine ground ball that rolled through the legs of rookie Australian shortstop Steve Hinton. The second batter, Chris Powell, lined a single to right field. The third batter, Hiro Shirahata, a former Japanese major leaguer, grounded to first base. Greg Wiseman scooped up the ball and tossed it over Hinton's head into left field. De La Nuez scored. 1–0. Mike Burton hit a sacrifice fly for another run. Late-arriving fans hadn't even sat down with a bratwurst and a beer. As the inning ended, Dukes trailing 2–0, the crowd booed lustily.

The team mascot, Earl the Duke, wore a black suit with oversize shoes and spats. His papier-mâché baseball head featured a monocle and a top hat. Earl the Duke stood around a lot, lethargically shaking hands and patting children on the head.

The Dukes rallied to tie the game in the bottom of the first, but the crowd stayed largely silent in the absence of motivational music. Finally, and inexplicably, the public address operator played the "Green Acres" theme song while the Sioux Falls pitcher was in the middle of his windup—a no-no in minor league parks. A few innings later he played a tape of mocking laughter when one of the Canaries struck out. Another baseball faux pas. After a fan complained Cushmore told the PA announcer to stop. A tough night.

"It's terrible," he said while touring the left-field grandstands. "This is a thousand."

"You're the owner?" one fan said. "What happened last night?"

Cushmore had to fib. "I think the rain held people back."

Standing in the nearly empty Hard Ball Cafe picnic area in right field, Cushmore sifted through recent events. He couldn't quite figure it out.

Presumably building on the first-season success, about a thousand fans had attended a "Welcome Dukes" function in the spring. Local TV coverage of the team included a half-hour special the day before the opener. Almost 2,000 showed up for an exhibition game. But Cushmore knew the team's marketing efforts had been weak. In the off-season two salesmen had been fired after making false promises to advertisers (who promptly ditched the club). The club lost $10,000 in revenues because it had to remove several fence signs hung from the brick facade in the far corners of the park that faced the outfielders, not the stands. Fewer promotional nights were scheduled. Group sales were poor. Preseason ticket revenue was down $30,000.

"I think I've been relatively supportive and encouraging, and I haven't done a lot of chewing out," Cushmore said. "There hasn't been a need to do that. Last night got my attention."

Cushmore believed Duluth fans had tolerated a losing team one season but might not do so again. He didn't think it was a crowd like in St. Paul, where fans would come, win or lose, for the pig and the haircuts and the fireworks and the goofball announcer. Duluth isn't quite as sophisticated—playing the Finnish national anthem wouldn't have anyone smirking as it did in St. Paul. And if the fans didn't come for the atmosphere, or to satisfy a first-year curiosity, that left the baseball. Fans support winners.

Cushmore kept one eye on the game, which was turning into a rout. Sioux Falls got a base hit. "He's struggling here. Rookie pitcher."

Another Sioux Falls hit. "We're having trouble getting out of this inning."

Cushmore already had asked himself whether he should have paid so much for the Dukes—a price he figured was 20 percent too high. But as someone with no experience in baseball, Cushmore concluded that he had had to pay up or risk losing out.

Another Dukes error, their fifth of the game. "We're throwing the ball all over the place tonight."

Another Sioux Falls hit. "We're in trouble here. Is that another run?"

It was, but the scoreboard operator failed to register it. "He's always late with the run." Cushmore made a mental note to correct the problem.

The inning ended, and the announcer reported: "For the Canaries, one run, three hits, one error, and two left on." Cushmore gazed at the field. "I knew this would not be a walk in the park. I knew this would be a lot of hard work. But I thought we'd have more momentum after the season in terms of fan support than there apparently is. It doesn't help that the club is getting off to a slow start."

The Dukes lost to Sioux Falls 8–3, dropping their record to one win against four losses. Cushmore planned to talk to Howie Bedell the next day about overhauling the team.

Todd Rosenthal

SEVEN

It's not New York, but it's not meant to be. If it was New York, you'd be in the big leagues. It's the minor leagues for a reason.

—Thunder Bay Whiskey Jacks
first baseman Todd Rosenthal

Along U.S. Highway 61, where Hibbing native Bob Dylan sang that he "left it," the shore of Lake Superior rolls through small towns with names bearing witness to the area's Germanic roots, like Tofte, and French ones, like Grand Marais and Little Marais. The area is remote, pickup-truck country, where the economy depends on the few months a year of fishing, hunting, and boating that support the tourist trade. The farther north you travel, the worse the weather gets. At the Canadian border, a sign reads, "WELCOME TO ONTARIO. WE'LL MAKE YOU FEEL INCREDIBLE!" With its seven-month winters, no one says how exactly that's possible.

When the railroad spread across Canada in the 1890s, Thunder Bay was dubbed the Golden Gateway of the Great Northwest, inspiring dreams of a Canadian Chicago and a Canadian San Francisco. The contemporary feel-good spirit of North America also saw fit to promote the region as an outdoor recreation center, but in reality Thunder Bay was a pretty grim place. The name was derived from an Ojibwa Indian word for the violent thunderstorms that echoed between Sleeping Giant and Mount McKay, which an army colonel declared the worst "of all known parts of the world." The angry weather moved poet Pauline Johnson to compose an ode to the town in 1898. It isn't exactly a Chamber of Commerce slogan:

When did you sink to your dreamless sleep
Out there on Thunder Bay,
Where the tempests sweep
And waters leap
And the storms rage overhead?

The gales screech down from the open West,
And the thunders beat and break
On the amethyst
Of rugged breast,
But you never arise and wake.

The climate no doubt had something to do with an observation by a visitor to Thunder Bay a few years earlier: "The number of saloons and drinking places in the village was astonishing. All seemed only too well patronized." In 1884 the town had no fewer than thirty-eight watering holes for its 6,000 residents.

One hundred ten years later, things hadn't changed much. Thunder Bay is a blue-collar town, barely scraping by with 12 percent unemployment thanks to a long, slow decline in the shipping, lumber, and mining industries on which it relies. The city lends an abandoned, half-constructed feeling. There is little foot traffic in the lone downtown mall. Empty restaurants abound. In the summer of 1994, across the road from Port Arthur Stadium, home of the Whiskey Jacks, the Dream World saloon advertised "STAGS—HOT TUB—SHOWERS. WATCH EXOTIC WOMEN OVER A LUNCH SPECIAL $3.99."

Thunder Bay has few claims to fame. Its name, of course, is one, but when the residents of the cities of Fort William and Port Arthur agreed to merge in 1969, they actually supported the name Lakehead. The city's most famous native son is Paul Shaffer, the droll, bald bandleader on David Letterman's late-night talk show. Thunder Bay also boasts the inventor of the gas mask, Capt. H. E.

Knobel, and a man who created, in 1917, what was claimed to be the first telephone answering machine.

The city seems an altogether unlikely place for a professional baseball team. The only one it ever had played just two and a half seasons in the Northern League in the 1910s. Other sports, from cricket to curling, are more popular.

If the idea of baseball in Thunder Bay struck the laconic locals as weird, the club's owner seemed even more bizarre. Ricky May is a southerner—from the American South—complete with a Dixie accent that confounded the residents he stopped on the streets and in corner stores during his first visit in the summer of 1992 to ask about their city.

Unlike those of Van Schley, Marv Goldklang, Harry Stavrenos, and even Bill Pereira, Ricky May's baseball résumé is skimpy. Miles Wolff had hired May in the early 1980s fresh out of the University of North Carolina as an assistant general manager in Durham. A year later, at age twenty-two, May inherited the GM's job. After two years he left to become an assistant athletic director at the University of Louisville, then director of sports marketing for Valvoline; then he opened two retail sporting goods stores in Virginia. An aggressive, cost-cutting small businessman, May over the years stayed in touch with his mentor. Wolff continually expressed his frustrations in Durham and one day mentioned his new Northern League venture. May said to keep him in mind.

Wolff's small circle of independent-minded baseball friends plucked the franchises with the greatest attributes. Sioux Falls had a quality stadium and eager-to-please public officials who kept tossing money at Stavrenos. Sioux City committed to building a ballpark. St. Paul was a big city, the league's flagship franchise.

But Thunder Bay was crucial. Wolff needed the city, which with 113,000 residents was certainly large enough to support a club, to pair geographically with Duluth. But who would be willing to risk money to start professional baseball not only in Canada, with its inherent currency problem, but in a recession-racked Canadian city that, save for watching the Blue Jays on television, had no connection to the sport?

Nobody, including Ricky May, had even heard of Thunder Bay.

Soon enough, though, May was flying into the city on a Bearskin Airlines twin-prop. The business venture was full of potential—for failure and success. Thunder Bay didn't have a clue about minor league baseball, but it followed the Blue Jays. The ballpark was falling down, but officials seemed willing to pay for repairs. The town was blue-collar, but it was a proud and hardworking populace (70 percent of residents owned their homes). The economy was languishing, but new opportunities were rising.

Thunder Bay reminded May of Durham in 1980. It was the field of dreams syndrome; you could build it your way and see if the people came. "It was one of those rare opportunities," he said, "where you could do it right the first time, do it your way, not have anybody in the community be able to say, 'Well, they used to do this,' or 'When the old ball club was here they did that,' or 'I don't want to talk to you because the last guy didn't pay his bills.' None of those things that you tend to run into when National Association leagues are expanding or shifting or moving franchises. None of that was here."

What Durham had that Thunder Bay didn't was a baseball history. Sure, the game had been played in northern Ontario as long ago as the turn of the century; a photograph from the early 1900s shows a streetcar billboard announcing a baseball game that afternoon at Current River Park, and a semipro club attracted crowds for a few years in the 1960s and '70s. But May was dealing with professional baseball novices. When he arrived after Thunder Bay received the franchise, he was asked repeatedly when the club would hold a tryout for the local boys to stock the team. Every new owner of a minor league baseball franchise wonders whether his club will draw fans. In Thunder Bay the fear was even more basic: If the city doesn't *understand* minor league baseball, how can it *support* minor league baseball?

Some towns fill baseball stadiums night after night out of some inexplicable longing for the game itself. You can almost predict whether a place will respond. Essential ingredients are history, a desire for inexpensive entertainment, a quality product, a fun atmosphere. In the 1980s, a number of American cities fit the description: Durham. Buffalo. Louisville. Salt Lake City. Peoria. Boise. Some volunteered to open their coffers for new franchises. Sioux Falls and Sioux City were writing checks before the league was a reality; in fact, their actions helped make it a reality.

In Thunder Bay officials were welcoming, but they didn't genuflect. In his first meeting with May and Wolff, the new mayor didn't volunteer to overhaul Port Arthur Stadium. It needed it. Built in 1952 for youth football and baseball, Port Arthur offers a lovely view of the grain elevators that take in wheat from Canada's western breadbasket for shipment south and east, but the stadium hadn't ever had any capital improvements. Water pipes leaked. The light towers were rotted; in 1988 Ontario Hydroelectric had condemned the lighting system. Paint peeled everywhere. The bathrooms were crumbling. Dugouts were in disrepair. In short, it was unusable.

In September 1992 the city council voted the new ball club a one-year lease and $210,700 Canadian for renovations. It seemed like a healthy amount, but in U.S. dollars it worked out to about $140,000. Enough for a new backstop and seats, sod, and a paint job. But not enough to remove the wooden light poles from the playing field. The locker rooms and bathrooms were so cramped that the visiting team changed at its hotel.

These careful Canadians in a struggling town wouldn't stand for pouring money into an unknown venture. Plus, here was an American businessman, with a funny accent at that, proposing to run a very visible part of the city's summer entertainment. (May had to work hard to avoid being labeled a carpetbagger; he encouraged the notion that he was barely making it in Thunder Bay, saying the weaker Canadian dollar cost the franchise $100,000 a year in expenses. But many locals still believed he was driving truckloads of money back to Virginia.) Local businesses didn't understand the concept of an outfield fence sign; they had never seen one. Everyone wanted to see results.

They didn't have to wait long. After starting their inaugural season with six straight one-run losses on the road, the Whiskey Jacks went home to learn whether Thunder Bay cared. They discovered

6,255 people in a stadium that seated about 5,500. Where did Ricky May put his Thunder Bay fans? Three deep along the outfield warning track. (A ball hit into the crowd was a ground-rule double.)

Credibility—and local pride in a butt-of-the-jokes town—soared when a Blue Jays announcer modeled a Whiskey Jacks hat during a telecast; the purple-and-teal caps decorated with a gray Canadian jay sold by the thousands. (May chose purple and teal because they were hot marketing colors. "It didn't matter if we were the Goats. We were going to be the teal and purple Goats. I knew it would sell.") The fans loved the on-field promotions May recalled from Durham. There were favorite players, and clubhouse groupies, and desperate cheers for a third-place team.

By season's end the Whiskey Jacks had the second-best attendance behind St. Paul, averaging more than 4,000 a night. Ricky May, a teetotaling Republican with a twang as southern as grits, was named newsmaker of the year.

The fans didn't particularly care that the baseball being played was independent. What was important was that teenagers took dates to Whiskey Jacks games, senior citizens gathered for a night out, and kids asked the players for autographs. Socially, the stadium was a popular hangout—a prerequisite for success in any minor league town. If you closed your eyes to the purple paint and your ears to the *eh?*s rolling off the Canadian tongues, Port Arthur Stadium had become a minor league ballpark like any other in North America.

Thunder Bay's 1994 season began with a three-game visit from the defending champion St. Paul Saints. "There wasn't anyplace else to be last summer," May said before the opening, taking a break from his frenetic movements around the stadium and dropping into one of the secondhand orange seats he'd purchased from an arena in Greensboro, North Carolina. "Now we'll find out if that's the case this summer or not."

The owner was counting on the fans to make it so. Reluctant to open the wallet too wide a year earlier, the city of Thunder Bay appropriated about $1 million Canadian over three years for more renovations, including lighting improvements that removed the poles from the field and increased the power to avoid the frequent brownouts that left outfielders in the dark. Season-ticket sales doubled to a thousand. Fence signs packed the outfield, representing businesses from the giant brewer Molson Canadian to Barewood Unpainted Furniture and Craftware. The local newspaper published a thirty-two-page season preview.

May was pleased, but he never stopped worrying. No detail was too small for the demanding owner, who barked commands at employees. Before a game a technician fixing the public address system shouted from the rooftop press box to see if May liked the sound. Informed there were no paper towels in the men's room during a game, May was off like a bullet down the corridor; someone had hell to pay. The second season would be the one to solidify the Whiskey Jacks as a fixture in town, and everything had to be right.

Opening Day 1994 offered a cloudless evening and temperatures in the low sixties in a town where darkness in summer doesn't fall until ten o'clock. Rock music from a local radio station and the thwack-thud sounds of baseballs hitting bats and gloves filled the pregame air. The team's new mascot, Jack, a purple, bug-eyed, bowling-pin-shaped creature, roamed the stands.

But Port Arthur Stadium wasn't filling; May had expected a sellout, and he got about 4,500. Games 2 and 3 would draw only 3,000 fans each. There was an easy explanation, one that also underscored a problem with baseball up north: Potential fans were watching the National Hockey League championship series between the Vancouver Canucks and New York Rangers. "There's NHL parties all over town," one usher said. (Still, more than 14,000 hockey fans showed up in Winnipeg for the debut of the Goldeyes.)

May, probably overreacting, was concerned that the thrill might be leaving Thunder Bay. "It's not what we expected," he told the local paper in a page-one story the day after the opener. "I can't figure it out. I hope it's the hockey game. I don't have a good answer."

Years before Wolff had taught May that there are two things you never promise in minor league baseball: a winning team and good weather. (May had also learned from Wolff to cut expenses at every turn. One example: the Whiskey Jacks provided an annoyingly small supply of batting practice baseballs to the visiting team. Hey, they cost $3 apiece.) The weather is inarguably lousy in Thunder Bay. Everyone accepted that. But fans also identify with a winner, and in independent baseball you can control winning and losing by assembling a better team.

After the Whiskey Jacks split the first two games against the Saints, May spent most of the final contest—the night of another NHL game—sitting in the stands with Wolff, who was touring the league with his family. The owner nervously eyed the small crowd, thinking about his bottom line. Unlike the other, deeper-pocketed, baseball-loving Northern League owners, who were in it as much for the on-field challenge as for the business potential, May was mainly concerned with making money in a suspect market. So when the Whiskey Jacks pushed across two runs in the bottom of the eighth inning to go ahead 6–5, the owner wanted a win badly. But not for the usual reasons. "Come on! One-two-three!" May said as the top of the ninth began. "It'll help the weekend crowds."

Among the anomalies of baseball in the frozen north, none was greater than T. J. Rosenthal, folk hero. Rosenthal became a fan favorite during the Whiskey Jacks' very first game—an intrasquad contest before the 1993 season. In the first inning he lined a single into left field. As he rounded first, legs chugging, Rosenthal's helmet flew off, and he dove into second base. From then on the blue-collar Canadians were in love with this suburban New Yorker whose father was a dentist and mother a psychotherapist. Every time he came to the plate, the fans would shout his name along with the public address announcer: *"Now batting for your Thunder Bay Whiskey Jacks! Number seven! TEE! JAY! RRRRO-sen-thal!"*

Rosenthal is a smart player, which is a backhanded way of saying that he makes up in intelligence and aggressiveness what he lacks in physical ability. Most players rely on their natural gifts. They always ran faster, fielded better, threw harder, and hit farther than the other kids. Others have to become students of the game in order to improve. Rosenthal is a student of baseball.

Todd Rosenthal—T.J. is a stage name—is fairly small, especially for a first baseman: five foot ten, 165 pounds. He doesn't hit for power. He isn't fast on the base paths. He can't cover much territory in the outfield, where he also plays. He doesn't have a strong throwing arm. In other words, Rosenthal has none of the checklist of tools that scouts mandate in tryout camps.

"I'm not sure they're completely wrong with that assessment," Rosenthal said one night. "But I think there's other things that play in games than just that. If it was home-to-first speed you'd be a track star, and if it was power you'd be a weight lifter. It's how you cut corners on the bases and read pitches. No one has an advantage in the ninth inning in a big at bat because they're six three and two-forty. It matters what your mental approach is to the game. So that's the kind of advantage I have to use if I want to stay in there."

Rosenthal is all about intensity. When he was eight his father stuck him in a league with older kids. Todd was the smallest on the team—and took home the all-star game MVP award. He attended Scarsdale High School, the most academically achieving in affluent Westchester County. Scarsdale is big houses filled with doctors and lawyers who commute daily to Manhattan. An ungodly percentage of the student body goes to Ivy League schools, so athletes aren't revered. When Rosenthal was named state athlete of the year by *USA Today*, his teammates and friends were shocked—not because they doubted Rosenthal's talent but because they wondered when anyone had noticed.

What was unmistakable was Rosenthal's work ethic. Extra ground balls in the infield. Extra flies in the outfield. Extra batting practice. Extra time talking about the game. Even when he watched baseball on television, he wasn't an idle viewer but a student. The long-haired teen listened to heavy-metal bands like Metallica and Anthrax and partied on weekends, but he knew where to draw the line. Sports were his priority. Basketball in the winter—Rosenthal was a fourth-team all-state guard who was recruited by some small Division I schools—and baseball in the spring. But his love always had been baseball. Before the Rosenthals moved to Scarsdale, they'd lived in the Riverdale section of the Bronx, ten minutes from Yankee Stadium, at a time when New York won back-to-back World Series championships. Scarsdale had no Little League program, but Rosenthal always envisioned himself playing baseball. "Even though there were kids who were a little better physically, athletically than me, even at that age I knew I wanted to be playing with commercial signs on the fence," he said.

"I could see it. I didn't know how far or how high I would be, but I just sensed myself being here. Even in college. My first year I was 155 pounds and I hit .412." (He quietly made second-team Big East, behind Mo Vaughn, the Boston Red Sox star.) "And I didn't really hit the ball hard. I was one of the country leaders, and I don't think a lot of the older guys were happy with the fact that I was hitting the ball so weakly. In my heart I knew I really wasn't hitting the ball far enough to get a contract. But in my mind it didn't stop me. I was going to do what it took."

Nick Belmonte, then managing the Salt Lake Trappers, was looking for a center fielder when he tuned in to a Big East tournament game on cable TV one day in the spring of 1992. He keyed on Rosenthal, whose coach at the University of Connecticut had moved him to the outfield, where, because of his size, he was more likely to get an opportunity as a professional. The lefty hit two tough sliders against a left-handed pitcher, pulling the ball. Belmonte was impressed. He called Rosenthal's coach, who talked nonstop about the player's love of the game.

When Rosenthal wasn't drafted, Belmonte invited him to fly out to Salt Lake (at his own expense) for a tryout. After two days Belmonte made a decision. He called Rosenthal into his office. Rosenthal already knew the rap. Too small, no power, no speed, no arm.

"Rosie, sit down. You know, we've got a lot of outfielders out there, and I know you're a good ballplayer, and the competition's tough and we still have some guys we're looking at."

Rosenthal's head slumped to his chest.

"The reason I brought you in here is I just want to tell you, you can play for me anytime. I want to sign you."

Rosenthal's eyes brightened. Belmonte told him to call his father. He shut the office door behind him but lingered outside to eavesdrop. He had just made a kid's dream come true, and he wanted to hear it.

"Dad!" Rosenthal breathed into the phone. Silence. "I made it!"

Every time Rosenthal batted—even during slumps—he just *knew* he'd get a hit. In Scarsdale, watching a Yankees pitcher named Brian Fisher throw ninety miles per hour, Rosenthal boasted that he could hit his fastball. "I'd miss the first thirty times, but then I'd smack the shit out of it," he said. Even in high school games Rosenthal patiently waited to see what a pitcher threw, often going deep into the count, and adjusted his swing accordingly. Mentally he was beyond his years on the field. He never felt pressure. And was he ever a clutch performer.

Late in the 1992 season, in the heat of a pennant race, the Trappers were playing a big game against Butte. Pitching for the Copper Kings was Scott Eyre, a prospect, and he was mowing down the opposition. About a dozen Trappers had whiffed, and Eyre had a no-hitter and a 1–0 lead through seven innings. But Rosenthal kept walking up to Belmonte in the dugout: "I can hit this guy. I'm gonna hit this guy."

In the bottom of the eighth, Belmonte had his first two batters bunt—safely, for base hits. With two outs and the runners now on second and third, Rosenthal stepped up, lefty against lefty.

"Aw, hell, Rosie," Belmonte told him, "you've been telling me all day you can hit this guy. Well, here you go."

Rosenthal bobbed his head as if to say, "I got it. I got it. No problem."

Bang. Line drive. Left field. Base hit. Salt Lake wins, 2–1.

Rosenthal was a competitor. On long Pioneer League bus rides, he'd always be the first in for a game of Trivial Pursuit. His nickname was Tank. He had shaved his shoulder-length hair to a crew cut, and he would run, crash, and dive around the field.

Early in the season, when Rosenthal was hitting about .390, Belmonte was trying to determine whether his new first baseman–outfielder was crazy or simply loved baseball more than anyone on the planet. At 2:30 one morning, after a game in Billings, Montana, the manager and two baseball friends closed down a bar and headed in search of an all-night diner.

The men walked past the motor court where the Trappers were staying, presumably asleep. Belmonte casually glanced over to make sure all the lights were out, only to see Todd Rosenthal standing in the parking lot outside his room, in nothing but boxer shorts, swinging a baseball bat. Belmonte watched for a minute before walking away in disbelief.

Rosenthal batted .305 in Salt Lake, but he got no offers from major league organizations and attended no winter tryout camps. Clutch hitting, patience at the plate, the ability to hit consistently to all fields—those are game skills that don't emerge in a two-day cattle call where coaches make snap judgments based on sprinting speed, arm strength, and power. Belmonte and his first-base coach, Dan Shwam, both left for the new Northern League, and Belmonte made sure Rosenthal was the first player signed by the fledgling league. Like the club's owner, Rosenthal had no idea where to find Thunder Bay. "It just sounded like a cool name. It sounded like I'd be wearing a cool cap, so I was psyched."

Rosenthal is the perfect independent player: scrappy, driven, confident, hardworking. He hit .309 for Thunder Bay, with no homers and twenty-six runs batted in. More important, Rosenthal had fun playing baseball—he learned not to worry about getting signed by an organization. It helped his psyche, but in the off-season no one called again.

"I do the same things every year consistently, but I guess there's parts of my game that what I'm doing on the field right now no one really needs," he said. "I guess that's why I'm back here." Instead of bemoaning his fate, though, as other players did, Rosenthal spent his time off evaluating his game. Should he weight-lift more to gain power? Run sprints every day? Play the outfield, where he was more likely to whet an organization's interest, instead of first base, where he was more comfortable and talented? Rosenthal settled on trying to "perfect, if you can perfect," his strengths. Shorten his swing to drive the ball better. Be even more selective at the plate. Swing at better pitches. Raise his batting average. In the first week of the new season, Thunder Bay signed a power-hitting first baseman, so Rosenthal would get some playing time in the outfield.

"I figure maybe another year of consistency, maybe someone will respect it," he said. "I'm not playing just to play in Thunder Bay. Whether it's get picked up or go to another country or something, someone will give you a job. There's always a job for a .300 hitter, you know? There's not many around."

Howie Bedell (© Howie Hanson)

EIGHT

We may lose again tomorrow, but not with the same guys.

—Yogi Berra

As anyone who ever played on a rotten team—*any* rotten team—can testify, losing is contagious. Each defeat builds on the previous one, and, in short order, the desire to reverse the trend is replaced by the fatalistic knowledge that you can't possibly win, that you or one of your teammates will do something to ensure another loss. Minor league baseball is hard enough mentally on players, who have to maintain a confidence that someday, someone would reward their efforts. Toss in the extra burden of playing on a miserable club and you've got an emotional Molotov cocktail.

By the end of June, the Duluth-Superior Dukes had a team batting average of about .240 and were scoring just over three runs per game— half as many as Sioux Falls and by far the fewest in the Northern League. Factoring out the odd game when the Dukes crossed the plate nine or ten times, the average was closer to two. Duluth's pitchers weren't exactly the 1970 Orioles, but their collective earned run average, around 4.50, wasn't the league's worst.

In baseball, particularly on a last-place team, one set of players who perform a task—say, pitching—shouldn't criticize another set of players who perform another task—for instance, hitting. The rule of thumb is you do your job and I'll do mine. *Never* taunt a teammate in a slump; some players won't even *talk* to a struggling player, partly not to anger him, but also not to catch whatever he's got. No one told that to the Dukes' pitching staff, which one night—during a game, no less—decided to address the club's hitting deficiencies. Which prompted a disagreement.

Andy Skeels, a veteran catcher who had played as high as Triple-A in the Yankees organization, was walking along the dugout as right-handed starter Tom Paskievitch loudly bemoaned the Dukes' hitting futility that night against an unimpressive pitcher. Skeels was a new-comer to the club, but his experience gave him the right to talk. He told Paskievitch that the hitters were doing their best, and, by the way, why don't you stick to pitching and quit ragging on your team-mates? Paskievitch, sitting on the end of the bench, told Skeels to shove it. Skeels grabbed him by the jersey. As Paskievitch stood up, Skeels pushed him over, the two players wrestling to the dugout floor. Howie Bedell was coaching third base at Wade Stadium. He raced back to the dugout to break up the fight.

There was a bright side to the incident. The Dukes may have been bad, but at least they cared enough to fight about it.

"Yesterday might have been the bottom" were the first words to pass Ted Cushmore's lips one night. The season was just three weeks old, but to the Dukes' owner it seemed an eternity. Duluth had a 3–15 record and was last in the league in just about every hitting category. Home attendance was barely 2,000 a game, also dead last. Earl the Duke was as lugubrious as ever. Cushmore felt like a cross between Casey Stengel of the '62 Mets and a poster boy for Murphy's law. No one here could play this game, and everything was going wrong.

Still, he was determined. He was missing his twelve-year-old son's Little League games. He hadn't played golf all summer. He wasn't sleeping well. The unruffled suburban corporate executive was feeling haggard. But no matter how difficult things got, there always seemed to be one more indignity waiting.

Cushmore took a vacation day from General Mills on a Tuesday when the Dukes were scheduled to play a doubleheader against Thun-der Bay. The city's responsibility for maintaining the field at Wade

Stadium ended at four o'clock, and, as usual, at five—one hour before game time—it began to rain. Because the Dukes employed just two groundskeepers, the club's general manager, Tom Van Schaack, was on the field unrolling the tarp while Cushmore sprinkled the magical Diamond Dust to soak up excess water.

Five minutes before game time, the Dukes' new left fielder, Greg Shockey, was stung by a bee and rushed to the hospital with a swollen throat. Cushmore didn't know it, so when the club's catcher and his .210 average strolled to the plate as the designated hitter that night, Cushmore wondered what was going on. "I'm ready to do a Steinbrenner and send a note down to Howie wondering why Shockey isn't playing."

To everyone's surprise, including the owner's, Duluth won the first game, 10–0. In the second game the Dukes sent their new pitching ace, Scott Freeman, to the mound, Cushmore having traded center fielder Steve Dailey to Winnipeg in a version of the deal that Nick Belmonte had proposed at the start of the season. In the bottom of the second, it started raining again. On came the tarp. After an hour play resumed. Now Cushmore was afraid the game wouldn't be completed by the league's 11:30 curfew, and he would lose his best pitcher for a turn in the rotation. For once, though, things fell into place. The Dukes won, 5–1, and had their first winning streak of the season. Cushmore left the stadium at 11:45 a happy man, relatively speaking. The Dukes were 5–15 but winners twice in one day.

Twenty miles south of Duluth, Cushmore's car began to sputter. And then it stopped. No gas. By the time help arrived, Cushmore had decided to forget about crawling into his own bed. He pulled into a motel in the town of Hinckley, less than halfway home, and spent the night. "I get up at five, put my pinstripe on, and go to General Mills as if nothing's happened," he said.

The very next evening the owner left the Wade before the end of the game against Thunder Bay for the long drive. The Dukes were winning, and he had an early meeting at General Mills the next day. It was a good night to duck out early.

This time the gas gauge was fine, but when he arrived at his car in a space reserved for Dukes employees—directly behind and perilously close to home plate—he discovered a baseball in his backseat. During games kids scrambled to the top of the grandstands and peered through the gaps in the brick to see whether a foul ball made contact with a car. The announcer read ad copy over the sound of breaking glass—"Uh-oh! Better call City Auto Glass! Seven-two-two zero-zero-zero-zero!" Picking shards of glass from the seat, Cushmore no longer found the ad amusing.

He tried to cover the gaping hole in his rear windshield, to no avail. OK, Cushmore thought, I can fix this tomorrow. He drove away, tuning the radio to hear the end of a Dukes victory. At the magic twenty-mile mark south of Duluth, the radio signal dissolved into a static hiss before the game had ended. Wind rushed into the car, but Cushmore kept driving. Rain began to fall. Beaten, Cushmore stopped once again in Hinckley for the night. The Dukes lost in twelve innings.

As sappy as it sounded, whenever things looked bleakest in the hell of his first season as a baron of independent minor league baseball, Ted Cushmore clung to the idea of the game itself. Wade Stadium was turning into a den of horrors, not to mention errors, but Cushmore considered it a second home. Knowing that the field and the players on it were his—metaphorically, anyway—wiped away the daily losses in the standings and the bottom line. After Duluth's first win Cushmore's favorite rookie, a University of Missouri standout named Rodney Weary, who went four for five that night, signed the game ball and gave it to the owner.

Even if he lost one hundred grand in Duluth in 1994—and it was looking as if he might—that moment might have made everything worthwhile. He owned something that he loved. Its success filled him with pleasure. Its shortcomings suffused him with dread—tempered by the fact that it was baseball, not cereal or flour or frozen pizza. Cushmore believed the words from *Field of Dreams* that he had hired someone to paint on a sign and had hung inside the red brick entryway to Wade Stadium:

People will come. They'll come for reasons they can't even fathom. They'll arrive at the gate, as innocent as children, longing for the past. They'll pay money for tickets without even thinking about it. For it's money they have, and peace they seek.

And they'll walk out to the bleachers, fit in short sleeves on a perfect evening. They'll find reserved seats somewhere along one of the baselines, where they sat when they were children and cheered their heroes. And they'll watch the game.

It will be as if they dipped themselves in magic waters. The memories will be so thick they'll have to brush them away from their faces.

One constant throughout the years has been baseball. This field, this game is part of our past. It reminds us of all that once was good, and could be again.

Cushmore felt he had profited the moment he signed the contract to buy the Dukes. He had spent twenty-eight years at General Mills, as regimented a corporate bureaucracy as any in America. He wrote memos, attended meetings, reported to committees, suffered through political struggles, waited for action to occur. With the Dukes he had finally broken free—no one to answer to, not even a major league parent. He could make whatever changes he liked, whenever he wanted. Most important, the business was baseball.

The freedom in operating a team is unique to the minors. "I think you just get spoiled working in the minor leagues," Miles Wolff once said. "You're so used to seeing an immediate reaction." But for farm club owners the freedom extends just to the business. It is only in independent baseball where a Ted Cushmore could have the free-ranging, all-encompassing power that could drive him to maddening anxiety and soaring euphoria at the same time.

"When I'm driving up here, no matter how tough things are, I get pumped," he said. "I can't describe it. It's the game. I love to throw and catch a baseball. I love to go down and take some whacks. I love to be around the players. I *was* a player. I played with a lot of players who signed. I wanted to be a big-league ballplayer—that's all I wanted to be, right through my last game at Colgate. When I walked out to left field—we were playing Cornell, it was after graduation—I realized this might be my last organized baseball game. I was crying. It was awful.

"The game just has a hook on me. When I'm standing around a batting cage, or a tryout camp, watching these guys hit, or having a catch with Steve Hinton, or having Scott Eidle throw a little b.p. to me, that's as happy as I get. I don't know what that's all about—and that is no reason to pay half a fucking million dollars for a baseball team." Cushmore erupted in laughter, a cathartic howl from the abyss. "But I think it might be why I did. And that's bizarre."

Ted Cushmore was getting good at dramatic opening lines. "This has been a living nightmare," he said by way of greeting a visitor to Wade Stadium on the afternoon of July 8. The Dukes were riding an eight-game losing streak since their doubleheader sweep of Thunder Bay. Their record was a jaw-dropping 5–23. At the box office Cushmore was having equal success; the previous night's rain-shortened game against Winnipeg had drawn just 1,381 fans, dropping the season average to 1,915 (compared with 7,221 in Winnipeg and 6,189 in St. Paul on the same date).

Then there was the front office. Cushmore still felt that, despite his motivational speeches, change wasn't occurring fast enough. The club's marketing efforts were abysmal. The Dukes were depositing $4,000 in the bank after every game instead of $10,000; Cushmore was projecting an $84,000 loss for the year. The sales staff of two couldn't recover accounts that had deserted because of first-season missteps—the false promises to advertisers and money-losing promotional deals the Dukes had cut with some accounts. Nothing was changing, and Cushmore blamed his general manager, whose dour personality he felt inhibited the marketing efforts the club needed.

Tom Van Schaack was back for his second year in Duluth and was known as a good stadium operator who lacked the interpersonal skills to make the club popular in the community. In 1993 much of that had been handled by the Dukes' talkative former manager, Mal Fichman, but it had fallen to Van Schaack now. In the mid-1980s, the general manager had begun his career working for Miles Wolff's Appalachian League franchise in Burlington, North Carolina, and Wolff had recommended him for Duluth and then encouraged Cushmore to keep him for continuity.

But as attendance slumped and problems mounted, Cushmore didn't care who had recommended Van Schaack. Whenever he was with his general manager, Cushmore felt his energy drain away. The franchise was suffering. So he made a move. Van Schaack was out. Frank Gahl, general manager of a Midwest League club in Appleton, Wisconsin, was hired. Gahl is a balding, exuberant promoter who admires Mike Veeck's offbeat approach. During his first week in Duluth, Gahl lugged an air tank to the ballpark and made balloon sculptures—Indian hats for the vendors, poodles for kids. He wanted Wade Stadium to be fun.

Changing general managers in midseason is rare in the minors. It's the GM who knows where the paper towels are stored, whom to call if the toilets back up, the first name of the local banker, how to coddle each advertiser. In the public eye replacing the GM also raises questions about the stability of the franchise. "It almost never happens," Miles Wolff said. "To find another competent guy to replace him in midseason is very difficult. You've got promotions planned—the *season's* planned. To bring in someone to finish it out is very difficult."

In Duluth the firing created dissension among Dukes staffers already depressed about the state of the franchise. They genuinely liked Van Schaack. They didn't see changing GMs as the answer. But Cushmore felt he couldn't wait any longer. Before the season he had delegated responsibility for the team's business and baseball sides. Now he was taking back the reins.

Cushmore took advantage of what, by local standards, amounted to controversy over the fate of the Dukes. The troubles were prompting whispers that he planned to pack up and move the team. In a way the adversity was a perfect opportunity for Cushmore to pump up fan support. He reminded the town that he had signed a five-year lease and wanted the city to take care of promises, like clearing pigeons from the rafters and painting the bathrooms.

"Absolutely not," the owner told the local paper when asked if he planned to move the club. "This is going to be as good a franchise as there is in the Northern League. Despite some of the difficulties we've had the past month, I'm very impressed with the core base of fans we have here. They're into the game. Dukes fans are clearly the best fans in the league."

It was also an opening for Cushmore to fall on his sword, which he did, obligingly. The memory of the poor Opening Day crowd hadn't faded, and Cushmore took the blame. "We assumed people would just show up. We didn't give them enough reasons to do so. Opening Day should be special, and we didn't make it special. That's not the fans' fault, and it won't happen again."

Privately, Cushmore was frustrated and angry. "This has been a joke," he said over a frozen yogurt one afternoon. "It's cost me a lot of money. It's cost me a lot of anxiety. It's cost me a lot of worry." It was just four o'clock, but he was yawning repeatedly.

The previous week had been typical. Cushmore brought his family to Duluth for the Fourth of July, but instead of relaxing at the park he was arranging Van Schaack's termination. There was a news conference the next afternoon. Then a staff meeting the following morning at Fitger's Inn, an old brewery converted into a hotel and shops, where Cushmore was shocked to discover the level of discontent with the move. That night around seven he drove home. The next morning he was up at 6:45 to fly to Washington for his father-in-law's funeral. After the burial at Arlington National Cemetery, Cushmore flew back to Minnesota. Up at five in the morning, he drove to Duluth to meet with his new general manager.

It was true that Cushmore wasn't planning to move the Dukes. But he couldn't afford to feed a money-losing franchise for two or three years. Cushmore had borrowed around $700,000 to buy and operate the team. But interest rates had been rising in 1994, increasing his bank loan payments. Even more troubling, Cushmore's principal asset, General Mills stock options, had been hurt as the company's share price tumbled from $69 at the time he had bought the Dukes to below $50 during the summer. (At least half the drop occurred in June after a recall of Cheerios and other General Mills cereals when the federal government discovered a shipment of oats sprayed with an unregulated pesticide. Cushmore's problems were converging: The tainted oats had been stored in Duluth.)

Cushmore didn't want to sell any of the club, but he might be willing to take on a partial investor who brought more to the team than money. "I really want to make it work," he said. "I really do. I want to make it work for the city. I want to make it work because I want something to do that I love. If I had to walk away from this, it would just tear me up. I would leave a big piece of me here. But we haven't done it right."

Cushmore had to balance his desire for the success of the Dukes franchise with the physical and emotional fatigue he felt. "I know I'm tired," he said. "I know I'm averaging three and a half hours of sleep. I know I never want to go through a period where I'm desperate—absolutely desperate—to win a baseball game."

After a 6–5 loss to St. Paul the previous night, the Dukes' record had fallen to 5–24, and the losing streak had reached nine.

Of the twenty-three players on Duluth's Opening Day roster in June, eleven were gone by the first week of July. Eric Parkinson, the veteran pitcher whose signing had tipped off the league that something was amiss in Duluth, was released. Gone too were Mike Hubel, the light-hitting catcher, and Greg Wiseman, the first baseman with the Mendoza-line batting average who hadn't played in a year. Jeff Bedell was relieved of his playing responsibilities but remained a full-time coach under his father, who himself was unofficially stripped of his player personnel duties.

Howie Bedell still wasn't able to work with Nick Belmonte, so Cushmore assumed the job of overhauling the Dukes. He consulted Bedell, largely as a courtesy, but nearly all the new players resulted from the owner's initiative. Still, Cushmore was a reluctant Branch Rickey. He wasn't entirely secure in his abilities as talent scout, but he quickly realized that with a little assistance he could do the job as well as the next Northern League owner. As Van Schley said, brain surgery this isn't. While the losing wasn't fun at all, day after day of defeat built Cushmore's confidence that he could repair his baseball team.

Sometimes he was a little too confident. One of the new players, Greg Shockey, recommended to Cushmore an LS-3 catcher named Mark Skeels, who had been released by the Marlins. When the owner called, Mark's brother, Andy, also a catcher, answered the phone. Andy was acting as Mark's agent but said he'd like to play too. A quick check revealed that Andy's numbers were better than Mark's.

"I think I want you instead of your brother," Cushmore said. But Andy loyally refused to displace his younger brother, so Cushmore asked whether the older Skeels could play third base. Andy naturally said sure.

The brothers drove three days from California to Duluth. In their first game Mark threw out three base runners. But within a week Cushmore—with the help of Bedell *and* Belmonte, though neither knew it—had landed a released third baseman named Bobby Perna. Andy Skeels played third as if he were standing in a minefield and had just two hits in sixteen at bats. Bedell and Cushmore took Andy out to the picnic area in right field. "Andy, we've got to send you home," Bedell said.

The twenty-eight-year-old veteran ballplayer looked at Bedell, then looked at Cushmore. "Well, guys, it sure was a long fucking drive for five games."

Batting .077 after a week and a half, Mark Skeels was released, too, but was re-signed two hours later when Dave Maize decided to retire rather than back up Jeff Grotewold, Cushmore's latest addition. A Triple-A catcher in the Twins organization who had played in the majors but had been released in the spring, Grotewold had been playing for the independent San Bernardino club in the Class-A California League. But he hated it and had quit a few weeks into the season.

No one in the Northern League knew this until Belmonte, tracking down some information on a pitcher released by the Phillies, heard from a contact that, by the way, a guy named Jeff Grotewold had just called looking for a job. Belmonte had heard of the catcher. Cushmore took it from there.

He called Grotewold in California to make sure the catcher understood the situation: It's an independent league, the team's been struggling, we really don't have a backup, you'd be a clubhouse leader. If you come out here, I'll want you to catch every inning, every day. Grotewold told him not to worry. It cost the Dukes' owner $1,200 to fly the catcher to Duluth and another $1,500 a month in salary.

Cushmore signed a new left fielder, Greg Shockey, and a new center fielder, Tom Coates. At third he replaced Andy Skeels with Perna, who had been released twice since spring training—first by the Cincinnati Reds and then by the Detroit Tigers, who signed him for just two weeks until another player came off the disabled list. Perna had been about to join the Seattle Mariners' Class-A affiliate in Appleton—competitively a step down. Thunder Bay's Dan Shwam had called Perna but gave up after he was told Perna was heading to Appleton. Duluth didn't quit so easily.

Belmonte already had spoken with Perna's father and raised questions about signing with Seattle. Why head to a lower classification where Perna already had succeeded? Why not showcase the talent in the Northern League? Could you trust Seattle when one of their executives said they saw and liked Perna in spring training—even though Cincinnati trained in Plant City, Florida, and Seattle in Peoria, Arizona? Howie Bedell knew Perna's father and also called him up to turn the screws and cinch the deal. Then Cushmore matched Seattle's offer of $1,400 a month, and the strong third baseman signed.

"Ted scooped Shwam. Until that guy was on the plane, Ted wasn't going to give up," Belmonte said. "This is all coming on Ted's insistence on turning this thing around. He's been very, very aggressive."

Cushmore kept moving. Belmonte recommended a pitcher named Dominic Desantis, who had played for him a few years earlier on a semipro team in Miami. Less than forty-eight hours after his release, Desantis's high school coach was on the phone with Belmonte. Sticking to the rules, Belmonte faxed Desantis's statistics to all six Northern League teams. When Cushmore called to inquire, Belmonte told him, "Desantis is your guy." Winnipeg, St. Paul, and Thunder Bay also expressed interest. But Cushmore went after him—fast. He did the same with a veteran pitcher named Dennis Wiseman.

Cushmore, of course, was acting largely because the demon desperation was whispering in his ear, but he was beating more experienced operators for the best available talent. St. Paul, for one, was interested in Coates, Wiseman, and Desantis, but Marv Goldklang was reluctant to shake up the roster of what still looked to be a solid team. (Van Schley favored new blood.) Cushmore had no such reservations; the Dukes were dead last. He may have stumbled in March, April, and May, but Cushmore was on a roll in June and July.

"He's beating out guys that aren't used to getting beaten out," Belmonte said. "The big boys of the league are losing out to Duluth.

When two or more teams are going after the same player, Duluth is getting better than their fair share in the recruiting war. I love it that he doesn't sit on it. He makes up his mind and he does it. Mainly he does it out of necessity—whoever we're talking about is better than what he has—but he gets the deal done. The negotiator is very convincing.

"The sad thing is," Belmonte concluded, "this is an expense that shouldn't have happened to this degree."

Saturday, July 9, and Sunday, July 10, were rare days in Duluth. After the ritual morning fog burned off Lake Superior, the sun emerged and never departed. Temperatures were in the low seventies. Rain or the threat of it had poisoned fourteen of the Dukes' first sixteen home games, but not this weekend. "Plenty of sunshine and cool," the *Duluth News-Tribune* promised. Tourists crowded the downtown harbor, skimming stones across the world's largest body of fresh water and watching the roadway rise 138 feet on the Aerial Lift Bridge that allows ships in and out of the Twin Ports.

Was the weather an omen? Ted Cushmore didn't tender the thought. He was seething over the team's bad luck—the one-run loss to St. Paul on Friday, a 6–4 loss to Thunder Bay on Thursday that had been halted because of rain after eight innings, just as the Dukes were coming back. He had a new GM who needed guidance and a mounting anger over Howie Bedell. Cushmore reached into his briefcase and pulled out a copy of Friday's sports section. "Bedell's tired of the losing" read a headline over a column by Bruce Bennett. "I'm tired of the constant change, the turnover, the losses," the manager was quoted as saying. "But this is my job. When I said this winter we were coming here to win, I meant it, but we're just not getting it done."

The column went on to describe Bedell as a tough competitor who didn't have any quit in him. Cushmore was a patient owner, and both were rookies in independent baseball. The two men had been misled, Bedell said, in putting together the team. And thus the buck was passed.

"All those tryouts and camps we had early on were a waste," he said. "I've found you can put together a club late, in mid-June or early July. A lot of good players become available then. But we spent a lot of time and money foolishly last spring traveling all over looking at players. What we should be doing is running a camp in mid-June or July and taking players as a league from it. But we were trapped. I was ignorant of what the Northern League was all about. Ted kept saying, 'It's a good league.' But how good? Now I know. We've made some changes and if we can get everyone together, we'll be all right."

Bedell said he had been told the Northern League was comparable to high Class-A or Double-A. "It's not. In those classifications you have prospects going to the major leagues. There are very few prospects in this league. What you have here are players who are very good, experienced, and play with determination. Therein lies the secret."

Bedell had learned one thing: Independent baseball bears no resemblance to organization baseball. But when Cushmore read his comments about the tryout camps, he was flabbergasted. They were "a waste," time and money spent "foolishly"? The league should hold camps in June and July? *After* the season had started? What could Bedell possibly have been thinking? Especially after he hadn't paid particularly close attention during the camps themselves—camps that Cushmore had helped pay for and paid Bedell to attend. (Bedell had left a camp in Fort Myers early to go fishing and traveled to but didn't attend another one in Houston.) "How do you think I feel?" Cushmore asked rhetorically. But he wouldn't bring it up with Bedell. It wasn't worth it.

When he hired Howie Bedell, Cushmore felt he had made a good choice. Bedell had the baseball résumé, of course, but that alone wasn't what won him the job. He could be terrifically friendly in conversation, telling amusing baseball stories in slow and deliberate tones. He appeared exceedingly polite and humble, with a broad smile and avuncular warmth that are rare in baseball. For six hours Cushmore had interviewed Doug Simunic, who liked the city and desperately wanted the job. Simunic had the independent baseball smarts to field a competitive team. But after a year of the quirky Mal Fichman, Cushmore wanted to present a serious but friendly baseball man to the community, and he didn't think the gruff, walrusy Simunic was right for the job.

But that was ancient history. Cushmore now just wanted to turn his team around. He would worry about Bedell later. "This team we're putting together is my team and Nick's team—and to some extent Howie's team," Cushmore said. "To his limited credit—very limited— Howie's been willing to make the changes."

Cushmore still was wearing his fatalism on his sleeve, but, like the weather, when he paused for a moment he could see a big difference in Wade Stadium. With the exception of Grotewold, who wouldn't arrive until the following week, the players on the field for the week-end series against St. Paul were the new and improved Duluth-Superior Dukes. The new general manager brought an aw-shucks-I'm-so-happy-to-be-here enthusiasm, parading around the park in one of his balloon hats, taunting the umpire, greeting fans, imploring the public address announcer to liven it up when he read the names of the Dukes' hitters. While Friday's rain-dampened crowd hadn't been huge—1,853—the Wade didn't have the funereal atmosphere of earlier in the season.

It was a good night. The Blues Brothers—a comedy act featuring John Belushi and Dan Aykroyd look-alikes who traveled around minor league ballparks—had fans dancing and singing. There was a new mascot, Homer Hound, a loose-limbed guy in a dog costume and a Dukes uniform, whose presence seemed to energize the previously comatose Earl the Duke. "He's alive, anyway," Cushmore said.

After St. Paul manager Tim Blackwell strolled to the mound to remove his starter, Joe Brownholtz, fans swayed in unison and waved to the departing pitcher as "Happy Trails" echoed through the ballpark. Another inning fans contorted their arms in the shape of letters to the Village People's campy 1970s gay-pride anthem "YMCA." If you were unaware of the team's record, or the front-office controversy, or the revolving-door clubhouse, you'd have thought that Wade Stadium was a terrific place to spend a summer evening watching minor league baseball.

Saturday's uncharacteristic weather produced a crowd of 3,328— the largest of the season. The fans saw a genuine pitchers' duel. St. Paul scratched out a run in the fifth on two Dukes errors and a single.

Duluth matched it in the sixth on a walk, a single, and a fielder's choice. The Saints threatened in the ninth but failed to score. The Dukes did the same in the twelfth. The zeroes lined up on the scoreboard.

"We might not lose tonight," Cushmore said in the middle of the fourteenth inning. "We might tie." Then, a minute later, "I really hoped we'd win so I could go to sleep. I'm beat."

The Dukes did their owner a favor. In the bottom of the fourteenth, Scott Eidle led off with a single. Newly arrived rookie second baseman Allen Williams sacrificed him to second. Then the light-hitting Dave Maize singled to center field. Bedell waved Eidle home, but the Yale alumnus was out by ten feet. Maize, however, alertly took second on the throw to home, and another newcomer, Tom Coates, rapped a single to right field to score the winning run.

Bedlam. The Dukes stormed from the dugout to greet Maize and Coates, clapping each other on the back and high-fiving. Streak over. Curse lifted. Whirlwind of roster changes validated. (But still the front office remained downcast. It was, after all, Frank Gahl's first day on the job, and the Van Schaack loyalists hadn't warmed to him, even making cracks about his balloon sculptures. Leaving an empty Wade Stadium after midnight, one Dukes staffer said, innocently enough, "See you tomorrow." Another replied, "You mean we have to come back tomorrow?")

The Dukes did it again on a glorious Sunday afternoon. Four runs in the bottom of the eighth—including a two-run single by Eidle, who before the game had rejected some gingerly worded hitting advice from an owner figuring the Yalie might listen to a former Colgate man—for another comeback win, 4–1, over the slumping Saints. A victory for a dominant relief pitcher named Dominic Desantis. A gate of 2,713 that pushed the Dukes' average attendance above 2,000 for the first time. And a beaming owner, who called his wife after the game to say he was leaving on the long drive home and for once left an upbeat message on their answering machine.

Vince Castaldo

NINE

We can't always guarantee that the ballgame is going to be good, but we can guarantee that the fan will have fun.

—Bill Veeck

FUN IS GOOD

—Sign in St. Paul Saints office

Sophomore slumps are a favorite cliché of sportswriters who want to cast doubt on an athlete's early promise. Miles Wolff feared one for the Northern League. The league president hoped the second year would solidify the circuit as a viable minor league, building on the respect it had earned in year one. He had goals. Improve the quality of the umpiring, unanimously considered abysmal in 1993. Ensure that the small-market franchises of Thunder Bay, Duluth, and Sioux Falls steadied their operations; Wolff couldn't afford another Rochester, literally and figuratively. Pray that a decent number of the 650,000 inhabitants of Winnipeg would support the first pro baseball team in the city since 1971, giving the league a second big market with St. Paul.

Could the league find sponsors? Would the cities continue to inject money into their stadiums? Would towns emerge for expansion? But the question that would determine whether the Northern League was here to stay or whether it was just another failed independent was this: Would fans in St. Paul, Duluth, Thunder Bay, Sioux City, and Sioux Falls back their teams now that the novelty of professional baseball had worn off? In farm system towns, clubs usually can afford to keep operating with low attendance. With the added burden of paying for salaries, equipment, health care, and insurance, the Northern League clubs couldn't survive a plunge in the fan base.

Credibility was another key to the second season, and Wolff was determined to force the majors to treat his league fairly. After the first year he was happy to see scouts in the stands and players getting a shot at a farm team roster, as did thirty-five Northern Leaguers—thirteen of whom had stuck, including second baseman J. D. Ramirez, a star Double-A second baseman in the California Angels system, and Kevin Millar, who was smacking homers for a Florida Marlins Class-A club. So Wolff didn't interfere when Harry Stavrenos sold two Sioux Falls Canaries to the Phillies for $1 apiece and gave away a third, just to give the players a chance. Or when two Cuban defectors signed by St. Paul late in the season were drafted by the majors without much compensation. (One, shortstop Rey Ordoñez, instantly became a top New York Mets prospect.)

Wolff was amazed at how cheap the big leagues could be. Organizations that spent a million dollars on a high school draft choice wouldn't fork over three thousand for a Northern League player. That was the price the league had set for its talent. It never got that much, not once. Over the winter the Montreal Expos tried to sign St. Paul pitcher Mike Mimbs without the Saints' permission— even though all Northern League contracts included a second year at the club's option. Finally, and reluctantly, the Expos agreed to pay $375 for the player, who would be their top Double-A pitcher in 1994. Someday the Northern League would land a stud prospect who would prompt a bidding war for his services among major league organizations. Before that day arrived, however, Wolff needed to make sure the league had established strict guidelines for selling players.

Then there were the copycat independent leagues. One was starting in Texas and Louisiana that seemed legitimate, despite its founders' lack of baseball experience. There were two potential flops in the Midwest—begun by men whom Wolff had rejected as possible owners, George Vedder in Duluth and Dick Jacobson in Rochester. The rookies-only Frontier League in and around Ohio was beginning its second year. Former Duluth-Superior Dukes owner Bruce Engel planned to form an indy circuit in the Northwest in 1995. There were rumors of a southern independent, too, as well as one in the New York area.

The Northern League owners were concerned about the proliferation of independents inasmuch as it meant competition for the best released players. In the spring the league had held its own, losing no one to the new Texas-Louisiana League, which was offering similar salaries. While Wolff wanted the Northern League to establish itself as the class of the indies, he felt a nexus of legitimate independents would only strengthen the message. "What we're trying to say is the big leagues are full of it, let's do it our own way," he said. "If there were four or five other leagues out there, it would be very healthy."

And if the majors ever made good on their repeated threats to eliminate the low minor leagues, the independents would be ready to fill the void. Still, if the new leagues were amateurish, the reputation of independent ball would suffer. As the dean of the indies, the Northern League needed to keep its distance from the upstarts.

But those concerns were all business. The baseball side of the league—the games on the field—had run without a hitch in 1993. The flagship franchise had captured the league championship. The players had enjoyed the summer. The mix of veterans and rookies had seemed creative, sensible, and effective. No one team had been an embarrassment on the field—and no one team had dominated, either. With the Northern League still enjoying a monopoly on the best independent baseball minds, Wolff was confident that the on-field show would continue to excel.

When more than 14,000 fans filed into Winnipeg Stadium on Opening Night in that city, and the magic number of 6,305 attended St. Paul's exciting debut, it seemed an unimpeachable thought that Northern League baseball would once again be wild, outside, and a great deal of fun for everyone.

Stephen Bishop had made the St. Paul Saints on potential alone. The coaches didn't figure him for a major role on the club, and the owners certainly didn't either. "Project" was the unanimous conclusion. Bishop was a raw talent, a sports car before the paint, racing stripes, and glittering hubcaps; it ran but didn't look very good in the process.

So it was no surprise that Bishop wasn't in the starting lineup when the Saints opened in Thunder Bay. His chance came the next night, when LS-1 slugger David Kennedy—who hit two homers to lead the Saints to their first victory—was tossed out of the game in the first inning for arguing a called strike three. Bishop replaced him.

When he came to the plate for the first time as a Saint, Steve Bishop looked ready. He always monitored his appearance closely. On his back was number 24, worn by his current favorites—Barry Bonds, Ken Griffey, Jr., Deion Sanders. Growing up in the East Bay, he'd idolized Rickey Henderson, another 24. (Bishop also was conscious of his black heritage. Twenty-four was the reverse of Jackie Robinson's uniform number, 42.) He wore his pants long, with the black socks barely visible. When they didn't fall right, he complained to the clubhouse manager for longer ones. Finally, black wristbands were an important touch. "If you look good, you feel good, and if you feel good, you play good." Plus, he said, "There could be a camera out there."

He did look good in his debut. Bishop took strike one. He fouled off strike two. He hit the third pitch up the middle, where the shortstop reached the ball but couldn't hold on. The official scorer generously gave Bishop a hit.

Despite a couple of swinging strikeouts—curveballs still troubled Bishop—he'd had a taste of playing and wanted to start. "I can hit!" he declared in the outfield before the home opener, almost like a kid begging the coach to play. The next night manager Tim Blackwell wrote on the lineup card: *Bishop 7*, the scorer's designation for left field. Bishop had two hits in four at bats, scored twice, stole a base, and drove in a run. The following evening Bishop went two for four again. The rookie had won a job. "I told you I could hit!" he said in the locker room.

Suddenly, Bishop's goals came into focus. Steal twenty bases. Bat .300. Get signed by an organization. He was slicing singles and a few doubles. With a torrid start—including a home run over a short

left-field wall in Winnipeg—Bishop was hitting .367 as the second
week ended. After five weeks he boasted a .330 average. Before a
game in early July, he looked at the lineup posted on the dugout
wall. "I'm hitting cleanup tonight!" he exclaimed.

One of the songs that Al Frechtman often tossed into the CD
player in his press box perch at Municipal Stadium was the Lovin'
Spoonful's "Do You Believe in Magic?" Along with Sammy's memorable take on the theme from *Shaft*, it seemed to work for the
Saints. It was uncanny. The comebacks had been multiple in 1993.
No one figured they wouldn't be in 1994. Opening Night was
burned in the hearts of every Saints fan. It was inevitable: The
season would be theirs.

Sunday, June 12, was a glorious day. Partly sunny, eighty degrees,
a light wind at game time. Owner Marv Goldklang, still in town
after the opener, roamed the field during warm-ups talking with his
new players. Nick Belmonte was in town, and he took Steve Bishop
aside to explain the difference between throwing a baseball from
third base and throwing one from left field. (An outfielder, requiring strength and accuracy, needs to extend his arm fully and throw
"over the top," from a twelve-o'clock position; an infielder, pressed
for time to beat a runner to first, can drop to the side a bit, ten
o'clock.)

Fans bought iced latte from a vendor wearing a backpack
equipped with a dispenser and hose. Fun could break out at any
moment. The Saints were trying new between-innings promotions.
One mocked the inexplicably popular computerized "races" among
different-colored cars or subway trains at major league parks. In St.
Paul three fans rolled tires from the first-base dugout around home
plate to third base to the theme song from the cartoon "Speed
Racer."

In the sixth inning, with Sioux City leading 2–1, Vince Castaldo
rocketed a two-run homer off a former big-leaguer, Joe Kraemer,
over the sign for Damianni's Pizza and Hoagies in right-center field.
But the Explorers immediately tied the game. In the seventh,
Bishop doubled to left-center, sliding to beat a throw to second

base. One batter later he scored on a single. In the top of the eighth, reliever Steve Morales, a rookie, couldn't hold the lead. Single, single, double. After an intentional walk, in came the Saints' projected closer, Jason Bullard. His first pitch ricocheted off the dirt and past the catcher, Nick Sued. Sioux City 5, St. Paul 4. *Shaft* time.

Bottom of the eighth. A walk. A sacrifice. A check-swing blooper by Leon Durham over the pitcher's mound. Kraemer couldn't find the ball, and when he did he kicked it. First and third. Then David Kennedy lofted a high fly toward the left-field corner that first looked like an out but kept floating toward the fence. "Oh, shit!" Goldklang cried. The ball traveled 321 feet down the 320-foot line. Saints 7, Explorers 5.

After recording two outs in the ninth, Bullard allowed a solo homer that Bishop watched sail away. But the next batter struck out.

Deficit. Comeback. Blown lead. Comeback. Blown lead. Comeback. Heart-stopping finish. A victory always in doubt. The fans— 6,122 appreciative ones—stood and cheered. Municipal Stadium had worked its magic once again. It was feeling a lot like 1993.

Rookies are supposed to be quiet pupils, humble and eager to work hard. Once Bishop had cracked the lineup, his attitude began to bother older teammates. They complained about rookie mistakes, like failing to hit the cutoff man, or, when he played first base, pivoting off the wrong foot. Bishop picked their brains, but they said that he didn't seem entirely interested in learning, that he didn't prepare himself mentally or physically for games, that he would work hard in practice only when someone was watching.

"Big League." That's what some teammates started calling Bishop behind his back. "He's the only guy on this team who doesn't think he should be here," second baseman Doug Kimbler grumbled. Bishop chewed out a groundskeeper one day. Very un-professional. And the pants! Bishop moaned for a month about needing longer pants. Lacking transportation in St. Paul, the rookie figured he could get a car from a local dealer just like Leon Durham. He even suggested doing a commercial with Durham—to the front office as well as his teammates. They marveled at his audacity.

But Bishop could play a little, as players like to say. Like everyone in the Northern League, Bishop was there for a reason: No major league organization wanted him. There were flaws in his game, in how he treated baseball, that needed correcting. If the Northern League were to be successful, players like Stephen Bishop would have to be taught how to approach the game.

Some older players wished they were in his position: "He's young enough that he's got an opportunity to still play in the big leagues," said twenty-seven-year-old center fielder Darius Gash, who had decided that this season would be his last. "He's got the makeup of a wonderful baseball player. He needs to work, though. He needs to lift some weights. He needs to shut down his extracurriculars a little bit and rest his body. You can't play a hundred sixty-two games going out every night. You can chase all the pussy you want to, but you can't drink every night and get laid every night and perform to the best of your ability. You just got to know when to and when not to. You have to be smart."

Bishop believed he practiced hard. Maybe not as hard as Vince Castaldo, who was all business on and off the field, or outfielder Benny Castillo, who shagged fly balls in practice as if it were a game, but who did? He had always performed well in baseball and felt there was no reason he shouldn't at this level.

Screw his teammates. If other guys smirked when Bishop wanted to interview a teammate on a local cable station—a half dozen players rejected his boyish pleas—so what? Bishop wanted experience for life after baseball. (He had started a modeling portfolio, cut a rap demo, and considered acting lessons.) If they didn't like his earrings or his nightlife, so what? "I'm here to play baseball, win a ring, and get into an organization. In that order," Bishop said. "I'm not here to win a popularity contest."

He was starting for the Saints every day. He was helping the ball club. No one could dispute that. Bishop believed that as long as he did his job on the field, the rest didn't matter.

The delicate balance of independent baseball, at least the way Miles Wolff had structured it, requires finding veteran players who are willing to serve as part-time coaches. The year before, the Saints had featured a thirty-three-year-old first baseman/designated hitter at the end of his career, Jim Eppard, who was happy to be a team leader. Leon Durham, who played the same two positions, also filled the role. They were riding out the string in baseball and helping a new venture take flight.

There are, of course, other personality profiles for independent baseball. Players who have tasted Double-A or Triple-A tend to be in their midtwenties, not at all prepared to quit the game. Vince Castaldo wanted another shot at Triple-A; he knew his tough-guy attitude had hurt his career, and he wanted a full season to work on the mental game while piling up big numbers. Darius Gash had a feeling he was done, but he came to the league to end his career respectably before taking a promised job with Boeing Co. in Wichita, Kansas, where he'd played in 1993. Shortstop Greg D'Alexander, in his fourth year of indy ball, craved a first opportunity in an organization. Kimbler and Castillo wanted another chance. They were serious players who knew what it takes to advance. They weren't in St. Paul to mess around.

"The hardest thing for me is that I'm accustomed to being around guys that know the game, that have played a higher level of baseball," Gash said. "Guys that know how to do this, how to do that, how to prepare yourself for a game mentally as well as physically. And you come here, and because you deal with guys who are right out of college up to veterans that have been in the big leagues, it's hard to combine all those personalities, mentalities, and come out with a gung-ho, let's-go-kick-somebody's-butt attitude.

"I feel sometimes that I'm a coach, and that's not my mentality, that's not my personality. I don't come out to try to tell people or to show people what to do. If anyone has a question for me, I'll do more than I can to try to help them, but I'm not the best player who ever played the game, so I don't think that warrants me trying to tell someone else what to do. I'm not a leader type. I think I am by the way I play but not by the way I talk. Because I'm quiet, I stay to myself, I try to prepare me to play and that's that."

In the affiliated minor leagues, the size of the city matches the level of play. Rookies are sent to Princeton, West Virginia, and Butte, Montana. As they age and improve, the quality of life of the places they play rises, too. Boise, Idaho, is a Class-A town. San Antonio, Texas, is Double-A. Indianapolis is Triple-A. Players gain maturity and experience as they graduate from burg to town to city.

Minneapolis–St. Paul is a major league town with the usual temptations: booze and women. Groupies latched on to Saints immediately, dancing and drinking with the younger players at a local nightclub after the Opening Day victory while the veterans ate at a communal table with their wives and girlfriends or had a few beers and talked. Every night players headed to Gabe's, the team bar, for pitchers of beer that often lasted until closing time. The veterans quickly identified the problem: Guys who like to party excessively—win or lose, but especially after a defeat—always signal trouble for a team.

The younger Saints banded together, apparently caring little whether they played in a major league organization, again or for the first time. The point was to play baseball another summer, get paid for it, and have fun off the field. That was why they were in the Northern League. "It's not important to them," Vince Castaldo lamented. "The game isn't as important to them as to some of us. To me, it's what I do, and I take pride in what I do."

There are eighty-two Class-A teams in the minors but only twenty-eight in Double-A, one per major league organization. Once a player arrives at Double-A, The Show is just a phone call or an injury away, so he learns to take the game seriously; mistakes aren't tolerated more than once. Players who haven't risen past A-ball haven't had the basic training of Double-A, so they don't understand the difference. It's all about maturity.

Unlike Stephen Bishop, who excitedly set his VCR to tape a Saints game and watch himself later, they had performed on TV. Before St. Paul's first trip to Winnipeg, which played on artificial turf, Bishop asked Castaldo, "Have you ever played on turf?" Castaldo just nodded.

The veteran summed up his feelings while downing a tuna sandwich and a Coke after a Sunday afternoon game. He glanced over at a long table of boisterous Saints. "There's too many young guys on this team," he said. Castaldo quickly got up to leave. He wanted to get to the gym to lift weights. He had a game to play tomorrow. He needed to prepare.

The same word was always used to describe Vince Castaldo: intense.

• During a preseason intrasquad scrimmage in St. Paul with no umpires, the catcher called a strike on a pitch about a foot outside. Castaldo walked across the plate, turned to face the offender, flipped over his bat, and smashed the handle on the spot where the pitch had crossed. Without missing a beat another player handed Castaldo a new bat. The catcher then called a second strike, using an umpire's exaggerated call. Castaldo looked at him and said, "Come on, we're not fucking around here."

• Still the preseason. The Saints coaches wanted Castaldo to play farther back at third base to increase his lateral movement. Castaldo was stationed on the infield grass. His reasoning? The grass was cut too high, slowing down the ball. "Let's cut the fucking grass," he said. "Game speed."

• In the bottom of the seventh in a 4–4 game at home against Sioux Falls early in the season, Castaldo struck out swinging. As the opposing catcher tossed the ball back toward the mound, Castaldo broke his bat on home plate. "FUCK!" Unmoved by a chorus of boos, he walked back to the dugout, kicked a garbage can, and yelled again. "FUCK!"

When a bat came flying toward the home dugout, helmet trailing close behind, it was, as people around the Saints would shrug and say, just Vinny being Vinny. It was also Vinny being Vinny when he tripled with the bases loaded on Opening Day, or homered in three straight games, or correctly guessed fastball to single home the winning run and cap a Saints win, or simply advanced the tying run during a rally.

There are two important parts of Vince Castaldo: his bat and his head. Both can be extremely hard. The first was the reason Castaldo should have been in the major leagues by 1994. The second was the reason he wasn't.

Vincent Perry Castaldo grew up Englewood, New Jersey, and suburban St. Louis, but he inherited the genetic coding of Brooklyn, where his parents were raised. Castaldo is tough. He rarely smiles. He speaks few words and keeps to himself. On and off the field he can flash a gaze that says, *Don't mess with me.* With his narrow face, jutting chin, and piercing stare, he could have entered a Sylvester Stallone look-alike contest.

Whatever brooding toughness Castaldo possesses he transfers to the baseball field. As an infant he crawled around the house chasing a ball. In Little League he threw temper tantrums after striking out, his father cringing in the stands. When he made six errors in a game as a sixteen-year-old, he carried the frustration around for days. It wasn't that Castaldo was immature. He was simply a perfectionist.

At the University of Kentucky, Castaldo impressed scouts his junior year, batting .370 and leading the Southeastern Conference in doubles. His coach predicted he would be drafted between the seventh and tenth rounds. Bypassed entirely, Castaldo brooded all summer. A year later he was chosen by Milwaukee in the thirty-second round, signed by the same scout who signed Pete Rose. (And told the same thing: "Kid, you're gonna make a lot of money in this game.")

In Rookie ball, with the Helena Brewers of the Pioneer League, Castaldo performed far better than the 884th pick of the draft is expected to. He batted .335, with eight homers and forty-seven runs batted in sixty-two games, moving from afterthought to prospect. At Class-A Stockton, California, Castaldo learned to pull the baseball. He ripped thirteen homers and drove in seventy-four runs. The organization loved Castaldo's hitting. His slightly crouched stance was reminiscent of one of his idols, Don Mattingly. His work ethic was equally painstaking.

Castaldo and his manager, Chris Bando, moved to Double-A together in 1992. For the first time Castaldo found obstacles in his path. The Brewers decided he couldn't make it as a third baseman and shifted him to the outfield. Castaldo didn't take the change well. When the club demoted a Triple-A outfielder, Castaldo wound up as a designated hitter, which he considered being half a player. And he no longer got along with Bando, who found Castaldo's hard edge—especially his profanity-filled outbursts—not the stuff prospects are made of. The two clashed, and Bando seemed to think Castaldo was trying to show him up. Bando was moving up to Triple-A in 1993. Castaldo read the writing on the wall. He asked to be traded.

"I was way too impatient," Castaldo said. "Everything that was thrown in my path I was pissed off at." Even though he had moved up the baseball ladder as fast as anyone but a stone-ass prospect, Castaldo had let his emotions get the better of his talents. It wouldn't be the last time.

The Expos acquired him in the Rule 5 draft and assigned him to their Triple-A club in Ottawa for the '93 season. Castaldo was the starting third baseman—until the club signed a six-year minor league free agent. That was the first perceived indignity. When his replacement took ill, Castaldo took advantage: "I was crushing." But as soon as the other third baseman returned, he was benched. When the player was released, Castaldo was the everyday third baseman again—until he hit an inevitable slump, when it was back to the bench. Triple-A players know they have to perform. But they also know that if you're not a prospect you might have to perform beyond reasonable expectations. Late arrivals like Castaldo who have some deficiencies to begin with—the Expos, reading the Brewers' reports, didn't rate his defensive abilities highly—are at a disadvantage.

"If it's a kid that's a high-round draft pick and everybody thinks is a big-leaguer and is a significant investment, he's going to play every day regardless of what he does," said Kent Qualls, then the Expos' minor league director, explaining Castaldo's limited playing time. "But at the Triple-A level, you're going to give guys a chance to work through it, but you have to have guys ready to help the major league team immediately."

Castaldo was demoralized. "I take this game in a more subtle way," he said. "I don't smile, but it's fun. I enjoy beating other people. I enjoy getting hits off another pitcher. I enjoy preparing well. It just wasn't there. I didn't have the right frame of mind. And if I don't have the right frame of mind, I can't play well."

Castaldo batted third in the lineup when he was producing. When he slumped he was dropped to seventh or eighth, lower than he ever had hit. In August, after a six-for-sixty stretch, he finally had a productive series on the road. His confidence returned. But when the club went home, Castaldo was still batting eighth.

During a doubleheader late in the month, a teammate said, "Man, Montreal just doesn't care about you." Castaldo knew it was true. His manager disliked him. He disliked his manager. The club treated him as not a potential big-leaguer but a roster filler. After a second called strikeout of the game, Castaldo deliberately argued with the umpire until he was ejected. He returned to the clubhouse and dressed. When his manager asked if he would be ready for the second game, Castaldo said he wouldn't be playing. The next day he announced he wanted to retire. No one in the Expos organization tried to stop him.

Vinny Castaldo stands six feet tall and weighs 185 pounds. He is well built but not imposing. Like most minor leaguers, he adheres to a neat and sensible dress code. Off the field he is polite and deferential, articulate and friendly—to those he respects. Castaldo doesn't waste his time on others, which is why he seems aloof to teammates and acquaintances. Life is like baseball, Castaldo believes. Why bother with people if they don't treat you as you would treat them? If they assume things about you by observing instead of asking?

Intense is the easy description of Castaldo. Serious is the more accurate one. "You reach a point where if you don't take it seriously, in a serious environment, it's a waste of time." Castaldo was talking about baseball, but it is also his approach to life. Don't waste time. Castaldo rose through the minors with precision because he took baseball seriously. He wasn't the most gifted athlete, but he worked harder than everyone else. In high school, in a slump, his father threw him batting practice in the morning before school. As a professional Castaldo worked harder than his team-mates. It didn't matter whether there were 2 games or 102 games left in the season. Castaldo never stopped working.

Over time he learned to channel his intensity so that a strikeout at the plate or an error in the field didn't affect the next at bat or ground ball. The bat throwing was merely how Castaldo released energy—it didn't mean he was a bad sport, or a crybaby, or even an angry young man. In fact, he is none of the above.

Still, the outbursts were visible to everyone at Municipal Stadium, where fans booed him out of a midwestern ideal of sportsmanship violated. But they also cheered every heroic moment, every clutch hit, recognizing that Castaldo was *the man*. In Section J behind first base, fans serenaded Castaldo when he strolled to the plate, his body swaying side to side, black stripes painted under his eyes to shield the sun, without a hint of a smile, as if pacing off steps before a Wild West duel. They sang to the tune of "Volare": "*Vin-ny Ca-stal-do. Woe woe woe woe. Vin-ny Ca-stal-do. Woe woe woe woe.*"

Before a game Castaldo talks little. He has a routine that he doesn't like disturbed. Castaldo is one of the first players to arrive at the park—around 2:30 for a 7:00 game. He usually takes early batting practice—regardless of his average—or "soft toss," where a player sitting on a bucket tosses a ball lightly while his companion raps it into a net a couple of feet away. After formal batting practice Castaldo retreats to his locker to read for a while. Then he stretches with the team, and later alone in the outfield. As the visitors finish their fielding warm-ups, Castaldo waits at third base, just in foul territory. The moment they're done, he steps over the white line to his position, the first player on the field. About twenty minutes before game time, Castaldo grabs his bat and wanders to left field, where he practices swinging, a solitary figure framed by the ads on the outfield wall. He works on his timing, his stride, his stance, his vision. The final ten minutes before the game, he sits quietly in the dugout, alone. As the national anthem plays, Castaldo bows his head and places his cap over his heart. All business.

Castaldo came to St. Paul with a purpose: to play well and return to an organization. He didn't drink or chase women. Apart from the fact that he lived with his girlfriend back home, he thought the partying was just dumb. It wouldn't make you a better ballplayer, and when your career was over you'd remember the lost opportunities and say, "I screwed up." Castaldo had been down that road once already.

After storming out of Ottawa, Castaldo did what was common to many players who quit abruptly: He reconsidered. Three days after returning to St. Louis, he told his angry father—who thought his son had torpedoed his career—that he had made a mistake. "Well, you can't go back," Tom Castaldo said. "You're going to have to figure out what you want to do. If your goal is to play, you have to put up with the nonsense."

When the Expos agreed to take Castaldo again in the spring, he was thankful because, away from baseball, he realized that all he wanted to do was play. "I always questioned was it worth all the bullshit you had to go through," he said. "After I left, I decided it was worth all the bullshit."

Montreal had forgiven, but they hadn't forgotten. They had a prospect slated to play third base in Ottawa, bumping Castaldo back to Double-A, where, at the end of spring training, the club decided to go with younger talent. At twenty-six Castaldo was deemed too old. His baseball choices boiled down to the Mexican League, where he could earn $4,000 or $5,000 a month but stood little chance of getting re-signed by an organization, or the Northern League, which he had heard scouts were watching.

For a salary of $1,200 a month, Castaldo signed with the St. Paul Saints. He knew the quality of play likely wouldn't meet his standards, but the important thing was to be seen, to prove he still burned to play in the majors. Castaldo hadn't relinquished the dream, but he realized now that he had no one to blame but himself if it didn't come true. He still threw bats, but he had grown up. "You end up finding out how things work," he said. "But if you want to play you have to deal with it. I didn't handle it well. If I don't get an opportunity to play in the big leagues, that's what I'll be bitter about. The way I handled it."

The one thing Castaldo handled quite well was Northern League pitching. He batted .500 in the first two weeks, with hits in each of the first fourteen games. After a month he had settled to around .375. He was second in the league in homers, second in RBIs, and in the top five in just about every hitting category. He was, as he liked to say, crushing, and carrying the Saints. On July 1, Castaldo had twenty-five runs batted in—sixteen more than the next-highest player on the team. He was responsible for seven of the club's seventeen homers.

The Saints, however, weren't carrying the league. They would win one, then lose one. Win two, then lose another. They won ten of their first sixteen games but lost five of their next six. They were no-hit by a talented Thunder Bay pitcher named Rod Steph. Everyone kept waiting for a streak that would propel the Saints past teams they considered their inferiors. Maybe it was true—St. Paul's lineup was better than most and no worse than any in the league—but the Saints found ways to lose.

Pitching was the key culprit. Marv Goldklang had been right when he said the staff was a big risk: No one could confidently give the club seven strong innings every fifth day, there was no proven closer, and the young middle relief corps liked to party. The blown leads against Sioux City erased by Vinny Castaldo and David Kennedy home runs were but a sign of things to come.

In Lewis and Clark Park in late June, the Saints led 5–1 in the eighth inning. A high throw to first, a homer off reliever Steve Jones. 5–3. More runners got on. With two outs rookie right-hander Duane Page appeared to escape—but his strikeout was also a wild pitch that allowed the batter to board first base. Then, with the bases loaded, Page walked home the tying and go-ahead runs. The Saints lost, 6–5.

Goldklang, who lived and died with every pitch, listened to Saints broadcasts via a special telephone hookup to his suburban New Jersey home. When Page threw his final ball four that night, Goldklang threw his portable phone against a wall for a strike.

Darius Gash was struggling. The speedy leadoff hitter was batting just .212. Veterans were precious in the Northern League; they had to produce. Leon Durham had been out of shape at the season's

start and then pulled a hamstring. He was batting .214 in just fourteen games. David Kennedy was struck by a pitch that broke his
left hand. The starting catcher, Nick Sued, a twenty-two-year-old
Dominican released by the Indians, was hitting .227, and it affected
his defense; the pitchers hated throwing to him. Not that the staff
could crow. Former Triple-A righty Scott Centala lost his first three
decisions. Returnees Ranbir Grewal and Jim Manfred had earned
run averages of 4.76 and 5.93, respectively. Van Schley moaned
about those two signings at every turn.

And the clubhouse karma was bad and getting worse. The Saints
already were having team meetings. The veterans complained
about the younger players. The younger players goofed around in
practice. On winning teams clubhouse problems can be overlooked.
On losing teams bad chemistry is explosive.

Mistakes abounded, the sort the casual fan wouldn't notice. Cutting off throws from the outfield that should go through to home.
Bunting directly at a fielder. Swinging with a three-and-oh count
against an out-of-control pitcher. Failing to move a runner from
second to third base with none out. Getting picked off base and
thrown out stealing—a Saints specialty.

And the mistakes didn't happen once but over and over, especially by rookies. "They don't learn," Vinny Castaldo said. "Our
mental approach to the game is pathetic," Darius Gash said.

Greg D'Alexander understood the problem. The shortstop had
played for nothing but independent teams. He had seen players
who on the one hand talked about "putting up the numbers" to get
back to an organization but at the same time didn't play to win
because they cared only for their numbers. They missed the connection. The Saints were missing the connection. "The only way
we're going to get back with an organization is if everybody plays
together and you win," D'Alexander said. "They're not going to
look at the last-place team. Even if they have some good players,
they're not going to get looked at if you don't win."

Still, the 11–10 Saints were only two games out of first on July 1.
Van Schley was itching to make roster changes before the club

deteriorated. His philosophy was If you're not producing, it's time to go home. That would wake up the team. Goldklang wanted to give his players more time. He had spoken with manager Tim Blackwell. "He seems comfortable with what we have," the chairman said. "Tim doesn't like to make changes for the sake of changes."

The approaches were the yin and yang of independent baseball. Schley was an activist, Goldklang and Blackwell more passive. Their backgrounds influenced their positions. In Rookie-level baseball, where Schley ran his successful Salt Lake Trappers, it's easy to shuttle ballplayers in and out—you have to because, unlike veterans, rookies have no track record. If a guy performs, great, you keep him. If he doesn't, there are plenty of others around. Schley also believed a timely cut is a terrific motivational tool: "My feeling is if you're not hitting .300 or have an ERA under 3.00, you should be worried." But that attitude doesn't always apply to veterans. Blackwell had to manage a team of varied skills and experiences. Coming from major league organizations, Blackwell believed in giving players a chance, and giving teams a chance to gel. When veterans slump, they often recover. It's just a matter of time.

Schley and Goldklang kept close watch on the release list. With Durham and Kennedy injured, they needed a first baseman. With the pitching erratic, they needed any live arm. A Triple-A power hitter, Mel Wearing, was released by the Orioles. The Double-A pitcher Dominic Desantis was available and recommended highly by Nick Belmonte. Blackwell said he wasn't convinced they were any better than what the team already had. (A couple of days later St. Paul made its first move of the year, signing a Cuban defector named Luis Alvarez, who had played first base and outfield, and hit for average but no power.)

Meanwhile, the Saints kept squabbling. While it isn't unusual to have cliques on baseball teams—as Gash said, "some guys are going to like rap and some guys are going to like country"—most players usually get along. On the Saints they didn't. Even insult-laden dugout banter, usually designed to provoke nothing more than laughter, had an edge. "Nobody likes anybody here" was how Doug Kimbler put it.

On the field the Saints were moving sideways. In the stands the St. Paul fans were as happy as ever.

At game time on the night of Wednesday, July 6, the thermometer read ninety-one degrees. It cooled gradually, the sort of carefree night one hopes will last forever. On that day major league baseball players decided not to set a strike date, not yet anyway. The Winnipeg Goldeyes sold the contract of pitcher Tim Cain to the Boston Red Sox for $3,000, the Northern League's first sale of the year (and the first time the majors had paid full price for a league player). During pregame warm-ups, Al Frechtman entertained fans with a recording of great baseball moments and songs—common in the minors—including a piece called "It's a Beautiful Day for a Ball Game."

The Minnesota Freedom Band performed the national anthem. Frechtman played "I Heard It Through the Grapevine" and a comical ode to the Garden State by John Pizzarelli called "I Like Jersey Best." In the top of the first, emergency starter Duane Page allowed five straight singles to the Sioux Falls Canaries after recording the first out. A throwing error made it 4–0.

"How many new people are here for the first time?" Frechtman asked the crowd. A smattering of applause. "Who do you know? How did you get tickets?"

The Saints scored three times in the bottom of the first. Frechtman played "Hallelujah Chorus" as sung by the Roches. An inning later Castaldo blooped the ball over third base on a three-and-two count to tie the game.

In the visitors' third Frechtman announced that Sioux Falls's Matt Davis was the "Tom Thumb Coca-Cola K-Man" of the evening. If Davis struck out—K being the scoring notation for a whiff—everyone in the stands was entitled to a free two-liter bottle of Coke from a local market. Opposing players hated the K-Man, believing it showed them up. Opposing front offices loved it, adopting some version of the promotion. Davis flied to center.

After the half inning two fans were escorted to the third-base line, where they placed their foreheads on a baseball bat, spun around ten times, and then staggered to a cellular telephone about fifty feet away while the crowd roared. The first one to call Frechtman won a prize. After the stunt Stephen Bishop swung at and missed three curveballs.

There were a few moments in the Northern League that placed the gulf between rookies and veterans, between experience and naïveté, in perfect focus. The teacher in the bottom of the fifth inning was Carl Nichols, the Sioux Falls catcher. Nichols had played in the majors because of his defensive skills. Stephen Bishop was the student.

After a check-swing single by Bishop, Nichols twice gunned the ball to first base, narrowly missing a pickoff. "Just a reminder," Frechtman interrupted, "now catching, number 33, Carl Nichols." Bishop stole second when Nichols dropped the ball while cocking his arm.

Second baseman Eddie Ortega singled up the middle with two outs. At third Tim Blackwell rotated his left arm in windmill fashion, sending Bishop home. He slid, left leg forward, right leg bent, arms splayed behind him. Nichols planted his left foot in front of the left corner of home plate and, as the ball arrived, collapsed his right leg to block the base entirely. Bishop's leg met Nichols's shin guard and went no farther. Side retired.

At the mention of "peanuts and Cracker Jack" in "Take Me Out to the Ball Game," composed eighty-six years earlier, reporters, broadcasters, scorers, and other press box hangers-on tossed bags of peanuts from their perch to the crowd. "You people are cheap," Frechtman said. "Go buy something."

In the seventh Castaldo smashed his bat on home plate after striking out.

Sioux Falls's Chris Powell singled into right field to open the eighth. Then the Saints made mistake number one. With Powell running, Rex De La Nuez bunted down the first-base line. David Kennedy, back from the disabled list, shouted, "Let it go! Let it go!" But the ball stayed fair. Pedro Guerrero singled, scoring Powell. Mike Burton grounded to Kennedy, who, attempting to start a double play, threw the ball into center field.

During a pitching change, Castaldo, angered by the constant mistakes, walked over to Greg D'Alexander. "How can you stand it?" he asked.

Frechtman announced the answer to his music trivia quiz: The singer of a version of "(I Can't Get No) Satisfaction" played a couple innings previously was Phyllis Diller.

The Canaries scored twice more before the inning ended.

In the last of the eighth, Bishop singled, Derrick Dietrich walked, and Sioux Falls changed pitchers. Frechtman played the ska song "Too Much Pressure." St. Paul police officers on duty at the stadium placed their hats on backwards to will the home team. They were called Rally Cops. The 6,218 fans, though, were atypically quiet.

"How many of you have only been to a baseball game at the Metrodome?" Frechtman asked. "Because you're acting like it." As if on cue, a train rumbled past the stadium, and the fans cheered more loudly.

Doug Kimbler popped out to the shortstop, tossing his bat in frustration toward the Saints' dugout. Another train passed. Nick Sued laced a line drive to left field, caught by Guerrero. Frechtman, imitating an organ player at a major league park, chanted the "Charge!" theme: *Bum, bum, bum, bum. Bum, bum, bum, bum. . . .* Benny Castillo struck out.

Frechtman cued up "Busted" by Ray Charles. Fans began leaving. "You know, a lot of people left last night's game because they thought we were going to lose, and we came back and won," Frechtman announced.

Not tonight. The Saints went meekly in the ninth, and into the night. But the fans left contented. Thanks to Al Frechtman, and Mike Veeck, and the staffers who devised the on-field promotions, and the reporters who tossed out peanuts, and the players from both teams, the fans had fun. They had participated in a glorious summer ritual—cheering for the home team—and they didn't feel ripped off in the process.

The Saints dropped to 15–12, a club with no confidence. The next weekend they lost two of three to last-place Duluth, the bullpen blowing leads in each loss. The Saints still were only two and a half games out of first place in a four-team race, but it was clear to the players and owners that the first half was over.

Van Schley wanted to overhaul the roster—now. "I think what the team needs is releasing about four guys," he said. "Nobody wants to do anything." Nobody meant Marv Goldklang, who preferred waiting until the right moves emerged.

In big-league organizations, winning at the minor league level is secondary. There's a higher purpose to farm teams: cultivating talent, slowly. (So what if the fans might have preferred to see a pitcher go for a no-hitter rather than be removed after reaching his pitch limit?) In independent ball instant gratification is the governing principle. Owners can't, at the end of a fourth-place season, say it was a terrific year because the shortstop got the necessary seasoning to help the parent team down the road.

Goldklang and Schley, lawyer and client, together had by far the most experience in the league running independent ball teams. When Miles Wolff was organizing the league in 1992, other prospective owners complained that St. Paul had cornered the market on indy knowledge. Schley volunteered to direct leaguewide scouting instead of work for St. Paul. After the season Goldklang let Schley buy into the Saints—the suddenly valuable Saints—at the original price, a share of the $50,000 franchise fee plus working capital.

They made an odd couple. Schley had his Malibu home and Hollywood friends. When visiting the club he shunned the Holiday Inn near the ballpark to stay at the historic (and nearly twice as expensive) St. Paul Hotel downtown. But he also was game for a six-hour road trip to Thunder Bay and wasn't above stopping for the night on the return in a town called Beaver Bay, in a prefab motel that boasted that Richard Gere had slept there. Players seemed comfortable around Schley. Goldklang, the hardworking Wall Street lawyer, cut a more corporate figure, flying in from New York to watch the team. He was chairman of the board, and the players knew it. Some called him "Mr. Goldklang." Schley was just "Van."

Despite their joint baseball investments, the two had never operated a team together. Schley had run the Salt Lake Trappers on his own, and Goldklang had owned a piece. The Fort Myers Miracle was Goldklang's club, and Schley owned some of that. With the 1994 Saints, they needed to divide the responsibilities.

Before the season it was easy. Schley chased the rookies and younger players. Goldklang, a skilled negotiator, dealt with older players and their agents. The chairman had the last word, but Blackwell had his ear. The manager, for instance, had wanted to re-sign Ranbir Grewal and Jim Manfred.

Once the season began the decision making became murkier. Blackwell and Goldklang together had won the inaugural championship. They made few moves in '93, largely because the team played well and had no clubhouse conflicts. The experience convinced Goldklang the manager needed control over player moves so his team knew who was in charge. The manager ran the clubhouse; players had to fear and respect him. "If a player thinks the manager has control over his baseball future, he's going to listen a little differently," Goldklang said.

Schley believed that ownership should control player moves, albeit with the manager's input. He felt managers develop loyalties that blind their judgment. Grewal and Manfred? They weren't *that* good, certainly not the two best arms in the country at the season's outset. Signing them had been an emotional decision based strictly on loyalty to the championship team. (Of course, Schley had also opposed signing Greg D'Alexander, who was having a terrific '94.) "We aimed for mediocrity, and we got it," Schley said.

Blackwell believed that the players responsible for the team's chemistry problems needed time to digest the often too-subtle message that they could be out the door if their attitudes didn't improve. It didn't help that none of the veterans had an inclination to lead, to take the young screwups aside and set them straight. But it was hard to blame the players. They wanted to get back to an organization, not coach. They weren't thirtysomething and ending their careers.

The Saints also had a fallback excuse: injuries. Durham's average dropped to .175 by mid-July. His struggles on the field limited his leadership potential on a team divided, as well as his coaching duties. Kennedy, Grewal, Gash, D'Alexander, and starter Mike Lewis all suffered injuries of one degree or another.

Even when healthy Gash was struggling. Goldklang considered releasing his projected spark plug but balked, saying there was no "countermove"—no one better to play center field. Schley felt the answer was simple: release Gash (and a few others) to shake up the team. You could worry about countermoves later. "If you're not producing, you're not going to get picked up," Schley said. "And if you're not going to get picked up, you're wasting your time."

Both arguments had merit. Goldklang didn't want his manager stuck with only seven or eight pitchers and a questionable center fielder. Schley was confident talented replacements could be found in short order. It was a push-me pull-you scene that couldn't be duplicated anywhere else in professional baseball.

The Sioux City Explorers, with two former major league pitchers, a harmonious clubhouse, and the same nine players and four starters in the lineup day after day under easygoing manager Ed Nottle, won nine of their last ten games in the first half to take the crown. They finished with a record of 27–13.

Doug Simunic of the Winnipeg Goldeyes, who had shot out to the first-half lead before folding, made four strategic moves with time running out in the half and his job on the line. Simunic released the league's stolen base leader, Ted Williams, because he was a negative force in the clubhouse; traded one of the league's top outfielders, Warren Sawkiw, for a rookie starting pitcher, Tim Bruce; and signed a third baseman and designated hitter, Pete Coachman and Jim Wilson, both of whom had major league experience. Simunic was thinking only about the second half.

The Saints, meanwhile, stood pat. They talked about moves and scouted available players but didn't make any substantive changes, instead waiting for a leaderless clubhouse of partiers, malcontents, and underperformers to wake up. During a lost weekend series versus Winnipeg when both clubs were out of the race, the Saints played to win in the hope of developing momentum for the second half rather than experiment with changes to set the lineup for the new season.

The rest of the league understood what was happening. Too many people—and consequently no people—were calling the shots in the big city. Indecision ruled the Yankees of the Northern League. "You're not going to make any moves, are you?" Simunic asked Schley. Nottle, during a visit to St. Paul, joked about the Saints' brain trust gathering on the field before games to assess the club's needs. Unlike the team's fans, Schley wasn't having fun.

The Saints limped in with a respectable but inadequate mark of 23–17, four games behind Ed Nottle's laid-back Sioux City Explorers.

Ed Nottle

TEN

*You spend a good piece of your life gripping a baseball
and in the end it turns out that it was the other way
around all the time.*

—Jim Bouton

The tattoo on Ed Nottle's left arm reads, "U.S. 502 Para-
troopers." The one on his right, "Eddie." His body is flab-
bier than when they were stenciled, but Nottle still has the
same spirit: a city kid whose rough edges smoothed only with time
and experience, a bar-stool raconteur who doesn't shy away from a
cold beer or a choice expletive, a fast and easy friend who believes
that life is only as complicated as you make it. Ed Nottle is a throwback to an era when baseball, and life, were simpler.

Nottle liked to show off the house in Sioux City where he lived.
The club's owner, Bill Pereira, had bought two new, adjoining, one-
story homes. Nottle's was neat and spare. A grip-and-grin photo
with the local Ford dealer, who lent Nottle a car for the season,
decorated one wall. A couple of baseball books were stacked on an
end table. The refrigerator held little but Coke and Coors Light.
Nottle's wife, Pat, was at home in Evansville, Indiana, where Nottle
returned when he had a chance. He had been married to Pat
twenty-seven years but had been married to baseball even longer.

"I made a decision the first day I was ever in a ballpark," Nottle
said, "that I'll never get out of it. That I love it and that's the end
of it. Family won't get me out of it. Lack of a family won't get me

out of it. I love what I do." All but one of Ed Nottle's thirty-plus years in baseball had been spent in the minor leagues, and the exception was a miserable year answering the bullpen telephone in Oakland. But instead of complaining, Nottle blamed no one but himself and prayed that he could stay forever in baseball. Why? Because he couldn't live without it.

It isn't the game so much, Nottle would say, but everything that goes with it. The uniform allowed Nottle to be himself—to tell stories at the local Kiwanis Club or raise money for charities with the husky piano-bar voice that earned him his nickname: Singin' Ed Nottle.

Now, after years in major league organizations, Nottle finally didn't have to bother with the endless paperwork and bureaucracy—a distaste that contributed to his failure to manage the Oakland Athletics and the Boston Red Sox in the 1980s—and could run a baseball team without a dozen front-office flunkies looking over his shoulder.

Nottle knew every bar in Sioux City, and the town knew and loved him back. Returning from a road trip after clinching the first-half title, Nottle found a sign on his front lawn painted in red and black letters: "CONGRATS X'S. NORTHERN LEAGUE FIRST HALF CHAMPS." That sort of warmth doesn't just happen. The major league clubs that employed Nottle didn't appreciate his gregarious side; the less attention, they figured, the better. But in the Northern League, not cultivating connections was unthinkable. And nobody was better at it than Ed Nottle.

After a game one August night when the mosquitoes were biting, Nottle climbed on a stage erected behind second base to sing a number with a local country band. "This is Siouxland!" Nottle shouted. "This is why I'm here!" Then he sang: "Yesterday is dead and gone. . . ."

Ed Nottle was an unlikely baseball prospect.

In the tough North Philadelphia neighborhood where he grew up in the late 1940s and '50s, there was no organized baseball. When they weren't causing trouble, Nottle and his friends played stickball, halfsies, hose ball, and other improvised city games that require no more than a broomstick and a Spaldeen.

At fifteen—just a few years after recovering from fourteen months in bed with rheumatic fever—Nottle was working in a bowling alley when he was hassled by a patron. Nottle borrowed the gentleman's car. He was chased by police, shot at, and finally caught. Sent to a reformatory, he enlisted in the military rather than face prison. It was the smartest move of his life, but he still had a lot to learn. A Japanese-American drill sergeant sent a smart-mouthed Nottle to an army hospital for two weeks. "From that time on I started being a decent human being," he said.

And, as it turned out, a decent ballplayer. Military teams in the 1950s were scouted heavily, and Nottle threw hard, despite a 130-pound frame, for the 101st Airborne Division club (organized by Gen. William Westmoreland). When he was discharged in 1959, Nottle found waiting for him a letter from Branch Rickey, Jr., and a plane ticket to Florida. Four springs later he was on the forty-man major league roster of the Chicago White Sox.

That marked Nottle's first major league disappointment. The White Sox were loaded with pitching talent—particularly a relief corps with stalwarts such as Don McMahon and Hoyt Wilhelm—but they perennially finished in the second division. Nottle was the White Sox's last cut four years running, and he never threw a pitch in the big leagues. But he hung on as a player-coach in the Texas Rangers system, eventually dropping the player part, then started at the bottom again as a manager in the Athletics organization.

Charlie Finley already had broken up his World Series champions, decimating the ranks of players, scouts, and coaches at all levels. Nottle managed teams with fifteen-man rosters. One year he managed a Double-A club, ran the A's' minor league camp, was East Coast pitching scout and spring training pitching coach. He threw every batting practice pitch and lost thirty pounds. His Waterbury team lost 182 games over two seasons.

After Finley sold the club, Billy Martin became the major league manager and fired nearly every baseball person—except Nottle, who was promoted to Triple-A and won Pacific Coast League division titles two straight years. When Martin was fired, Nottle was one of two finalists for the job. The Athletics hired Steve Boros instead but wanted to give Nottle a coaching job with the big team. Finally, the majors.

Nottle expected to be named a dugout coach. At the news conference, he was announced as bullpen coach, a lowly, thankless position. Adding insult to injury, twelve hours later Nottle learned that as the club's fifth coach he didn't qualify for the majors' generous pension plan. It was the worst experience of his career. The next year he chose to return to Triple-A. The following winter the Athletics fired him.

The Red Sox called. In the middle of Nottle's fourth season in the organization, managing Triple-A Pawtucket, Rhode Island, the Red Sox axed manager John McNamara. General manager Lou Gorman dialed Nottle's hotel room—the PawSox were on the road—and told him to wait by the phone. *In the bag*, Nottle thought. But as Nottle waited, Gorman learned that Jean Yawkey, the parochial owner of baseball's most parochial franchise, had decided to hire Joe Morgan as interim manager, because he was from New England.

Boston offered Nottle a major league coaching job, but Nottle stubbornly refused, figuring that Morgan, whom no one confused with Sparky Anderson, wouldn't last long. But Morgan's Red Sox won their first game, and their second, and their third. After the nineteenth straight victory, Nottle knew he was through, and he started acting like it.

Nottle hated filing postgame reports with the front office, as minor league managers are required to do. After a few beers he'd call the club's answering machine at three in the morning and offer unexpurgated comments. He often ignored requests to scout other teams. ("I didn't sign on as a scout, I signed on as a manager," he said. "I have enough trouble twenty hours a day taking care of my club.") Once, after begging the Red Sox for two years to release a particular player, he sent the front office a note: "If you won't cut the guy then at least have him neutered so I won't have to coach his fucking kid in twenty years." The message wound up on Mrs. Yawkey's desk.

During what he knew were his last months in Pawtucket, Nottle was asked by Gorman to send up a left-handed pitcher. The Red Sox were six and a half games out with a month to play and already had eleven pitchers on their staff. Nottle wanted to promote Dana Williams, a .320-hitting outfielder with speed who might help in a key situation.

"You want a left-handed pitcher from me who isn't helping my club and you haven't used your ninth, tenth, and eleventh pitchers in a month," he told the GM one night. "What are you going to do with this guy?" But Gorman persisted. Nottle called him an hour later and repeated his concerns. Finally, at 1:30 in the morning, Nottle called Gorman at home. "How dumb can you sons of bitches be up there? You've got a chance to win. You're only six and a half out." The next morning the Red Sox activated Dana Williams. It was Nottle's last proud moment. A few weeks later he was canned.

But Nottle had thriven in Pawtucket. His boys-will-be-boys approach suited Triple-A. (Nottle never understood early curfews and warnings against drinking a few beers or chasing women. Youth, talent, and notoriety were all these kids had. The organizations didn't pay them well, so how could they run their personal lives, too?) Nottle also showed that he could handle a locker room full of reporters. And the beer-and-a-shot town took to his relaxed style, his storytelling, his charity work, and his singing. In Oakland, Nottle had cut an album of old standards, backed by members of the Oakland Symphony. In the off-season he sang at retirement homes, bars, Chamber of Commerce events—anywhere to raise money for a cause.

Nottle's major league dreams were never about managing a team to a World Series title. Instead, he dreamed about singing for charities, hitting every bar in Kenmore Square around Fenway Park. Boston supports a child-assistance program known as the Jimmy Fund, and Nottle envisioned scaffolding on Fenway's legendary Green Monster, a major entertainer, a television audience, and millions in donations. "I dreamt of all those things. You're not supposed to, I guess. But I can sing. Why the fuck wouldn't I think about it?"

That didn't mean that Nottle neglected his teams, or the game itself. He was always preparing to manage the Red Sox. He'd think,

"How can I get Jim Rice in the frame of mind to be pinch-hit for? In Fenway Park?"

"If I had got the call, I was ready," he said.

But it was the late 1980s, the dawn of a politically correct era. Baseball's rulers believed they needed more organization men and fewer hard drinkers. "I doubt if the powers that be wanted an Ed Nottle in Boston," he said. "I never thought you had to be a baseball genius to manage in the big leagues. I thought you had to be damn good with the media and damn good with the community to not kill yourself. And I am damn good with both of them.

"Every once in a while, as soon as the camera goes on, you'll see [Dodgers manager Tommy] Lasorda run over to second base and act like he's teaching someone to turn the double play. Well, fuck, he never turned a double play in his life. If you want somebody to teach how to turn the double play, it's not going to be Lasorda, a left-handed fucking pitcher. Yet that's the role they play. Lasorda's role is to handle the media when things are going tough, to handle the community, to bring Sinatra in once in a while. To take the onus off of a losing team. They don't allow you to be Lasorda in the minor leagues. That's why I love independent ball."

Ed Nottle and Bill Pereira made a strange couple. Nottle was a street-smart kid from Philadelphia; Pereira was a privileged son of one of California's most famous architects. Nottle was a free spirit who managed his ball club according to few rules; Pereira was a politically conservative entrepreneur who brought a tight business discipline to his club. Nottle raised a beer glass whenever he could; Pereira raised Arabian horses. But for all their differences, Pereira and Nottle were perfect for each other, and for Sioux City, and for the Northern League.

In Bill Pereira, Nottle found a kindred spirit who understood that the best way to run an independent club is to let the manager run it. Pereira didn't listen to every inning of every game, wasn't deeply involved in player moves, and didn't scrutinize each at bat or inning pitched. He left that to Nottle. Pereira was involved in baseball because it was fun—and because there was enormous opportunity to implement ideas, effect change, and make money.

To Pereira, the game wasn't a career but another in a line of entrepreneurial ventures. His involvement had begun when he wanted to publish a book of photographs of the minor leagues, but after visiting ballparks and watching games he concluded that the bush leagues were just that. "It looked like a dumb business," he said. But if minor league baseball was so poorly run, Pereira realized there was room for improvement. In October 1987, as the stock market was crashing, Pereira bought half of the Northwest League's Boise Hawks for $250,000. He was another rich businessman buying into the minors. But he had a plan.

William Pereira, Jr., grew up in Los Angeles, the son of the man who designed California landmarks, including the Transamerica pyramid in San Francisco. The baseball of his youth was the Pacific Coast League, whose teams could and should have constituted a third major league. Pereira remembered how the PCL signed top talent, sold players to the majors, and drew big crowds.

After graduating from Stanford, Pereira wrote for *Newsweek* but abandoned journalism for business. He was twenty-nine when he rounded up $10 million in financing to start an airline, Air California, which shuttled passengers from Orange County to San Francisco. Two years later he sold AirCal for a small fortune. In the next two decades, Pereira formed an ad agency, bought a farm and raised Arabian horses, learned photography, and moved to Sun Valley, Idaho. Life was good.

In his first season as owner of the Boise Hawks, Pereira's club played in a dilapidated park used by a high school team. With ample money to spend on his new toy, Pereira negotiated a sweetheart land deal and built a stadium with $2.2 million in cash. He broke ground in February 1989, and the independent Boise Hawks were playing baseball there three months later.

With the new stadium attendance doubled almost overnight. (As did operating costs, so Pereira affiliated with the California Angels.) Over time he developed one of the minors' most sophisticated franchises. When Wolff needed an owner for Sioux City, Pereira fit the bill: He was smart, progressive, successful, had built a stadium, and had operated independently.

Wolff called the Sioux City Explorers a "twenty-first-century operation." In the relatively backward minor leagues, it was.

Pereira held a weeklong training seminar for employees every winter, at which he distributed two marketing manuals as thick as telephone books to everyone—including Ed Nottle. Whereas St. Paul's offices were clutter and chaos, Sioux City's were distinguished by the hum of computers, fax machines, and laser printers. An Apple Macintosh sat on every desk, and employees in Pereira's far-flung sports empire—he and his partners also owned a minor league hockey team and a team tennis franchise—communicated by electronic mail. Pereira toted his PowerBook everywhere.

A central computer system tracked ticket sales, ad revenue, souvenirs, and concessions—every aspect of events management. The $100,000 computer program included linear regression analysis, Pereira noted proudly, to forecast sales results. Next year, he said, the system would chart concession sales as they happened, enabling the club to adjust prices during a game. Peanut sales lagging? Drop the price in the sixth inning.

"There's a natural resistance in the minor leagues to computers," said Pereira, a commanding presence with a Cheshire cat grin and a basso legato voice that makes him sound like John Wayne. "You've got a lot of guys that have been in baseball a long time, or an owner that's trying to keep costs down and just keep his head above water while his franchise goes up in value."

To run a profitable operation, Pereira believes you have to apply sound business practices. Doing so doesn't sap the romance from the game, it only brings it up to date. And it paid off. In Boise his club posted some of the best per capita ticket and concession revenues in the minors. Sioux City's were right up there.

But like the team's corporate style, Sioux City's $4 million Lewis and Clark Park was all about organization. In the press box, on yet another Apple computer, a technician clicked on musical sound bites and noises. Each Sioux City player had his own song; every time second baseman Lance Robbins came to bat, a few bars of "Rockin' Robin" played. The same few bars. Tweet, tweet. Except for the game itself, an evening at Lewis and Clark Park had all the spontaneity of professional wrestling.

But it was clean, efficient, and, to its entertainment-starved fans, fun. Waiters took seat-side orders. Garbage was collected during the game. There was plenty of parking, bathrooms were spacious, the press box huge, and mixed drinks available. The stadium even had four skyboxes. Promotions were plentiful, like What's Your Beef Night, to celebrate the local industry, and David Letterman Night, since the late-night talk-show host had made Sioux City— where the CBS affiliate didn't carry the program—the "home office" for his infamous Top 10 List. (The Explorers flew in Mujibur Rahman, the suddenly famous Broadway souvenir store owner and Letterman regular, signed him to a contract, taught him to throw a baseball, and started him against an unamused St. Paul team. After one pitch Rahman's career ended, but the gag made highlight films from coast to coast.)

In the summer of 1994, no one was complaining in Sioux City. The down-at-the-heels town had just been ranked 175th on *Money* magazine's list of best places to live; Sioux Falls was tenth. But Sioux City had the first-half champion Explorers. Stopping in a diner near the ballpark for a postgame bite, Pereira found all the waitresses and busboys wearing Explorers T-shirts. He was thrilled.

For all the elaborate computer programs and business plans, Pereira deep down cares about the baseball. He doesn't pump his fists and yell like Marv Goldklang, but Pereira wants badly to win. The Explorers made it easy to relax after cruising to the first-half title, in the process showing the more aggressive organizations, i.e., St. Paul, how to get the job done.

The owner and manager shared a philosophy: Find players who fit the league's talent level, who understand that their careers had been derailed, and who want to stick around for a couple of years so the city can adopt them, as in Pereira's beloved Pacific Coast League. "If we have musical chairs in the clubhouse all the time, players never bond to the community, fans don't bond to the players," Pereira said. "That to me is as important as winning or losing or anything else."

Nottle received "a thousand fucking faxes" from players and agents in the off-season, but he assembled the team on advice from old baseball friends—former roommates, farm directors, assistant general managers. He looked for quality players, not according to their statistics but according to their personalities. He found St. Paul's constant search and emotional debates over players amusing. "I'm going to ask for a bonus for all the travel money I saved the club," he joked. It would have been a large one: Van Schley's expenses in St. Paul totaled $20,000 for the year.

The Explorers returned fourteen players from 1993 and, to create a local attraction for fans, signed three from the Sioux City area, including a backup third baseman who had worked as a groundskeeper at Lewis and Clark Park while playing semipro ball. Pereira would have brought his entire team back if he thought they could produce. In Boise, Pereira had seen the effects of organizational pressure on players. He wanted to minimize that on his independent club. "Most of these guys have already been victims of 'perform or else.' They've already been kicked out of organizations, and that tells me they don't react well to it," Pereira said. "What they have to feel like is that they're wanted. And if they go through some extended periods of adversity, that doesn't mean they're going to get booted out.

"I think this is pure labor—people engaged in this sport simply to do it, with very little thought to what they're being paid or where it's leading them. It's just for the love of what they're doing. We have a large percentage of our players who know they're not going to get back to an organization. They're here to continue to play the game. They want to get a ring. All those pure goals. We have more players like that and fewer who are here as a means to an end." The owner could have included his manager in that category, too.

When he met Bill Pereira at the 1992 winter meetings, Ed Nottle had been out of baseball for two years, living at home full-time for the first time in his marriage. He managed a bar, delivered ice, and worked other odd jobs. He refused offers for steady employment, because he knew he'd quit if baseball called. It was torture. "I've daydreamed all my life, and suddenly I had nothing to daydream about," he said.

Nottle had done things his way in baseball, never afraid to speak his mind. It had gotten him fired, but he couldn't change. In a game that was becoming increasingly corporate, where the rising young managers were clean-cut and earnest, Nottle was an anachronism. He had never kissed up to scouts and farm directors and front-office types, so he didn't have great contacts. Plus, his career had been relatively stable—only four organizations in all.

But Miles Wolff wanted Nottle's experience and energy in his new league. Philosophically, if not stylistically, Nottle fit well. In Sioux City, Ed Nottle could be Ed Nottle—throwing batting practice, schmoozing with fans in the parking lot, signing whomever he wanted, speaking at Kiwanis and Optimist clubs, patronizing the local bars, singing at charities, and traveling in winter to towns sixty miles from Sioux City to meet the locals, fostering goodwill that would pay off when the townsfolk came en masse to a game the next summer. "I don't think anybody loves all of it the way I do," Nottle said. "There is no phase of this business that I don't like. I joke with my wife. I say, 'I've been married thirty years. If I can stay in ball I'll be married a hundred years.'"

In a career of near-misses, Nottle was entitled to a helping of bitterness and anger, but he passed: "I'm only bitter about Ed Nottle. Baseball hasn't kept me from changing things. If I hadn't wanted to manage in the big leagues, I probably would've gotten four or five years (as a coach) in Oakland, four, five years in Boston. Ten years in the big leagues when you retire is ninety grand a year. And I would have made good money all that time.

"Baseball didn't keep me from doing that. Ed Nottle did. That's why I feel so bad for my family. I got no bitch against baseball. How could I bitch against Oakland, for instance? They ended up letting me go. But they got me in the big leagues. The fact that I wasn't smart enough to stay there ain't their fucking problem."

While he talked Nottle enjoyed a greasy breakfast—the only

kind he eats—in a St. Paul diner during a road trip by Sioux City. Two eggs and hash browns washed down with four or five cups of coffee. He called the waitress "hon," which even in the ultraliberal Twin Cities seemed innocently old-fashioned, not sexist. He also insisted on picking up the tab.

Nottle had quit smoking a few months earlier, but only because it was affecting his singing voice. He was a two- or three-pack-a-day man for forty years but boasted that he never coughed or hacked. (His wife said that when Nottle dropped dead of a heart attack she'd write that on his headstone.) Nottle picked the vegetables off salads and dumped five packets of sugar in his iced tea. On the field and off he always walked; after all, he liked to say, he was a pitcher, not an athlete. When he couldn't find a parking space close enough to the shopping mall entrance one day, he simply left the car out front.

Nottle's approach to baseball is as uncomplicated as his approach to life. He doesn't believe in overmanaging, or creating a revolving door of players, or developing attachments to his charges—he's seen thousands in his time. Baseball to Ed Nottle is the garbage can in the locker room loaded with beer and ice, good stories, and good conversation. It was almost passé in 1994, but after a game Nottle would sit in his uniform, throw back a few, and talk with whoever was around about baseball, life, whatever.

Except to his family, Nottle offered no apologies for his minor league career. But as a caring man in an uncaring business, he sometimes wished it were different: "I think an organization ought to sit down once in a while and say, 'Oh yeah, we've got so and so, he's been with us twelve years. Let's figure out something to do. He's heading to forty, fifty years old. He's given us half his life.' But they don't. I'm not sure that they owe you something, but there should be something there. Because it's not easy to do. Very few people have twenty-five, thirty-five years in this business without having made it—and I absolutely don't consider coaching for Oakland in '83 making it. I consider that probably the low point of my fucking mediocre career.

"I never ever missed b.p., never missed games. What I did do is miss sleep for thirty years. Everything I've ever done has been on my own time. And I don't know who the fuck anybody is to tell me—when you're not paying me what you should, when you're giving me no goddamn pension, when nobody gives a rat's ass what happens to my family—who the fuck are they to tell me what to do on my own time? When I'm giving them fifteen hours a day of their time."

A few months after Boston fired him, Nottle returned to Pawtucket to fulfill a promise to sing at a charity. The event raised $40,000. To end the show, Nottle sang "My Way." "It was so perfect, because my way got me fired. I know that. But here I am still at it." Nottle laughed. "And tough shit."

Howie Bedell and Ted Cushmore

ELEVEN

The weather's cold, my club's bad, my knee hurts, I can't putt no more, I'm off my diet, my wife's nagging me. Other than that, everything's great.

—Don Zimmer

The veteran players summoned to rescue the Duluth-Superior Dukes at midseason were like emergency relief workers racing to the site of a major earthquake: Everyone believed they could help, but no one expected any miracles.

The two dramatic wins over the slumping St. Paul Saints had lifted Ted Cushmore's spirits and raised the notion that perhaps the Dukes wouldn't be so bad in the second half of the Northern League season. At least for a moment, and at least in public, Howie Bedell played Dr. Pangloss to Cushmore's battered Candide. "The mentality is such that we can always come back," the manager said after beating the Saints. But reality proved somewhat more complicated.

Despite the addition of veteran Dennis Wiseman to a rotation anchored by a steady right-hander named Tom Paskievitch, the pitching staff needed two more effective starters, and the bullpen couldn't close out a game. Jeff Grotewold arrived out of shape and with a sore arm that limited his ability to catch, and Cushmore quickly wondered about his temperament. After Grotewold drove in the winning runs in Duluth's one and only road win in the final game of the first half, Cushmore congratulated him. "I don't win

179

for owners," the catcher snapped, draping his arm around Howie Bedell. "I win for my manager." Tom Coates was ineffective in center field and was soon replaced by Ted Williams, the veteran base stealer cut by Winnipeg. The club's two Australians had skipped town for seventeen days to play for their country in the Pan-American Games, and replacements were proving tough to find. (A bus carrying a backup infielder broke down en route to St. Paul, where the player was to meet the club. Instead of $19, Cushmore had to shell out $97 to get the light-hitting Tito Frias into a Dukes uniform.)

The uprising against St. Paul was a mirage. The Dukes went on to finish the first half with eight losses in their last nine games. That left them 8–32, nineteen games behind Sioux City. A reporter for the local paper noted that the Dukes had the third-worst mark in all professional baseball, their futility surpassed only by the Puebla Parrots of the Mexican League and the all-women Colorado Silver Bullets.

The split-season format has been used sporadically in minor league baseball over the years. The intent is simple: to renew fan interest halfway through the summer. With an eighty-game schedule and just six teams, one club could run away with the title quickly. By splitting the season into two forty-game races, every team, even one as bad as the Dukes, theoretically has a second chance.

Cushmore would have been satisfied with .400 baseball in the second half, a 16–24 record. When it became clear that despite the overhaul the Dukes personnel still was too thin, Cushmore was reluctant to tinker further. Whatever morale existed had been sapped by the losses and the revolving-door clubhouse. Players who had been in Duluth from the season's outset believed they were next on the list to go. Bedell, a forty-year baseball man who felt he had been cast aside by a know-nothing owner, began questioning Cushmore's actions. Cushmore contemplated firing his manager but feared that would only deepen the trouble in the clubhouse and the stands. He was growing more distant from the team daily.

So it didn't boost anyone's spirits when the Dukes promptly lost the first four games of the second half. But it wasn't just the fact of the losses, that they all but committed the Dukes to last place for the remainder of the season. It was how they were achieved that made the owner wonder. Cushmore asked himself: What's the worst we could do? Zero wins? Could we go 0–40? Two wins? Four wins? Yes, that seemed reasonable. A 4–36 record in the second half and 12–68 overall. That would be the absolute bottom.

On the first day of the second half, the Dukes kicked the ball around in an error-filled 11–4 loss to the Thunder Bay Whiskey Jacks at Wade Stadium. Cushmore called Nick Belmonte at his South Florida home to vent his frustrations at 2:45 A.M. Eastern time—after all, it was only 1:45 in Minnesota when he returned home.

The next night, Saturday, July 23, was ideal for baseball. Clear skies, warm weather. Three thousand enthusiastic fans in the grandstands. Both teams dressed in old-time outfits for a turn-back-the-clock night—the Dukes in baggy uniforms from the 1930s, the Whiskey Jacks in replicas of the Fort William–Port Arthur team of the 1910s. In the top of the eighth, with the Dukes leading 7–3, Bedell brought in his left-handed closer, Paul Romanoli, and Thunder Bay sent righty after righty to the plate. Grotewold signaled for fastballs and Romanoli shook his head and demanded to throw curves. After a few hits the veteran catcher gave up. "OK, big guy, you just throw whatever you want. I'll be back here."

As the Whiskey Jacks drew near, a palpable gloom descended on the stadium: Everyone knew the Dukes would lose. The game-winning hit came on a Paul Romanoli curveball. Thunder Bay 9, Duluth-Superior 7.

The starter on Sunday gave the Dukes reason to hope. Tom Paskievitch, in his fourth year in the minors, was the team's only consistent pitcher. With a sidearm delivery and crouched motion that resembled Charlie Hough's, Paskievitch threw hard and with control. The previous winter he'd had high hopes. Despite elbow surgery the Marlins selected the righty from the Padres organization in the Rule 5 draft. Paskievitch was destined for Double-A. But when he showed up for spring training out of shape and a few pounds overweight—he had spent the winter caring for his insomniac newborn daughter while his wife attended classes—the pitcher was demoted to Class-A. After a brief promotion he was released.

Paskievitch felt he hadn't been given a chance—just five outings in Double-A, the first on the very night he arrived for a road game after having driven from suburban Chicago to his home in Erie, Pennsylvania, then on to meet the team in Binghamton, New York. Paskievitch didn't want to leave baseball on a bitter note. He had something to prove to himself, so he accepted $1,000 a month from the Dukes—$600 less than he was making with the Marlins.

In Duluth, Paskievitch was Mr. No-Decision. He seemed to pitch just well enough to leave the game tied; when he gave the Dukes a lead, the bullpen inevitably blew it. One night he outdueled Oil Can Boyd of the Sioux City Explorers, taking a 3–0 shutout into the ninth. After yielding a single, Paskievitch induced a sure double-play grounder that was muffed by the second baseman. Bedell then removed him from the game—to Paskievitch's anger and bewilderment—and the Dukes lost 4–3. Another night Paskievitch pitched Duluth to a 3–1 lead after six innings, when the game was suspended by rain. When play resumed the next day, the Dukes surrendered six runs in the top of the eighth and lost. In more than fifty innings pitched, Paskievitch's earned run average was below 2.50, but he had just three decisions, two of them losses.

Against Thunder Bay, Paskievitch cruised through seven innings with a 3–1 lead. It could have been bigger but for some curious play by the Dukes. In the seventh Duluth loaded the bases with none out. With a rookie pitcher on the mound who had walked the previous two batters, conventional wisdom suggested putting on the take sign until the pitcher threw a strike. Instead, Steve Hinton, the Australian shortstop who was struggling at the plate, hit a high-and-tight first pitch on the ground for an easy force play at home. Bedell, coaching third base, gave the next batter the green light to swing with the count three balls and one strike. He popped out. The next one worked the count to two balls and no strikes. Another logical take situation. Instead, he popped out. Inning over.

In the eighth Paskievitch contributed to his woes with a throwing error that led to a couple of runs and a 3–3 tie. Still, he hadn't lost. In from the bullpen came Dom Desantis for a rare appearance.

Since he'd been signed the righty had been used sparingly. Bedell said Desantis was sore-armed and ineffective, but it was a catch-22; he wasn't pitching enough to become effective. (Desantis had started twenty-eight games the previous two seasons in the low minors. In Duluth he was used as a setup man for a closer with a grand total of two saves, on a team with eight wins.) Against Thunder Bay, Desantis induced a pop-up to short left field. A Keystone Kops combination of Hinton, third baseman Bobby Perna, and left fielder Benoit Belanger converged on the ball, which inexplicably dropped in for the go-ahead run.

After the game Belanger told a reporter that he could have reached the ball but just didn't and didn't know why. When Paskievitch read that in the newspaper the next day, he decided it was time to go home.

Duluth was becoming what independent baseball operators fear most: a joke. It's hard to maintain credibility before major league scouts and your fans—and credibility is crucial to any fledgling league—when infielders fail to make routine putouts, an increasingly hostile press wonders whether the whole team is quitting, and the manager is openly second-guessed by his owner and his rivals.

Losing was hurting attendance, Cushmore was sure of that now. But it could have been worse. Duluth and Superior boasted a core of dedicated fans numbering 1,000 to 1,500 who showed up rain or shine, win or lose. They gyrated to "YMCA" and shouted out the number of the auto glass repair shop—"Seven-two-two zero! zero! zero! zero!"—after a foul ball sailed into the parking lot. They cared about their Dukes, which they had made the town's team.

Cushmore had worried that the Duluth fans would support only a winner, but they came to see an unrepentant loser. It was still a fabulous market, he reminded himself occasionally. His new general manager took to the public address microphone and asked fans whether they were from Duluth, Superior, or out of town. Inevitably, the applause broke down in thirds.

Cushmore knew that *more* people would have shown up even for a .500 club. With St. Paul in town, Can Cooler Night attracted

3,400 to the Wade. In honor of the Saints' mascot, the Dukes roasted a pig in the parking lot. The stadium had energy. Breaking even required about 2,500 a night; the Dukes were drawing under 2,200. Still, in Rochester the previous year, fewer fans had turned out for a winner. That city didn't deserve a club. Duluth did.

Cushmore couldn't bear the fatalistic thought that in his only season as a baseball owner he had allowed the club to go under. By the end of the year, he figured to have sunk $800,000 into the Dukes—including a projected operating loss that had ballooned to more than $100,000. He needed comforting. He called Miles Wolff, who was concerned because without Duluth, having a team up Highway 61 in Thunder Bay didn't make any sense for the league. Cushmore flew Harry Stavrenos up from Sioux Falls for a one-day pep talk/seminar. He grilled Mike Veeck and Marv Goldklang in St. Paul, where Cushmore still shared a block of season tickets. Everyone felt that he was overreacting, that his investment would be fine.

It was small consolation that, thanks to loyal fans and the advice of colleagues, his franchise wasn't collapsing. Against his better judgment, Cushmore had become too wrapped up in the team's on-field failures. After the two wins over St. Paul—the highlight of the season—the Dukes lost thirteen out of fourteen games. Cushmore was embarrassed and depressed. On the rare nights when the Dukes would win, he was stunned. "Six–nothing in the eighth. Dukies," Nick Belmonte reported one evening in St. Paul, where Cushmore was watching the Saints play Sioux City. "I like it!" Cushmore replied. But disbelief quickly took over, and the Dukes owner leaped from his seat and shouted after Belmonte, who was walking away. "Are you serious?"

Since he had seized control of the player personnel side—much to the manager's disgust, although Bedell concealed it in public, for now, behind a cheery exterior—Cushmore had nowhere to hide. He was getting advice from all angles, when all he wanted was to win a few games. When you care, independent baseball is hard. When you are a rookie yourself, doubt begets insecurity begets anxiety.

"I'm flying guys in all over the place and I'm still losing," he said in late July. "Miles is telling me to settle it down. Nick is telling me to keep going. I am going to make one more change." The change was to sign a veteran shortstop who had just finished playing in the Mexican League to fill in for the missing Australians. After the player arrived—using a plane ticket paid for with Cushmore's frequent flier miles—he took a look at the team's record, said he had an offer to play in Venezuela for $4,000 a month, and left town.

The player moves ended there, at least temporarily, but bizarre episodes continued. When Paskievitch quit, he told Cushmore he missed his wife and daughter. In reality, the pitcher fled Duluth as if it were on fire. He had wanted more money—teammates with similar experience were making an additional $400 a month. A promise from someone—Cushmore said it wasn't he—to fly his wife to Duluth never materialized. And, worst of all, the Dukes couldn't make even routine plays. In short, he was frustrated, and day after day of losing had pushed him over the edge.

On the night Paskievitch arrived home, Cushmore called to thank the player for being part of the team. The next day Paskievitch was watching a major league game on television. The pitcher's mound was perfect. "I want that," he told himself. "I want a chance to do that." Over the tearful protests of his wife, who wanted him to quit baseball, Paskievitch decided to return to Duluth. He received a $75-a-month raise. Soothing tensions, his father, wife, and daughter drove to Duluth for ten days.

Twentysomething ballplayers with uncertain futures can be expected to face retirement reluctantly. Far stranger was a manager of a team with eight wins in more than forty games who believed he had done nothing wrong. After the Dukes dropped the opening series of the second half, Bedell asked Cushmore for a job commitment for 1995.

Howard William Bedell grew up in a blue-collar household in Pottstown, Pennsylvania. His father operated a press at a clay products company. His mother was a hostess at a Howard Johnson's. Their Quaker beliefs meant no sports on Sunday. The athletically talented Bedell didn't even try to sneak away to play ball. "I was kept on the porch and in the yard," he recounted.

Bedell found plenty of outlets. His high school baseball team won forty-eight consecutive games, a feat enshrined in the Baseball Hall of Fame. He set state records in football that stood for decades. In 1957 Bedell left college in his junior year to sign with the Milwaukee Braves, and he moved up the minor league ladder. In 1961 he led the Triple-A International League in hits and a year later ran off a forty-three-game hitting streak.

But like so many players, Bedell didn't make it in the majors, although he did have a moment to remember: In 1968, after a call-up from the Philadelphia Phillies, Bedell hit a sacrifice fly that snapped Don Drysdale's all-time scoreless streak at fifty-eight and two-thirds innings.

The next year, at age thirty-three, Bedell was managing in the Phillies organization. Five seasons and two pennants later, he entered the club's front office and was director of minor league operations when Philadelphia won the 1980 World Series, after which he was fired. He moved to Kansas City for six years, including one as a major league bench coach under an old friend, manager Dick Howser. He worked for the Seattle Mariners, with a year as first-base coach. Bedell joined the Cincinnati Reds as minor league director. He lasted two seasons—including another World Series title—before he was fired. In 1993 he managed a Class-A club in Bend, Oregon, for the Colorado Rockies before he was fired again.

When you erased the firings, as any good résumé does, Bedell's appeared impressive. So when he was steered to Duluth through Tom Leip, the Northern League's executive director, Ted Cushmore was interested. Wolff believed an established major leaguer like Howie Bedell would lend a different stamp of respectability to the Northern League.

Bedell may have come to the Northern League as an organization man, but he too had deeply held gripes with the majors. He was starting to feel like a dinosaur, part of a generation that grew up before free agency and seven-figure bonuses for high school seniors. Bedell saw owners and front offices rushing top prospects through the system to save development costs instead of allowing the cream to rise to the surface.

The game had changed. In Cincinnati he was forced to hire a twenty-seven-year-old assistant with no baseball background to help run the farm system. (Jim Bowden went on to replace Bedell and later became the Reds' general manager.) Bedell saw the baseball families he respected leave the game—the Carpenters in Philadelphia, the Yawkeys in Boston, the Griffiths in Minnesota. He complained that in his last job, with the Rockies, the front office had interfered constantly with his ability to work with young players. The club favored a handful of expensive prospects, and Bedell was expected to focus on them. He couldn't stand the "interference" from the organization. The gradual banishment from organized baseball made Bedell a bitter man. "It's become a more bottom-line industry," he said. "Minor league clubs are being cut off. Development opportunities have been cut off. Scouts have been let go. People that have been very successful working with talent have been let go. What you're doing is constantly pushing players beyond a certain point. They never really get settled. They never really find their talent. As soon as a guy hits .310, they want to move him to another classification because it'll get him to the major leagues, and if they get to the major leagues faster there's less dollars invested in that individual."

Like many in baseball, Bedell figured that the spiraling costs would lead organizations to cut where it's easy to cut: the low minors. Independent baseball would make a comeback. Wolff encouraged Bedell to join his league. Ed Nottle told Bedell he would enjoy the experience as no other in baseball.

As the season wore on, the gulf between Howie Bedell and Ted Cushmore grew as wide as the gap between wins and losses. The second-half mark of 0–4 became 2–6 became 3–15 became 8–21. Cushmore couldn't accept how bad his team was. He had hired an experienced baseball man to do a baseball job, and it didn't get done. So he stepped in.

Bedell admitted that he hadn't researched the league's talent level closely enough, and for someone with no experience in independent baseball that was a mistake. When he jogged out to the third-base coaching box, certain his team couldn't possibly win, Bedell felt miserable. So when Cushmore approached him about making changes, he was supportive. "On the limited knowledge I had coming in, I rolled the dice thinking I could go ahead and at least have a nucleus and we could make our adjustments in June or whatever," he said at midseason. "The reality was that I under-pegged it. Ignorance in a court of law is not acceptable, and I don't consider it acceptable in my business either.

"I can't make an excuse for having selected fifteen or twenty guys who couldn't play here. It basically was my responsibility to do it, even though some others offered. I've got to say we just got into something we didn't know about." (Bedell often referred to himself in the first-person plural.) "Once we got stung a few times it was too late."

But Bedell also clung to the belief that he had been misled: The tryout camps are important, rookies play a major role, it's a Class-A league. As the losses piled up, and the strain built, Bedell retained a positive attitude with his players, some of whom grumbled behind his back about the curious on-field decision making and lost respect for their manager. But Bedell's story began to change.

The spring doubts about Nick Belmonte gave way to grudging credit at midsummer for helping make over the ball club. But as the wheels slipped off the wagon, Bedell said the replacement players weren't that good anyway. By August he was deeply resentful that his authority to shape the club had been usurped. Once the season was lost, Bedell said that he shouldn't have let it happen, that he should have put his foot down and demanded control over the roster.

As for the players from the last-place 1993 club he had re-signed, well, Bedell claimed Belmonte had endorsed them. (Belmonte said he hadn't.) The rest of the roster? It was unfair and counterproductive, he said, to single out a few bad moves—Eric Parkinson, for instance—or point fingers at who signed whom.

Bedell's opinion of Cushmore changed as well. In June, Bedell endorsed the owner's involvement in overhauling the club; by late

August, Cushmore was just another meddlesome businessman with no baseball experience who had bought a plaything, like the characters he had worked for in the majors. Cushmore was getting too much advice—and bad advice at that. Belmonte's interference had poisoned a potentially positive relationship with the owner. With the Rockies, Bedell had complained about front-office interference that kept him from doing his job. That was his lament in Duluth as well.

Maybe Howie Bedell, once he grasped the Northern League's talent level, could have turned the Dukes around on his own. Maybe his major league contacts would have yielded more than Eric Parkinson and Greg Wiseman. Maybe it was unfair to second-guess his on-field decisions. Maybe given a second year, with the accumulated knowledge of the first, Bedell indeed could put together a winner. Maybe. But Cushmore couldn't afford to find out. He told Bedell he was planning to restructure the franchise. He planned to hire a player personnel director to work with the manager. He wanted a clean slate. Bedell's services wouldn't be needed in 1995.

The owner felt he had made the right decision. When Bedell submitted a $450 bill for a team pizza and beer party the next weekend in Thunder Bay—after telling his players he had picked up the tab—Cushmore had no doubts. The season had a month to go. The personnel changes had ended. Fans hadn't deserted the Wade. Bedell wouldn't be back in 1995. Ted Cushmore figured he had hit bottom and could begin looking ahead.

Stephen Bishop

TWELVE

If you don't catch the ball, you catch the bus.

—Yogi Berra

Ever since he was a Little Leaguer in the San Francisco suburbs, Stephen Bishop had started for every baseball team he
joined. Sometimes he struggled to win a job, as in college,
but when he got into a lineup, he made sure he stayed there. Only
an injury kept him from a full season of success with the Idaho Falls
Braves, but he was proud of his .382 average anyway, and he could
say he wasn't benched for any reason.

In Idaho Falls, Bishop was in the zone: He knew he would hit
whatever the Pioneer League pitchers tossed his way. Willie Stargell told Bishop that when he saw a curveball coming to whisper to
himself, "Up the middle." *Thwack.* Up the middle it would go.
Even more encouraging, Bishop learned to drive the curve to right
field. He was becoming patient at the plate, a mark of an improving
young player.

Slumps were alien to the well-built athlete. Bishop often complained about the adversity he overcame to play in high school,
college, and the pros, but whenever he played he succeeded. His
first month as a St. Paul Saint followed the pattern. He overcame
doubts to make the team, then won the starting left-field job and

was stroking the ball to all parts of Municipal Stadium with confidence.

But the Northern League isn't Rookie ball. Pitchers with some experience know to feed younger players a steady diet of curves. After his first tour of the league, Bishop began seeing more and more pitches that sliced down and across his tall, right-handed frame as they approached the plate. He was demonstrating classic rookie behavior: lunging at curves out of the strike zone, taking others for called strikes. "Up the middle" had vanished from his vocabulary.

Like many athletes Bishop is analytical, to a fault. He wondered why he swung at pitches he knew he should take. Tim Blackwell threw change-ups and curves in practice to teach Bishop to wait for the ball. But with his energy spent concentrating on the curve, Bishop wasn't belting fastballs with any authority—and he knew that if he couldn't hit a fastball he'd never advance in the game. It was a vicious circle. Bishop thought constantly about his shortcomings but didn't know how to take the steps to change them. "I just want to do so well I'm my own worst enemy half the time," he said as his average began dropping in early July. "I'm trying to find out what I'm doing wrong. No one can tell me."

With so many players on the field for practice, Bishop found it hard to get the attention he felt he deserved. Leon Durham had hitting troubles of his own and wasn't helping. (That's a problem with a player-coach who is more concerned with playing than coaching, as was the case with Durham.) The other veterans didn't seem eager to assist. Blackwell had to think about the whole team. The focus was on winning, not instruction and development. And Bishop didn't know it, but he had been labeled a whiner. It was either produce or perish.

By mid-July, Bishop's average dipped below .300. Marv Goldklang labeled his early production "soft"—meaning the rookie had few extra-base hits and drove in few runs. Bishop admitted he wasn't playing well. After starting thirty-one games in a row, he was benched.

The signs weren't good. The Saints had signed a center fielder fresh out of college as a backup to Darius Gash, who was still in a funk and seemed likely to be released. The team had made a few minor moves—cutting catcher Nick Sued and backup first baseman Bill Blanchette. Bishop was growing worried, too. The self-confidence that sounded like arrogance and alienated his teammates— contributing to their reluctance to help—itself began to erode. "If you're not playing every day, that means there's room for you to get sent out of here," Bishop said. "If that happens, that would be terrible."

The Saints opened the second half of the season with a three-game road trip to Winnipeg, a city in the province of Manitoba on the banks of the Red and Assiniboine rivers that took its name from two Indian words: *win*, meaning muddy, and *nipee*, or water. Winnipeg's skyscrapers rise like stalks of wheat sprouting from the surrounding prairies. The city has opera and ballet, a downtown that mixes steel-and-glass towers with turn-of-the-century warehouses. From its incorporation in 1873, Winnipeg has thought itself more sophisticated than other western cities, a grain-trading center that calls itself the "Bull's Eye of the Dominion." Residents boast that the architects of its train station also designed Grand Central Station in New York City.

Winnipeg fancies itself American in many ways—in the late nineteenth century, its leaders debated whether to join Canada or the United States—so it's natural that baseball has a stronger hold there than in other Canadian cities. In 1903 Winnipeg was a founding member (and first champion) of the Northern League. Winnipeg teams in an outlaw minor league in the 1940s included black players, and one club was even managed by a black. The city fielded a Northern League team on and off (reclusive Hall of Famer Steve Carlton pitched there) until the Goldeyes, named for an indigenous fish, folded in 1969. The city's last fling with professional baseball came in 1971, when a Triple-A club known as the Whips went out of business after a season and a half.

During the minors' rebirth in the 1980s, local businessmen tried to lure another Triple-A team to the city, but Winnipeg was deemed too far out of the way. One of the baseball boosters was

Sam Katz, the son of Holocaust survivors, a local rock 'n' roll promoter who resembled another Canadian, the musician Paul Shaffer. When Miles Wolff was hunting for cities, Katz was the man to see. His style screamed Los Angeles—cellular phones, cowboy boots, gaudy shirts—and like a strong-willed Hollywood agent Katz pulled Winnipeg's cultural strings. He wanted to be the man to return baseball to the city. When Katz dawdled during the formation of the Northern League, Wolff turned to Winnipeg's stadium authority to negotiate a lease. Katz intervened. If he didn't revive baseball in Winnipeg, no one would. Rebuffed again in 1993 by Triple-A, he finally agreed to join the Northern League.

After Ted Cushmore passed on Doug Simunic, Katz hired the Rochester manager. By the end of the first half, it looked as if Simunic wouldn't survive the season. The club went 16–24, finishing ahead of only Duluth. Simunic's team lost nine of its last ten games, during which the manager threw in the towel and overhauled his lineup. The rest of the league was angry at Simunic. Seven of Winnipeg's last nine losses were to Sioux City, and the Goldeyes' pitiful effort sealed the title for the Explorers.

In Simunic, Winnipeg had a total baseball animal. He was forever complaining to whoever would listen about some rule or decision that placed his club at a competitive disadvantage. St. Paul had all the money. Sioux Falls had the talent. His owner was a baseball neophyte. He was a one-man show. The deck was stacked against him.

Now he had given the rest of the league even more reason to dislike him: He tanked the end of the first half. Simunic didn't care. He was preparing his team to win. So what if other clubs had revenge in their hearts? "We're going to go up there and beat his fat ass," one manager said.

Behind his screw-everybody posture, though, Simunic was just another insecure coach who always worried about his next job. Growing up near Pontiac, Michigan, where his father was a carpenter and his mother drove a school bus, Simunic was a football-baseball MVP, but he doubted his chances of becoming a professional athlete. "I was always kind of a large guy," he said.

Large in the sense of . . . "Fat."

Signed as a free agent, Simunic rose to Triple-A as a good defensive catcher in the Cleveland organization in the early 1980s. But he never got a call-up. After extending his playing days in Canada, Italy, and the failed Senior Professional Baseball League, Simunic survived two years as a Rookie ball coach with Los Angeles, but if you didn't bleed Dodger blue your life span in the organization was short. When Simunic heard about the Northern League, he pestered Miles Wolff and then Charles Sanders, the de facto Rochester owner, until he got the managing job. But after leading Rochester to the playoffs, Simunic was out of work when the team folded. After the poor start in Winnipeg, his head was on the block again. It was no wonder that Simunic always rocked back and forth nervously while sitting on the dugout bench.

A jowly face and droopy mustache, a balding pate and overhanging gut don't inspire confidence in Doug Simunic. He isn't charismatic like Ed Nottle, doesn't cut an All-American profile like the well-built father of four Tim Blackwell (another catcher who *had* played in the majors), doesn't carry a résumé as long as Howie Be-

Doug Simunic in Winnipeg Stadium

dell's. Simunic is just a blue-collar guy—he drove a United Parcel Service truck in the off-season—from a blue-collar family who grappled for a home in organized baseball. "You wouldn't know how many times I've pounded on the door and scratched and clawed begging for a job in baseball," he said, "because that's all I know."

But Simunic's desperation was something of a ruse. As much as any manager in the Northern League, he knows baseball. He can play the aggrieved innocent, but he always has a master plan; later in the season Simunic buddied up to Bedell and talked the Duluth manager out of making a trade that would have helped rival St. Paul. The lesson with Simunic was simple: Don't be fooled by appearances. The bellyaching, tobacco-chewing, fat guy might not be ambassador to the city, but he could kick your ass on a baseball field.

Simunic's approach to independent ball was fairly simple. In October he obtained the list of six-year minor league free agents and called the ones he figured were near the end of their careers to see whether they might be interested in playing independent ball if nothing else worked out. When spring came the players, newly released, would remember who'd called first. Over the winter Simunic scoured the list of players cut by organizations and contacted friendly agents. He called a few college coaches, too, in search of rookies.

Possessed by insecurity, Simunic worked harder than anyone else in the league. He liked doing it alone. "I think that's the way it's got to be done, because I know what I need out here on the Astroturf," he said one day, rocking in a folding chair on the Winnipeg Stadium field. "I knew I needed some power, I knew I needed to get some pitching. My front office doesn't know that. I'm standing next to it every day. I'm watching it. So I know what I need."

To start the second half, the Winnipeg Goldeyes swept three games from the St. Paul Saints.

Players could smell the end coming. For Darius Gash, the whiff of the inevitable was in the air. The Saints had signed a rookie center fielder, Elgin Jeppesen, and on some nights Gash moved to left field. His batting average had increased, but only to .238. His on-base average—a leadoff hitter's main benchmark—was less than three in ten.

"So when do I go on waivers?" Gash asked no one in particular in late July. The previous night he had been lifted for a pinch hit-ter, and it wasn't Leon Durham but Eddie Ortega, a slap-hitting second baseman. It was the ultimate indignity.

Marv Goldklang arrived in St. Paul on Friday, July 29, for a peri-odic checkup on the Saints. Van Schley was back from California with his wife and eight-year-old daughter, Hannah, who liked to lead Saint Paula, the pig, on a leash. After the disappointing, in-jury-laden first half, the Saints had evened their record at 3–3, sweeping Thunder Bay at home. Still, Schley said, it looked as if the team was playing poorly enough to justify change.

Some St. Paul veterans were tired of losing games in the same fashion: blown leads and repeated mistakes. Better players always want to win, regardless of the level of baseball at which they find themselves, and the core of the St. Paul club was no different. They felt the club had the talent to succeed but not the comportment. There was deadwood, and it needed to go.

"Is that Van's kid?" Vince Castaldo asked.

"Yeah."

"Is Van here?"

"Yeah."

"Good. Maybe we'll make some changes."

While players shagged batting practice fly balls, Schley, Gold-klang, and Blackwell rendezvoused on the third-base line outside the Saints' dugout. Through an agent friend Goldklang had landed an eleven-year veteran first baseman named Matt Stark, who had played with the Blue Jays and White Sox and had just returned from another big league, in Taiwan. Stark is a quiet, imposing figure of 250 pounds who spits tobacco juice, calls everyone "hog nuts," and knows how to hit. In '93 he tore up the Mexican League with thirty-one home runs. He had signed and arrived. Now what? When should we activate him, Goldklang asked, and what's the countermove?

"Right now the first guy to go is Gash," Blackwell said.

Not only hadn't the switch-hitting outfielder begun to bat with any consistency—he was abysmal from the left side of the plate—but he was reluctant to take instruction. Blackwell said Gash never recovered from the disappointment of being released by the Padres.

"When do you want to make that move?" Goldklang asked.

"Before he gets dressed," the manager replied. "I think it's necessary to go ahead and do it rather than get him dressed. I know some of the other times I've pulled guys off the field, and I'd rather not pull him off the field."

"Let's just do it," Goldklang said.

Goldklang and Schley had been unable to find a veteran pitcher through the normal channels, contacts and the list of released players. At home plate during the previous series against Thunder Bay, Blackwell made an offer to his counterpart, Dan Shwam, who needed an outfielder. Darius Gash and Steve Morales for ace pitcher Pat Tilmon.

"He said no?" Schley asked.

"He said, I've got to think about that. He didn't say no flat out."

"He's slow to pull the trigger."

The Northern League is unlike any minor league in that trades happen. There is no major league front office deciding when to unload or swap players, with the manager and club owner simply accepting whoever is sent their way. Miles Wolff had hoped the trade winds would blow fiercely. But teams were cautious, and few deals materialized. The Saints felt aggrieved: No one would deal with the flagship franchise out of fear they'd help St. Paul win the league. The other owners, suffering an inferiority complex in the face of the St. Paul brain trust and market, balked at even lopsided offers. So the Saints figured they'd throw in more to the Thunder Bay deal.

At Schley's behest the team had flown in two more rookie outfielders—bringing to three the complement of neophyte newcomers. It made Stephen Bishop and Vince Castaldo wonder, for very different reasons, what was going on. Why are they signing outfielders when the problem is pitching?

In their sidelines conference—which Sioux City's Ed Nottle, who filled out the lineup card with the same names every day, watched in bewilderment—Blackwell said he liked the new rookies, Craig Gronowski and Brett Feauto, even if he still didn't have their names straight.

"Have you seen enough to say you want to sign 'em?" Goldklang asked the manager.

"I've seen more of Brett, uh, Feauto? I've seen more of him than I have Gronowski."

"We've got the option to maybe think about signing both of them," Schley said.

"The option is to sign one and keep the other for a couple days on a tryout basis," Goldklang said. "That's one way to do it. In which event we have to take one of our players and either release him or [put him on the disabled list]. It's a question of when you feel you've seen enough to activate this guy."

"If we kept both probably Nick [Belmonte] could get Jeppesen a job in Thunder Bay. They need a rookie outfielder," Schley said. "Everybody wins in this deal."

Now they were getting somewhere.

"There we go," Blackwell said. "We could throw Jeppesen in that trade for Tilmon."

"For six innings," Goldklang said, "he's the best pitcher in the league."

"I'll use him for those six innings," Blackwell said.

The decision then was which of the rookies to activate. They had been with the team a few days, happy to have jobs but wondering whether they would play.

"You could flip a coin," Blackwell said. "Just seeing what I saw in the cage, their approach to hitting is much better than Jeppesen."

"You want to make a move before the game?" Goldklang asked, deferring to the manager.

"Let me see what Rob and Leon say."

Let me see what Rob and Leon say. Everyone on the Saints had a say. While Blackwell consulted with his assistant coaches, Rob Swain and Bull Durham, Goldklang and Schley retreated to the stadium office to pressure Shwam. A quick phone call dashed their plans: The Thunder Bay manager didn't want Gash or Jeppesen. He'd consider an offer of pitcher Steve Jones plus someone else for his third starter, Brian Ahern.

"You can't make a trade in this league." Goldklang sighed. "Dan'll never make a trade."

"No, he sounds like he will," said Nick Belmonte, who had just arrived in St. Paul.

"He needs an outfielder," Goldklang said.

Schley had an idea. "Bishop?" he said. "He's not a bad ballplayer. Bishop and Jones. . . . Bishop, Jones, and one other guy."

"The key thing would be to make it fair and you'd get your veteran pitcher," Belmonte said.

"Bishop, Jones, and Gash," Goldklang said. "Final offer."

"That's very fair," Belmonte said.

"Bishop, Jones, and Gash for Tilmon or Ahern," the chairman repeated. "And tell him we've got to know right away."

Belmonte went to an upstairs office to call the Thunder Bay manager. He tried to sell Shwam on Steve Bishop. But ever diplomatic about brokering deals to avoid the appearance of favoring St. Paul, Belmonte added, "But please, Dan, don't rush to help these guys out."

The Saints wanted to activate Stark, the new veteran, so they had to release a veteran to clear a roster spot. Blackwell summoned Darius Gash into his locker-room office, which doubled as a supply closet. Gash knew what was coming. Hell, he'd had the same conversation with the Padres just a few months earlier.

"It had to end sometime," Gash said a few minutes later, dressed in his street clothes. "If I died a millionaire from ball, it'd still have ended sometime."

When Stephen Bishop realized he wasn't starting that night—and one of the newly activated rookies, Craig Gronowski, was—he strolled to the relative solitude of center field shortly before game time. Under the cover of music filling the ballpark, he unleashed a string of expletives into the summer air.

When Bishop was benched, he stopped caring. This wasn't the

majors, where players know their roles and are paid handsomely for filling them. It was indy ball. The point was to play your way *out* of the league. Every man for himself.

So whenever the Saints rallied, Bishop sat silently on the bench. When a teammate homered, he didn't stand for the obligatory high fives. If other players thought him arrogant, so what? He wasn't a cheerleader. That was his personality. Take it or leave it.

Bishop privately was angry that two black teammates—Gash and that same day Jeppesen—had been cut. "They're releasing all the black guys," he said in frustration. "I'm next." Bishop was indeed on the trading block, though he didn't yet know it.

Blackwell had decided that Bishop's attitude had become a detriment to the club. After Bishop's center-field outburst, the manager dispatched Leon Durham to talk to the rookie. The former major leaguer hadn't been much help with the young hitter on the field, but his mental experience could be useful. It was a role the better veterans had to play in the Northern League. Oil Can Boyd, for all his oddities, was turning out to be a valuable instructor in Sioux City. Jeff Bittiger, who'd played for the 1991 World Series champion Minnesota Twins, doubled as ace and pitching coach in Winnipeg. Dann Bilardello, the Winnipeg catcher and former major leaguer, wanted to manage someday soon. Miles Wolff had hoped the league would be an incubator for coaching as well as playing talent. When the older player had the right attitude, the system worked.

Durham offered Bishop some obvious but sage advice: You have to learn to cope with the disappointment of not playing; in jock terms, "keep your head up." Your attitude is jeopardizing your future, Durham told him. After a second talk on Saturday, Durham told Blackwell he felt strongly about keeping Bishop. The Saints could add Durham to the circle of decision makers. Bishop stayed.

He seemed to be a quick learner. On Saturday, Bishop, his cap on backwards to spur a rally, was the first Saint out of the dugout during a ninth-inning comeback. The next day he apologized to Blackwell and during the game warmed up the pitcher between innings and swung a bat in case he was summoned to pinch-hit.

But appearances were deceiving. Bishop still didn't play—he had batted just once in the last six games, at the end of a 12–4 blowout win. He was in a slump, yes, but still hitting .286. Why didn't he get a chance to play out of it, like others? What had he done wrong? And why were the Saints signing college kids to play the outfield? When he asked, Bishop was told the team just wanted to win. Well, he had started thirty-one games in a row. The Saints hadn't lost thirty-one in a row, had they? "I want out of here," he finally said. "If I can't play on an independent team, release me so I can get signed somewhere else."

Forty-five minutes before Saturday's game against the Sioux City Explorers, the brain trust gathered again, this time in the shuttered office of general manager Bill Fanning. In the minors general managers are responsible for business operations—not player personnel, like their major league counterparts. But Fanning saw the players on a daily basis, had strong opinions about their personalities, and could offer some input. He joined Goldklang, Schley, Blackwell, and Swain behind closed doors.

Thunder Bay wouldn't trade. The club's owner, Ricky May, quashed any deal for a pitcher, fearing he would lose his top starter, Rod Steph, to a major league organization before the year ended. The Saints were back to square one.

They had signed Stark, giving the team what was, by Northern League standards, a fearsome lineup: Castaldo, Durham, and Stark in a row. Bull was starting to hit—three for four with a homer and two RBIs on Friday in a 6–5 win. But pitching remained the crucible. Schley again raised his pet peeve: Ranbir Grewal. Let's cut him, he said. Blackwell refused. Grewal's ERA was down to 3.99 pitching in relief, and he was a stable clubhouse presence. Schley was frustrated. He and Goldklang proposed another trade: Steve Jones and Eddie Ortega to Duluth for pitcher Dominic Desantis. That too would be rejected, by Howie Bedell.

At least the Saints were winning a few games.

On Saturday, trailing 4–1 in the ninth inning, Al Frechtman

loaded "Theme from *Shaft*" into the CD player, and the Saints responded. Gronowski walked. Ortega singled. Doug Kimbler walked. Greg D'Alexander singled. In an instant, the score was 4–3.

In the grandstands behind home plate, Vince Castaldo's parents had flown from St. Louis to watch their son play. They spent a weekend every summer visiting their boys. (Vinny's younger brother, Gregg, was a Class-A shortstop in the Orioles system.) Castaldo's mother wore a button that said, "Vinny the Hit Man." She showed off baseball cards of her sons protected by plastic folders and stored in her handbag. When Vinny came to the plate in the bottom of the ninth with the winning runs on base, she clapped her hands above her head and cheered.

Castaldo ended the suspense quickly. He lashed a fastball from closer Barry Goldman more than 380 feet over the left-center-field wall. After touching home Castaldo was mobbed by teammates. He raised two fists above his head and pumped once, then again. Tim Blackwell kissed Castaldo in the dugout, and the third baseman doffed his cap and raised his right arm to fans demanding a curtain call. They were singing his name to "Volare."

After the game, walking through the parking lot with his parents, Castaldo told his father that he wasn't swinging well. A lesser player would have been basking in the afterglow of his crushing three-run, game-winning, bottom-of-the-ninth home run before a sellout hometown crowd, but Castaldo was analyzing the three hitless at bats that had preceded it, including two swinging strikeouts.

Tom Castaldo, as soft-spoken as Vinny is intense, understood how his perfectionist son approached the game, and didn't try to steer the conversation toward his game-ending heroics. Instead, he suggested that Vinny wasn't keeping his front shoulder down—and then laughed at the idea that he was giving Vinny advice. "Hey," his son interrupted in deadly seriousness, "I wouldn't be here without him."

The glacier, as Van Schley said about the Saints' reluctance to make roster moves, had broken. Gash, Sued, and a couple of unproductive younger players had been sent home. The addition of Matt Stark was, like the portly former catcher himself, huge. Schley persuaded Goldklang to call up Dan Zanolla, a rookie pitcher who had excelled on the Saints' "farm team" in Ogden.

But the moves were like shoveling snow in a blizzard. The problem didn't go away, and the Saints didn't improve. St. Paul's performance underscored a weakness that was apparent even before the season started. It was the answer to a fundamental baseball question: How do you get to the playoffs? Pitching, pitching, pitching. Even with the Northern League equivalent of Murderers Row, the team couldn't be expected to score seven runs every night.

Schley moaned through August as the Saints played mediocre baseball. They scored the requisite seven runs in a game against Sioux City but surrendered eight, losing in thirteen innings. They blew a 3–2 lead in the ninth against Sioux Falls. They scored seven the next night against the Canaries, only to yield twelve. They relinquished a seventh-inning lead at Sioux City and lost 5–4. Winnipeg, meanwhile, with its new lineup stacked with veterans, continued to dominate. By midpoint St. Paul stood at 11–9. Winnipeg was 16–4. With every St. Paul loss, the numerical and psychological spread widened.

Schley wondered why the Saints were waiting to make further changes. A Triple-A-caliber pitcher, Julio Solano, who had played in The Show, had become available, but Goldklang delayed signing him because he was a closer and the chairman was holding out for a starter. "Why, I don't know," Schley said. "We're five out. It's almost over."

Players, Vince Castaldo prominent among them, were growing increasingly disenchanted and impatient. Castaldo was glad that his roommate, Darius Gash, had been cut (believing that Gash had lost the desire to play long ago), but he wondered why other moves had stalled. Where was the pitching? What about the problem children on the Saints? The manager complained that he was running a baby-sitting service. Why then, Castaldo thought, didn't he do something about it? Why were these guys still around? They were a cancer on the team, the veterans said. A cancer on the team.

With the Brewers and Expos, Castaldo had paid the price for

complaining. On the Saints, he was the star, the de facto team leader, and he couldn't stand his teammates' failure to make routine plays. He didn't expect everyone to hit .300 and knock twenty homers, just behave like professionals on the field, in the clubhouse, and away from the park. "It's just the little things that I'm sick and tired of seeing every fucking night," he said. "It's worn on me." Castaldo's feelings toward the rookies were as subtle as one of his clutch homers or thrown bats. "Either they suck or they don't care," he said.

The older players liked their manager, but they knew not to mistake Tim Blackwell for Vince Lombardi. Blackwell was the best on-field manager in the league, they believed. He understood game strategy. Veterans responded well to his approach. They knew how to prepare to play well. But younger players need discipline, attention, instruction, in short, a kick in the ass. The veterans had seen their manager fail to get the rookies in line. They were fed up.

During a road trip to Sioux Falls and Sioux City, the older players decided that if management wouldn't make changes to help the team win, the players would force them to. It was indy ball. The veterans knew they had nothing to lose. Most felt empowered for the first time in careers that had been governed by fealty to a parent club. Plus, they were reading about their major league counterparts who had just walked out on strike. "It's a little different from the [affiliated] minor leagues," Castaldo said. "We can do what we want. Without us, they're not much."

So while the Saints were blowing leads in Sioux Falls, eight older players requested a meeting with Blackwell. They had identified the morale killers on the team: Duane Page, Steve Morales, Steve Jones, and Stephen Bishop. The veterans had a message: If those players aren't released, we won't play.

It was a difficult position for management. Players can't dictate who plays and who doesn't, who makes the team and who's released. That the Saints players even felt they had the ability to make such demands suggested that the club's cockpit had been hijacked. Forget for a moment that they may have been right. The inmates running the asylum? Not in baseball.

Marv Goldklang hadn't wanted to make any cuts without a

"countermove." Now Blackwell faced the real possibility of a walk-out by his starters if he didn't succumb to their demands. The problem was that Blackwell didn't disagree with them; he even had told his mutinous veterans he had hoped they would say something about the rookies. The hell with it, Goldklang said. His team had just been swept in Sioux Falls and was fading in the pennant race—though still clinging to a thread of hope with six head-to-head meetings with Winnipeg remaining. Three of the four players—Page, Jones, and Bishop—weren't considered important performers on the club. If they were sent home, maybe it would be the nudge the Saints needed. "This is probably something we should have done earlier," Goldklang concluded.

After traveling to Sioux City, Blackwell called Page, Jones, and Bishop, one by one, to his room at a motel called the Riverboat Inn and said the team was making some changes and they would be released.

Van Schley learned about the cuts after the fact. He was feeling more and more marginalized in the decision making. Schley was shocked that the ball club had sunk to the point where a group of players could think they had the power to order the front office to cut certain teammates—and worse, that Goldklang and Blackwell had done as told. "How not to run your player personnel," Schley snapped. "It looks like panic. You don't make releases when you're losing. If you have a guy who's a problem, release him when you're going well. A release can be a very strong psychological message. Then you've made your statement."

When Bishop was cut by the Atlanta Braves, he accepted the decision meekly. That was what his buddy, major leaguer Tony Tarasco, had advised. With an organization, you couldn't question why you weren't playing or why you were released because the temerity might earn you a bad reputation and jeopardize your future with another club. But this was independent ball. If you didn't ask, you'd never know why.

When Blackwell told him he was gone, Bishop didn't question the reasoning. In a way he was relieved it was over. He had begun with high hopes—making the team, earning a starting role, taking the championship, winning awards for his play. Now he was disappointed. But not in himself; Bishop never stopped believing he could play the game. He was pissed off at the Saints. He had been released twice in less than a year. This time he would find out why. At least make them say something.

After reaching the motel elevator, Bishop did an about-face. He walked back to Blackwell's room and popped the question. Your production plummeted, the manager replied. We needed to make a change. You can play a lot of positions, but your production went down.

Blackwell didn't mention Bishop's attitude, and the rookie continued to deny anything was wrong, in spite of what the teammates who had sabotaged him believed. Bishop said that the day his batting average fell below .300, he was benched, never given an opportunity to redeem himself on the field.

"I didn't have a bad attitude," he said. "I didn't say anything, really. I'm not that type of person. They couldn't deal with it. I'm not a cheerleader. I'm not happy sitting on the bench. If I'm not happy, I'm not happy. My thing is to take care of me first, then my friends, then other people. I wasn't dogging it at all. I was going about my business. I still came out early. I tried to get back in the lineup. I tried to improve my swing."

Then came Bishop's inevitable conclusion. It was a young and frustrated athlete's easy rationalization. It was also true: "They just didn't like me."

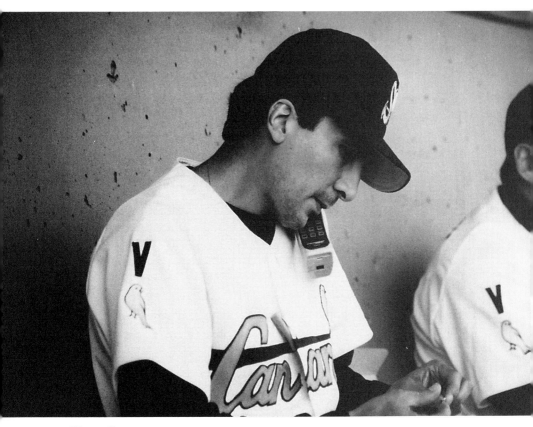

Harry Stavrenos

THIRTEEN

A baseball manager is a necessary evil.

—Sparky Anderson

Harry Stavrenos, the owner of the Sioux Falls Canaries, sat in a small office beneath Sioux Falls Stadium, the ballpark that unexpected city largesse had converted from a candidate for the wrecking ball into a cozy, pristine, and up-to-date facility. The Canaries were at home for two games in early August against the rival Sioux City Explorers, and the owner was in town to watch. He had also attended the previous night's game at Lewis and Clark Park in Sioux City. And he would board the team bus after the next day's game for the overnight ride to Winnipeg.

Stavrenos was fatigued. He dragged on a cigarette and undressed. The club owner would rather have been at home near the beach in laid-back Santa Cruz, California, with his wife and two children, who were under the age of two. Instead, he was road-tripping with his independent league team. He was in the public eye, which he hated. (Stavrenos boasted that he hadn't been on television the last three years in San Jose, where he was president and part owner of a Giants farm club in the California League.) And he was catching grief from the rest of the Northern League, which thought he was on an ego trip. Can you believe Harry? was the refrain heard around the league.

"He who is his own attorney," Mike Veeck said, "has a fool for a client."

That bothered Stavrenos more than anything. The last thing in the world he needed was the aggravation. Anyone who knew him understood he wasn't after publicity, or struggling to fulfill some fantasy-camp dream. He honestly believed he didn't have an option.

Stavrenos tugged his white sanitary stockings above his knees and pulled on the black stirrups over them. He twisted the tops of the socks to one side and left them there. (Steve Howe taught him that. The socks never slipped.) Cigarette dangling from his lips, Stavrenos put on Sioux Falls's all-white home pants and thick, black belt. He wore a T-shirt and a black windbreaker beneath the home jersey, which said "Canaries" in light blue script across the chest, a yellow bird perched on the end of a black baseball bat. The uniform bore the number 2, and his name was spelled out in capital letters across the back.

Stavrenos, the owner, had a game to manage. "I'll tell you the truth," he said. "I don't give a fuck what anybody says. Who cares? If we win it, it'll shut 'em up."

Harry Stavrenos had managed a baseball team once before.

The year was 1986. Major league baseball had a new commissioner named Peter Ueberroth, the entrepreneur who turned the Los Angeles Summer Olympics into a corporate-sponsored profit machine. Ueberroth was cracking down on drug use. The game indeed had problems. Three Kansas City Royals had been imprisoned on drug charges. A trial in Pittsburgh implicated twenty-three players in a drug ring. Suspensions were common. Fearful of angering the new commissioner, major league clubs steered clear of anyone with a drug-tainted past.

Stavrenos had arrived in San Jose four years earlier. The grandson of Greek immigrants, whose father owned parking lots in Youngstown, Ohio, Stavrenos had just finished fifty-one weeks as a coffee salesman for the big local company, General Foods. But he didn't want to sell coffee. He wanted to return to baseball.

His first job in the game had been as an intern with the Miami

Amigos of the Inter-American League, the failed independent Triple-A circuit around Latin America. A friend from the Amigos wound up managing an independent club in Macon, Georgia, the following year. Stavrenos loaded his Dodge Dart and took a job as assistant general manager of the Macon Peaches. In five months the Peaches had four presidents, the last a baseball warhorse whose ignorance of the ways of the South was exceeded only by his boorishness. One time he scolded two old-timers who had worked at the stadium for thirty years for failing adequately to clean up bird droppings on the seats. Another he scheduled a press conference on a Sunday morning, not a great idea in the Bible Belt. Stavrenos quit the $300-a-month job midway through the season and went home, selling coffee in Youngstown until, through a baseball connection, he was offered the job of general manager in San Jose. He quit General Foods one week before his paid vacation and stock options would have kicked in.

At the time the San Jose club was a cooperative, receiving loaners from a few major league organizations. The yuppies of Silicon Valley didn't care about the team at all, with fewer than a hundred fans coming to a run-down ballpark some nights. Stavrenos secured a working agreement with the Montreal Expos and promptly made his first mistake. He changed the team name from the historically relevant San Jose Missions to the San Jose Expos. The city had one more reason not to care about the club. When the Expos packed up after a year, Stavrenos revived an old name, the San Jose Bees. A Japanese club supplied a few players, as did various major league organizations. Stavrenos bought a small piece of the team for $5,000.

In 1986, the club fully independent, Stavrenos needed to do something to make the Bees interesting, so he opened the club to wayward major league players—the drug policy be damned. Over the course of the season, Stavrenos hired sixteen ex-big-leaguers, including eight who'd had drug-related problems. The headline act was Steve Howe, then serving one of his eight suspensions from baseball. The club was known in the press as the Bad News Bees. Out of print they were the Bad *Nose* Bees, referring to a certain white powder. Rehab stories abounded. "I went the devil's road," third baseman Todd Cruz said, "cocaine and alcohol."

Stavrenos began the year as the club's president, general manager, and, out of necessity created by a last-minute cancellation, field manager. He removed the uniform for good after he was suspended for allowing Howe to pitch the day Ueberroth banned him for failing another drug test. (Howe denied any use but tested positive again later in the summer and was kicked out of baseball, again.)

The spectacle of the Bad News Bees drew a crowd. A media horde turned out for Opening Day. A CBS News crew arrived by helicopter to report on the team. One night Bees players climbed into the stands to stick up for Stavrenos in a fistfight prompted by taunting fans.

Through it all Stavrenos defended giving the troubled players another shot. He liked the idea of bumping chests with the major leagues. He was young, only thirty-one years old, and having fun. "If I find anybody else who I think can help this club, I'd sell my car to get him," Stavrenos said at the time. "We're an independent team. They're trying to make me out as a bad guy for trying to build a ball club without help."

That season, the Bad News Bees, cellar dwellers the three previous years, managed to finish ahead of one club. Attendance, meanwhile, rose 63 percent. A year later, with fewer ex–major leaguers and less notoriety, the Bees posted the worst record in organized baseball, 33–109. Independent baseball isn't easy.

Stavrenos ran the Bees as an independent for six seasons, but the game's financial realities forced him to sign a working agreement with the Giants. He had a cordial relationship with San Francisco over the years but hated the bureaucracy of baseball. Signing Steve Howe and Mike Norris and Todd Cruz and other bad boys had been one way of getting back at the big leagues. Owning—and managing—the Sioux Falls Canaries was another.

Stavrenos stood out among Northern League owners. He doesn't come from money like Bill Pereira or Van Schley, or have a Wall Street pedigree like Marv Goldklang, or the cerebral tendencies of Miles Wolff, or the corporate experience of Ted Cushmore, or the lineage of Mike Veeck. Stavrenos has street smarts. He is the son of blue-collar ethnics, graduated from a respectable midwestern college (Bowling Green), and worked his way up through the minors. Long midwestern vowels and slow, breathy, colloquial speech sometimes make Stavrenos sound like a stoned teenager. Entirely unpretentious, he is the kind of guy who will say anything, about anybody, at almost any time, and not worry about it.

He has style. Stavrenos drives a metallic blue Cadillac Seville from the late 1970s and wears black high-top Converse Chuck Taylor basketball sneakers. When he dresses up, the outfits are often all black and wouldn't seem out of place at a convention of two-bit hoods.

Stavrenos also has heart. After his grandfather arrived in America, like many immigrants he informally abbreviated his name, from Panayoti Stavrenos to Pete Steve. His father legalized the Americanized version, and into adulthood the sports-loving son was known as Harry Steve. Like many second-generation Americans, he doesn't speak much Greek, but he cares about his heritage. Shortly before his father died in the late 1980s, Harry Steve legally changed his name to Stavrenos (pronounced STAH-vri-nos).

With more than a decade in minor league baseball, Stavrenos knew every aspect of the game. In many ways he combined the skills of the St. Paul triumvirate of Veeck, Goldklang, and Schley: He could run a ball club's business operations, negotiate with the majors, and scout players. In Sioux Falls, Stavrenos assembled the team entirely on his own. Many of his players came from California or had played in the California League; one, former major league catcher Carl Nichols, had played in San Jose a decade earlier.

His manager was Frank Verdi, a cantankerous career minor leaguer whose first season in professional baseball was 1946. Verdi's fifteen-year playing career is notable for one reason: He is the only player in major league history to have been announced as a pinch hitter but recalled to the bench in his one and only big-league appearance. Frank Verdi's playing record in the *Baseball Encyclopedia* consists of a string of zeros.

As a player-coach, Verdi earned another distinction: He helped American baseball leave Cuba forever. On July 26, 1959, a Cuban holiday, Castro loyalists packed Gran Stadium for a Triple-A International League game between the Havana Sugar Kings and the Rochester Red Wings. Pistol shots occasionally rang out in the raucous ballpark. Verdi was coaching third base for Rochester when he was grazed by a bullet in the head. Fortunately, he was wearing a plastic helmet liner. "If that bullet was two inches to the left, the boys on the ball club would have had to chip in five dollars apiece for flowers," he said at the time. After the season, as the rift between the United States and Cuba grew, the International League decided that Havana was too volatile a place for a team and moved the club to Jersey City.

Verdi always seemed to cut it close. Among other stops he spent sixteen years managing Triple-A clubs for the Yankees, Mets, Orioles, Astros, and the old Washington Senators, but he was never promoted to the big leagues.

Stavrenos wielded the sharpest pencil in the Northern League. His club's expenses were under $500,000 a year, less than half those of St. Paul. Rather than fly players in at the beginning of the season, he encouraged them to drive (they needed a car anyway, he would tell them) and paid the league rate of ten cents a mile. Cost cutting extended to the manager: Stavrenos employed Verdi from spring training to the end of the season for about a third of what St. Paul paid Tim Blackwell and Duluth paid Howie Bedell. When the Northern League held its first tryout camp in Fort Myers in February, Stavrenos didn't even send his manager, who lived only a couple of hours away.

It was a mutually satisfactory arrangement. After more than forty years in baseball, Verdi had little interest in scouting players (or in attempting to place them in organizations after the season). When Stavrenos offered him the Sioux Falls job—his first managing post since 1985—Verdi was happy to handle the on-field duties and nothing else. During spring training the owner would send his manager brief sketches of each player. Verdi took it from there.

Stavrenos sometimes worried about Verdi. His manager was sixty-eight years old, a gruff baseball man who sat on a folding chair at the end of the dugout during games. He said he wanted to manage until he died.

In 1994 he almost did. In early July, on the road in St. Paul, Verdi complained of chest pains. But he kept managing. When the pains recurred, the Canaries' team doctor conducted a stress test on Verdi's heart. Verdi failed the test and was admitted to Sioux Falls Hospital. Tests revealed severely blocked coronary arteries. After successful quadruple bypass heart surgery, his season appeared over.

Stavrenos's choices were limited. His first-base coach had just left Sioux Falls for a college coaching job in California. His pitching coach was Bob Beattie, a former minor leaguer living in South Dakota who had just retired as an analyst with the state labor department. Stavrenos didn't feel comfortable turning the club over to him. He could have hired a manager from within the league—a couple of coaches were interested in the job—but they wouldn't know the club or its chemistry. Stavrenos did. Putting on the uniform was the easiest solution, and his real reason, not saving a few thousand dollars, the charge circulating around the league. "I knew going in why I signed these guys, and I know a lot of them personally," Stavrenos said. "I didn't think they'd feel uncomfortable with me around. If someone had given me a better alternative, I would have taken it."

In independent baseball Stavrenos didn't need an alternative. It was his club. If he thought he could manage, he was entitled to manage.

With the exception of first-half champion Sioux City, which had every reason to feel relaxed, Sioux Falls was the most laid-back team in the league. Its two former major leaguers set the tone. They were at peace with the fact that their careers were mostly behind them.

Thirty-eight-year-old Pedro Guerrero, the fifteen-year Dodger and Cardinal with 215 career homers and a .300 batting average, returned to the Northern League for a second season because he loved the game. A five-time National League All-Star, Guerrero didn't need the money; he had done well enough that his real desire was to own a club—possibly the Canaries—one day, and he no longer hoped for a phone call from an American League team seeking a designated hitter. That was why he had agreed to play for Stavrenos in 1993, but the possibility was all but gone a year later. Now it was just for fun.

Guerrero, as *Sports Illustrated* put it in a story about the independent circuit, led the league in cellular phone calls from the dugout. He could be found smoking cigarettes between innings in the tunnel beneath the stadium, talking about his golf game, or happily instructing younger teammates.

Guerrero didn't ride the bus on road trips. As part of his deal with

Pedro Guerrero

Stavrenos, he flew to the faraway destinations and drove his black Mercedes on shorter hauls—all at his own expense. "I am the only man in the history of professional baseball who is paying money to play," he said. Guerrero batted close to .400 much of the first half and was in the top ten all season. The onetime World Series MVP could still hit a baseball.

The other former big-leaguer on the Canaries was thirty-one-year-old Carl Nichols, who had played parts of six seasons with the Astros and Orioles. Unlike Guerrero, Nichols, with a .204 career average in just 186 at bats, was never an All-Star. He was, however, a member of the 1988 Orioles team that lost twenty-one straight games to begin the season.

Nichols is quiet and reserved, and while bitter that he never got a chance to play regularly in the majors, was glad to be on the field. He could gun down base stealers at will; he was a perceptive defensive catcher who still possessed major league skills.

The youngest of ten children (he has twenty-five nieces and nephews, including the St. Louis Cardinals outfielder Ray Lankford), Nichols grew up in the rough Los Angeles neighborhood of Compton. Baseball helped keep him out of trouble—"that and the extension cord my father kept in the closet," he joked.

From age eight Nichols knew he wanted to play professional baseball. In Little League he was so much bigger than the other kids that his mother had to carry around his birth certificate to prove his age to disbelieving coaches. A scout talked to one of his older brothers about him when Nichols was eleven. He was a good student in high school, but when the Orioles picked him in the fourth round of the 1980 draft, Nichols chose minor league baseball over a college scholarship.

"I had the focus from day one," he said. "It kept me out of trouble. It kept me from hanging with the wrong crowd. There were a lot of distractions. A lot of guys in gangs, doing drugs, selling drugs. I know a lot of kids who got killed for absolutely no reason, just being with the wrong people. I was pretty mature growing up. I was able to see beyond today."

But in pro ball Nichols's career quickly hit a snag: The Orioles drafted another catcher in the second round. Nichols saw little playing time his first three years in the minors—years when he could have been in college. In 1986, at the end of his second Double-A season—his best in baseball with fourteen homers and seventy-two runs batted in—Nichols received a September call-up to the Orioles. For the next five years he bounced between Triple-A and the big leagues but never won a starting role in Baltimore or Houston, where he was traded in 1989. Even there, with weak-armed Craig Biggio behind the plate (Biggio later was converted into a Gold Glove second baseman), Nichols rode the bench. He suspected that his quiet demeanor contributed to his lack of playing time. Nichols never asked why he wasn't in the lineup and appeared to the coaching staff to be sullen and uninterested, a common misinterpretation of subdued black athletes made by white coaches.

Nichols has his memories. He made The Show. He beat the Reds one night with a bases-loaded single off closer Randy Myers with two outs in the bottom of the ninth. He gunned down Lenny Dykstra twice in one game and picked Kirk Gibson off first base. He *knows* he threw out Rickey Henderson, even if the umpire called him safe. But Nichols never batted more than fifty-one times in a season in the majors. "I never had a chance to fail," he said.

When the Astros released Nichols after the 1991 season, he returned home to Milwaukee, playing three or four times a week in a beer league the following summer, hoping for a call from an organization that never came. Stavrenos remembered Nichols from a couple of seasons he spent in San Jose. The catcher was happy for a chance to play professionally again, back to eating at McDonald's every day and jamming his imposing, 215-pound frame into bus seats. No regrets. No reason to criticize the big leagues.

Nichols, who was leading the Northern League in runs batted in as the 1994 season wound down, had accepted his fate and, unlike many of his teammates, harbored no unrealistic expectations. After the season he didn't plan to hound major league offices for a playing job; he expected to call his career quits. He might work again at the post office or drive a newspaper delivery truck back home, as he had the previous winter, spending time with his wife and two children before trying to land a coaching job. The maturity that had saved him on the streets of Los Angeles showed in another way now.

"You just have to learn to face it, that's all," Nichols said. "When I came here last year I was wondering if I could still play. This year I came back and tried to enjoy myself a little more and do more than I did last year. I can't worry about things I can't control. I proved to myself that I can still play. If nobody wants to give me a chance, that's not a reflection on me. I'll see what happens. I don't take it personally."

Having Stavrenos in charge made Sioux Falls even more relaxed. He doesn't stand on protocol. He isn't gregarious or domineering, with employees, players, or friends. He isn't an imperial owner, so his players don't feel a need to bow and scrape in his presence. He is Harry to everyone, and would have been even if his last name wasn't so difficult to pronounce.

But Stavrenos does have a fiery Mediterranean side. A troublemaker as a kid and a hothead as an adult, Stavrenos isn't afraid to mix it up. Near the end of the 1993 season, the St. Paul Saints were in town. Stavrenos was in the stands. Leon Durham crushed a fly ball down the right-field line, high above the fence and the foul pole. Everyone in the stadium but the umpires appeared to realize that the ball was foul by about twenty feet. As Durham trotted around the bases, the first-base umpire signaling home run, Stavrenos leaped from his seat, jumped onto the field, and sprinted toward the umpires, who were ready to call a cop to escort the unruly fan. Miles Wolff had to suspend Stavrenos for the rest of the year.

The memory of that incident was burned into everyone in the league, who laughed at its retelling. So when Stavrenos took over for Verdi, heads were shaking. Would the players take him seriously? Would it hurt the league's image and credibility to have an owner managing? Stavrenos wasn't Connie Mack, after all. Some of his colleagues worried about the message that an owner-manager—even one who knew baseball as well as Stavrenos—sent to players, fans, and baseball at large. The league had to be serious. It wasn't a playground. Not having genuine, professional managers demeaned the product.

"I didn't buy a ball club for my alter ego," Mike Veeck said. "This isn't Walter Mitty. I'm in this because I love what I do and I know that what I do is important. It helps people get their careers back on track here. It helps people in the stands forget what's out there. It gives me a chance to do something that connects me with my lineage. So I want this league, I *need* this league to survive for very personal, very emotional reasons. Because of the independent and wildcat nature of all this, we suddenly think it's our own personal OK Corral."

Stavrenos knew what he was doing on the field, but he didn't push it too far. He let Bob Beattie coach third base—usually the manager's job in the minors. Carl Nichols called the pitches. Mike Burton, the first baseman, set the infield defense on bunt plays. But Stavrenos played a role, too. He ran the pitching staff, even if opposing managers sometimes wondered. With Sioux Falls trailing 6–1 one night and his pitcher getting hammered, Stavrenos strolled to the mound—but he had no one warming up in the bullpen. Only after he returned to the dugout was a reliever summoned to get ready.

Stavrenos had a talented team in Sioux Falls, perhaps the best all-around club in the league. The Canaries played .600 baseball in the first half, finishing with a 24–16 record, three games behind Sioux City. The same pattern was repeating in the second half, only this time they were chasing Winnipeg. The new manager took over with Sioux Falls at 4–2. After losing four of their next five games, the Canaries rebounded, despite or because of Harry Stavrenos, and they stayed in contention all the way.

But the owner-manager felt persecuted. He was angry about being bad-mouthed around the league. He felt it was unjustified. After all, Miles Wolff had approved Stavrenos's decision to manage. And the team was no disgrace. But Stavrenos felt he was held to a different standard.

Thirty-one peaceable games into his tenure, Stavrenos was ejected from a home game versus Winnipeg for arguing balls and strikes. Five pitches later Nichols, who despite his understated manner is a verbal agitator on the field, was tossed for the same offense. In the newspaper the next day, Stavrenos called the sequence of three straight balls with an oh-and-two count—the fourth pitch resulted in a two-run single that helped the Goldeyes win the game—the worst he had ever seen but said he felt vindicated because his respected catcher also was ejected. The Northern League office fined Stavrenos $300. The manager maintained that the penalty was ridiculously unfair. It was his first ejection—and no other manager in the league, including St. Paul's Tim Blackwell, had been fined after getting booted. When the league's executive director sent Stavrenos a fax saying that if Verdi hadn't been sick he would have been suspended for three games, Stavrenos was outraged.

It was enough to make Stavrenos consider selling the Canaries. He had spent much of the summer advising Ted Cushmore in Duluth—Northern League owners knew it was in their collective interest to make sure each franchise was successful—and he contemplated buying a piece of the Dukes and running their player personnel. The Sioux Falls franchise was worth more than $1 million, Stavrenos figured. He owned 76 percent of the team, which he'd established as a limited partnership—and had just $18,000 of his own money invested. Selling the club would be a bonanza.

But Stavrenos was loyal to Sioux Falls and the league. As the Northern League's charter member—he had signed a lease even before franchises had been awarded—Stavrenos didn't want to look like he was taking the money and running. He genuinely liked Sioux Falls and felt honored to be a principal owner in any venture organized by Miles Wolff. Despite the temptation of reviving Duluth, Stavrenos figured he would keep Sioux Falls. For the time being, he was busy managing a contending club.

In Sioux Falls one August night, the Canaries fell behind Sioux City 7–2. His eyes shielded behind sunglasses, Stavrenos nervously chewed sunflower seeds in the dugout. But a young relief pitcher shut down the Explorers while Sioux Falls mounted a comeback. Trailing 7–6 in the ninth, with runners on base, Pedro Guerrero stepped to the plate, only to ground out and end the game.

Stavrenos was angry about the loss, which dropped the club further behind Winnipeg, and still a little defensive about his managing abilities. ("I didn't make any mistakes, did I?" he asked.) That night Stavrenos had pushed the right buttons but simply lost. Sitting in front of his locker, he lit a cigarette and began packing for the overnight trip to Winnipeg. He rolled up a Canaries T-shirt and stuffed it into a travel bag. He grabbed a pillow for the bus ride.

Over breakfast that day he had bemoaned the notoriety of managing and the indignance of his Northern League colleagues. But Stavrenos had to admit he savored the challenge. He obsessed about winning the second-half title. He was enjoying the job, even the road trips, where he could leave his worries behind, sleep until eleven o'clock, relax in the afternoon, and wear the uniform at night. Ever the antiestablishmentarian, he also liked getting a rise out of his fellow owners and managers. It made you wonder whether his complaints weren't one big ruse. "Funny things happen," he had said with a smile, "you know?"

Sioux Falls Stadium in August 1994 (© Buck Miller)

FOURTEEN

When you ain't got nothin', you got nothin' to lose.

—Bob Dylan

O n August 12, 1994, major league baseball players walked off the job, through a door held open by management. Almost two years earlier, at the game's annual winter meetings, big-league owners had spent an eye-popping $260 million on free agent contracts—$125 million in one day alone. Embarrassed by their excess, baseball's barons blamed the charged atmosphere of a hotel packed with untrustworthy brethren, ravenous player agents, and a wolf-pack press for their loss of self-control. And they wouldn't let it happen again. They decided not to attend the winter meetings in Atlanta the following year. Instead, the check writers gathered in January 1994 in the relative safety of Fort Lauderdale, Florida, for a meeting at which any talk of baseball, the game, was unwelcome. Instead, the discussions were all business. Baseball's owners had traded a week of free publicity about player moves for more stories about the sport's comical financial and political condition.

The majors didn't have a commissioner, and the owners weren't eager to hire one. They already had agreed to pay Milwaukee Brewers owner Bud Selig $1 million a year to remain in the job on an "acting" basis. The owners then angered purists by adding central divisions and an extra tier of playoffs, and began a debate over sharing revenues to assist small-market franchises. Revenue sharing would save baseball's financial house of cards from collapse, leading owners said. Even George Steinbrenner favored divvying up the wealth, although he couldn't hide his true feelings. "This is social-ism at work and baseball is still a free-enterprise sport," he declared. After much posturing and compromise, the owners passed a reve-nue-sharing plan—but they linked it to the implementation of a cap on player salaries.

In March, fifteen months after the owners decided to reopen labor talks, they finally sat down at the bargaining table. Issue num-ber one: the salary cap. Players' response: Forget it. As a historic, can-you-top-this season unfolded on the field, negotiations reached an impasse. Newspapers counted down the days to a strike. Fans grumbled. Forty-seven percent of those surveyed in an ESPN/Chil-ton telephone poll blamed the players for the impending work stop-page and 34 percent the owners. In the same poll one-quarter of respondents said they would consider boycotting baseball when it returned.

Once the strike began the minor leagues suddenly became the only professional baseball in the nation. The *independent* minor leagues were the only professional baseball not tainted by associa-tion with the majors. And the Northern League was the class of the indies. By the transitive property of baseball, the Northern League suddenly offered the purest form of the game anywhere.

But the league had little to gain by bashing the majors, sitting ducks though they were. It still needed the interest and cooperation of the big leagues to fulfill its players' dreams. Five Northern League contracts had been sold to organizations, all pitchers. Tim Cain of Winnipeg went to the Boston Red Sox and Rod Steph of Thunder Bay to the Cleveland Indians. At Van Schley's invitation, Gary Hughes, the Florida Marlins scouting director, flew to Sioux Falls for a weekend. He left with three new pitchers: the Canaries' Jamie Ybarra, and Dan Zanolla and Mike Lewis of the Saints. Three of the five signees fetched $3,000 and the other two $1,000; the Northern League was beginning to get fair value. Some organiza-tions, though, persisted in trying to shortchange the league. After refusing to pay, the Seattle Mariners directly contacted two play-ers—Greg Shockey of Duluth and Mike Hankins of Winnipeg—to try to talk them into jumping their contracts. When Miles Wolff found out he told the commissioner's office to instruct the Mariners to quit tampering illegally with Northern League players. Strike or no strike, the majors, it seemed, would never learn.

While the affiliated minor leagues were busy fending off ques-tions about whether their games would come to a halt (they wouldn't), the Northern League just played baseball. Miles Wolff worried that the strike would cool fan interest in baseball generally. But Northern League fans were as devoted as ever, and in St. Paul or Sioux City or even troubled Duluth, it was easy to forget about the big-league shutdown. The Northern League owners didn't have to worry about the stability of their product. Or so they thought.

Late-August games for teams out of pennant races are thoroughly without meaning. The Duluth-Superior Dukes had little incentive to keep playing. Players could quit, as Tom Paskievitch had, but that would jeopardize their baseball futures. Not that most of the Dukes had a future in the game. Scouts weren't exactly beating a path to Wade Stadium.

The Dukes played because that was what they did for a living. They were professional baseball players, and most were glad to have the opportunity. Technically, they also had made a commitment to play when they signed the Uniform Player Contract of The North-ern League Inc.: "The Club hereby employs Player to render, and Player hereby agrees to render, skilled services as a professional baseball player for all games of the Club in The Northern League Inc. during the 1994 Season from and after the date of this Con-tract." The contract didn't specify how skilled the services had to be or mention an exemption for players who unwittingly had wan-dered into the baseball Twilight Zone that was Duluth in 1994.

After the team's second nine-game losing streak of the season dropped their second-half record to 3–15, the Dukes went on what for them was a tear: they won five of eleven. The last of those victories came over the St. Paul Saints, and the Dukes were heading for win number nine the following night at Municipal Stadium when rain halted the game in the third inning. It was Tuesday, August 23, eleven days after the start of the major league strike.

League rules prescribed that the game be made up as part of a doubleheader the following day. But if both sides agreed to a different course of action, that was fine, too. Mike Veeck looked in the stands, looked at the calendar, and realized that there were no more games to offer fans to compensate for the rainout. He had three choices: Refund everyone's money and play the doubleheader the next day; stage a "split doubleheader"—one game beginning at noon and the other at six on Wednesday, requiring separate admissions; or play the game on Thursday, an off day for both clubs.

The first option left ticket holders out of luck and denied the Saints the gate revenue for one night. The second was exhausting for players and staff. The third satisfied the Saints' front office and the fans but denied the players their day off. Veeck needed to decide fast. The Saints already were refunding tickets when Veeck asked Howie Bedell and Ted Cushmore in the tunnel leading to the visitors' locker room whether they would be willing to play on Thursday. Both men agreed, Cushmore figuring he might need a return favor one day. Miles Wolff approved the plan. The Saints would cover the Dukes' expenses for the extra day in St. Paul.

Veeck called the local television stations in time for the ten o'clock news to announce that the rainout would be played Thursday at noon.

Fifteen minutes later Bedell walked into Veeck's office. The Dukes won't play on Thursday, he said. They won't relinquish their off day. And a group of players had committed to a golf tournament to raise money for a sick child and to a baseball clinic in Duluth. The Dukes will forfeit rather than take the field, Bedell said.

When Veeck heard the word *forfeit*, he knew there would be trouble. A league that can't fulfill its schedule is no league at all. The Northern League's credibility depended on the sanctity of its promise to present baseball to paying customers. If the Dukes didn't take the field, the Northern League was no better than a semipro circuit or a weekend beer league, where games are canceled when a club can't find a ninth man.

Cushmore had already left Municipal Stadium thinking the issue was decided. When he arrived home Veeck called, and the Dukes owner had another headache. Cushmore had indeed forgotten that some of the Duluth players were to join a golf outing to raise money for a group called Save the Wade. But a sick kid? The money was to help defray the cost of restoring Wade Stadium, not to pay medical expenses for a boy named Wade.

As was natural in his endless summer, Cushmore worried. He called the Dukes' locker room and pulled Bedell from the shower. Veeck already had reminded the manager that he had committed to play Thursday. With Cushmore on the line, Bedell agreed it would be unwise to allow players to tell the league when they were available for a game. Bedell talked to some players and called Cushmore back to say he would field a team on Thursday, but it would be better if the owner stayed away from the clubhouse tomorrow. The players weren't happy.

Teams that don't win—can't win—take on personas. They can be feisty and fun, objects of affection for fans who love an underdog, like the 1962 Mets. Or they can be volatile and surly. In an independent minor league, when players realize their careers are near an end, where they've spent a tumultuous season making little money, always wondering when they'll be released, and losing all the while, frustration is bound to boil over into rage. The Dukes, losers at the time of fifty-three out of sixty-nine games, needed an outlet for their frustrations, and they discovered it in their precious day off.

As Cushmore drove to the stadium on Wednesday, he didn't foresee any problem. The crisis had been averted, he assumed, when Bedell persuaded the Dukes to play. Cushmore arrived at 4:45. He walked across the parking lot and around the team bus. Nothing seemed out of the ordinary until Jeff Grotewold climbed down and approached the owner. "The players want to talk to you," the catcher said.

Wrong place, wrong time. Cushmore was surprised the players were on the bus, and he detected anger in the former major leaguer's voice. He knew getting on the bus was a mistake. But he boarded anyway.

Bobby Perna led the verbal assault. "What gives you the right to take away our fucking day off?" the third baseman began.

First baseman Andy Hartung jumped in, demanding to know why Cushmore hadn't included the players in the decision-making process. Grotewold wore a satisfied smirk on his face.

For fifteen minutes the players shouted obscenities at the owner and recited a laundry list of complaints against the club. "They're just stacking up the money here," Perna said. No one spoke up in Cushmore's defense. (Later, Tom Paskievitch reminded his teammates that in a major league organization they would be released on the spot for challenging management's decision on when to schedule a game. Players showed up at the ballpark when told.) Finally, the ringleaders kicked Cushmore out to hold a team meeting.

"Get the fuck off the bus," Grotewold told the man who had given him a job when his career was all but over. "This is our fucking team, not yours."

The Dukes voted seventeen to seven to boycott the makeup game.

Ted Cushmore was shaken. As he entered Municipal Stadium, Cushmore wondered what had happened. Why was this club turning against him? What had he done? The Dukes owner was angry, hurt, and, above all, disappointed. He had bought an independent league team because he loved baseball, and now he was realizing how unseemly the business of the game can be. Young men who should have embraced a reprieve from the working world—an opportunity that Cushmore had passed up many years earlier—were bitter and spiteful over the state of the losing team.

Cushmore separately asked Mike Veeck, Nick Belmonte, and Miles Wolff whether there was anything extraordinary about scheduling a rainout on a day off. The Northern League, they told him, had more days off than any other minor league. The Dukes had twelve during the eighty-game schedule. Veeck said his Florida State League team had about eight off days—and played nearly twice as many games.

Was it the missed golf tournament? Unlikely. Players aren't wed-ded to fund-raising events. That left only the debilitating season. Cushmore didn't deny that shuffling the personnel so aggressively had hurt morale and generated clubhouse angst. (By year's end forty players had worn a Dukes uniform, tops in the league; the names of the dearly departed were written on swatches of tape stuck to a clubhouse door under the sign GONE FISHIN'.) But that was part of baseball, especially on a team that won eight of forty games in the first half. The players suddenly had grievances with the club owner, claiming that they hadn't been treated well, that promises had been broken.

Cushmore couldn't say for sure, but he strongly suspected that Howie Bedell had set him up. Their relationship had become super-ficially cordial and curt. Behind Cushmore's back Bedell called him "the cereal salesman," referring to his job at General Mills. When one of the Dukes asked Bedell why he wasn't playing, the manager said it was Cushmore's decision. Bedell continued to blame the owner's interference. "I told him a number of times, get a uniform, come on and manage it," the manager said bitterly. (Cushmore denied that Bedell ever issued the challenge.)

Bedell also believed he was an outcast in the league, detecting "snobbishness" toward major league organizations. And he was de-fensive about his last-place team. "You take apart the job we did on the field, and it has been an intelligent, documented, well-thought-out job," Bedell said near the end of the season. "I don't know how you can question it." So when it came time to choose between the players and Cushmore, it wasn't difficult to figure out whose side Bedell would take.

Why had the manager suggested that Cushmore avoid the ball-park before Wednesday's game? Did he know the players planned to revolt? Had Bedell, who'd agreed to play on the day off without a whimper, dumped all the blame onto the owner when he discov-ered his troops were unhappy?

Cushmore walked to the field and found Bedell and the Dukes' coaches in the dugout waiting for the players to finish their meet-ing. When Cushmore described what had happened on the bus, Bedell, ever the smooth talker, expressed his condolences and promised to meet with the team. The owner cleared out before the players arrived.

While leaving their hotel that morning, a few of the Dukes encountered some of the St. Paul Saints. The Duluth players said they were considering a walkout. And if they didn't walk, they expected more money to play.

The Saints' record wasn't nearly Duluthian, but the club was out of the pennant race nonetheless. Expectations had been so high— St. Paul being St. Paul—that when the team failed, the players' fuses suddenly shortened. They had their own beefs with management. They didn't particularly want to lose a precious day off either.

Hell, the Saints once again thought. This is independent baseball. We can do something about it. Collectively, they carried around years of resentment from their treatment by major league organizations. They already had been released one or more times. What could the Northern League do to them that the majors already hadn't? After beating the Dukes 4–3 in the regularly scheduled game Wednesday night, the Saints invited Mike Veeck into the locker room for a meeting.

Bill Veeck had been a players' owner. He stood apart in an era when major league bosses, thanks to the reserve clause that bound players to teams for life, treated players like so much chattel, forcing them to take pay cuts after productive seasons. (Branch Rickey slashed Ralph Kiner's pay 25 percent even though the slugger led the league in homers. "We finished last with you," he said. "We could've finished last without you.") Veeck even spoke out against the reserve clause—heresy and treason in the halls of baseball power. Now Mike Veeck, ever his daddy's boy, faced a locker room filled with players who were angry with him. It had never before happened to a Veeck.

The players sat on benches and stood beside their lockers. Tim Blackwell leaned on a ladder behind the club president, joined by his coaches. Marv Goldklang was in New York, unaware of the proceedings. Van Schley was in town but wouldn't set foot in the clubhouse. No one had leaked a word about an impending labor problem to Veeck.

Vince Castaldo and Matt Stark were the main spokesmen: The Saints have decided, they said, that to play on Thursday we want $200 a man. Grievances, some real, some exaggerated, poured forth. Friends and relatives received bad seats; Castaldo said that his parents were assigned to a top row near a light pole, to be rescued only by a member of a teammate's family. (Veeck explained that the club was short eighty seats a night because of renovation troubles.) Players weren't adequately compensated with merchandise or money for public appearances. (Veeck was unaware of a problem.) The front office treated the players shabbily, without respect, as if they were morons. (Veeck disagreed.)

Veeck asked the team to work with him to save the game. He tried to explain that the decision to play Thursday had nothing to do with squeezing an extra gate out of the season. The Saints didn't care about the revenue, he said. They simply had no way to honor the rain checks. Accommodating St. Paul's incredibly devoted fans was his top priority. He offered the players $75 each in compensation and left them to discuss it.

When Veeck returned five minutes later, the players said they were sticking to their figure. Two hundred or the show didn't go on.

Veeck composed himself. "I know that you're going to talk about me when I leave here," he began, "and say that I am less than manly, because I am going to give in, I am going to acquiesce, I am going to give you what you want. But I am going to do it because I love this league and because this is the best thing that's happened, not just to me, but to all of us."

Then he looked at Leon Durham and Jim Manfred and Greg D'Alexander, veterans of the Saints' championship season, and said, "Tell them what it was like here last year."

Veeck left via the dugout and strolled to center field for one of the occasional conversations he held with the spirit of his father. The air was still that night, the American flag hanging limply by its pole. "Did I do the right thing?" Veeck asked. He didn't get an answer.

Veeck walked to the infield, where a Saints employee tossed him a nonalcoholic beer. He returned to center, talking with Dad some more, questioning the ideals that governed the club, the league, his family. Had he compromised his integrity by succumbing to the players' demands? He wandered toward the Mr. Tire billboard in left field. Twenty-five minutes had passed since the clubhouse meeting.

Leon Durham and Matt Stark approached Veeck and said the players wanted to talk again. Veeck walked alone down the line, not speaking, wondering what they could possibly want now.

While Veeck was communing with his father, Vince Castaldo sat before his locker and considered what the players had done. In his anger he thought about, as players inescapably do, the lopsided power structure in minor league baseball. The club was making half a million, three-quarters of a million dollars a year, he figured. Every penny because of us. We make peanuts here. But he also felt badly for Veeck, whom the players genuinely liked. Veeck wasn't the problem in the front office. Castaldo struggled with the knowledge that he had upset a decent man. He couldn't in good conscience accept the club's money that way. We made our point, he concluded. We should play. Castaldo persuaded his teammates that refusing the cash was the principled thing to do.

"It's not about money," Vinny Castaldo announced when Veeck returned to the locker room. The team had just wanted to air its complaints. The Saints would be on the field the following day.

The Northern League was created with a message in mind for major league baseball. It would demonstrate that you could operate a professional baseball league in which the owners, players, cities, and fans all have fun. Now Duluth's players had voted to walk. St. Paul's had held a gun to Mike Veeck's head. The league couldn't even control a workforce supposedly desperate for a chance—any chance—to play. If the season-long pressure on Ted Cushmore wasn't enough, now he had the reputation of the entire league on his shoulders. Would his team play or wouldn't it?

Howie Bedell had been in baseball too long not to understand the circumstances. He wished the makeup game hadn't been scheduled for the day off, but then he also knew that minor leaguers can't control the schedule. So when the Dukes arrived in the locker room after browbeating Cushmore before Wednesday's game, Bedell urged them to play. He said they'd had every right to invite the owner onto the bus, but no matter how they felt about him, their conduct was inappropriate. You're professionals, Bedell reminded the Dukes. If you don't play it's a breach of contract. The players made no promises.

On Thursday morning Ted Cushmore pulled into the parking lot at Municipal Stadium at 11:45, close enough to the 12:05 start to avoid encountering the players. The team bus wasn't there, and the owner still didn't know whether his ball club had shown up for the makeup game. But when he looked on the field, he saw Dukes.

Cushmore walked over to his manager. "Three guys called in sick," Bedell announced.

The ringleaders of the bus ambush didn't show up. Grotewold, Perna, and Hartung—three players whom the Dukes had recruited at midseason to help turn the club around, who were to supply experience and maturity, who batted third, fourth, and fifth in the lineup. But they were nearing the end of disappointing seasons and possibly the end of their careers; playing for the Dukes, they realized they weren't likely to be picked up by an organization. Some of their teammates felt they had just snapped.

Cushmore released Grotewold outright and suspended Perna and Hartung indefinitely without pay. He was embarrassed and upset by the bus incident, which he considered reason enough to dismiss the malcontents. Failing to show up for the game was unforgivable. Grotewold, Perna, and Hartung were the team's three best players, but Cushmore didn't care if they were Ruth, Gehrig, and DiMaggio. They were gone.

Howie Bedell disagreed. Despite the verbal abuse of the owner and the three players' personal strike, Bedell maintained that they should have been suspended for one game, tops. And, he told Cushmore, maybe these guys wouldn't have walked out if they knew I was returning as manager. Cushmore couldn't believe Bedell's audacity but said nothing. Instead, he began counting the days until the season's merciful end. "I keep waiting for the bottom," he said, "and it keeps eluding me."

Ted Cushmore didn't get pumped up driving to Duluth anymore. He didn't take batting practice or linger on the field before the first pitch. He didn't wander the stands chatting with fans. He didn't listen to games on the radio. He dreaded the descent every morning from his bedroom to the fax machine in his home office to learn the result of the previous night's game.

Cushmore was bitter about Howie Bedell. The manager had changed from willing participant in reshaping the club after its abysmal start to a name-calling malcontent who claimed he had been "misled" by his owner and league officials. Cushmore felt that Bedell had failed and didn't have the guts to admit it.

In Duluth fans knew nothing of the behind-the-scenes soap opera. The newspaper reporter who covered the Dukes, Bruce Bennett, was a backer of Howie Bedell, as he had been of the previous manager to guide the club to last place, Mal Fichman. The reporter ripped Cushmore for letting Mike Veeck talk him into playing on Thursday, accusing the greedy St. Paul franchise—which controlled the league, of course, he wrote—of simply wanting to collect another pay date. Bennett never talked to Cushmore or Veeck, and he wrote glowingly about Bedell. To no one's surprise, the story sounded as if it had been dictated by the manager: "[Cushmore] wants to run the show, but too many of his moves have backfired," Bennett wrote. "He hasn't learned the biggest lesson of club ownership yet: Hire baseball people and let them run the baseball business."

Cushmore couldn't stand the journalistic pinpricks; he had never before been criticized in the press. He was already angry enough that Bedell had bamboozled the players into believing the owner was their enemy, but he felt that Bedell had snowed the press and public, too; fans were circulating a petition urging the Dukes to rehire the manager of one of the worst teams in professional baseball. Now Bedell was trying to take down Cushmore and the franchise with him. The owner wouldn't let himself believe that once Bedell left town few would remember him.

The run-in with the players had been a final indignity that left Cushmore feeling vulnerable. He had witnessed the seedy side of baseball, the reality that fans can happily ignore: that some players are jerks, that managers can be manipulative, that your relationships with the club can be as raw and divisive as a marriage gone sour.

Before leaving town the three Dukes who had led the revolt took out their anger on a teammate who'd changed his mind about joining the walkout. They broke seven of Greg Shockey's bats and defaced a dress shirt in his locker with threats and obscenities. Cushmore was stunned.

Miles Wolff knew independent baseball would have its minefields. The Northern League's first season had run smoothly on the diamond. The second had proven tumultuous. It wasn't surpris-

Miles Wolff and Ted Cushmore

ing. Players were in the league for many reasons other than ability. They had been kicked around by the system. Among them were boat-rockers and clubhouse lawyers, complainers and agitators. Baseball is a complex game made even more so by human dynamics.

But it changed every year. That was the beauty of the league, and that was what Wolff and Goldklang and Schley and Stavrenos and Belmonte—everyone who mattered—told Ted Cushmore. Intellectually, Cushmore accepted that he should chalk up the year to experience and move forward. He stood by his decision to take the risk and buy the team, and he didn't want to settle for a season of failure. Emotionally, though, he was drained. "I thought owning an independent league ball club in a small town . . ." His voice trailed off. "I guess I *didn't* think about it."

Cushmore didn't talk to Howie Bedell for a week, and he spoke only briefly with his soon-to-be-ex-manager just before the Dukes' last home series of the year, a three-game weekend set against St. Paul. The owner skipped the first game of the series on Friday evening, September 2. He didn't want to be a lightning rod for criticism, from Bedell, the players, or the press.

At least the fans had remained true. On Saturday the Dukes drew their second-largest crowd of the year, 3,341 strong. They cheered when a season–ticket holder named Rosemary Stratioti sang her usual bellicose, off-key version of "Take Me Out to the Ball Game" during the seventh-inning stretch. They danced to "YMCA." The front-office woes, even the team's record, didn't matter.

Cushmore arrived with his wife, Carol, and their son, Chris, shortly before Saturday's game. Wolff was in town, wearing a black golf shirt embroidered with the Northern League logo, an eight-pointed star with a capital N at the top, and gave the rookie owner a pep talk about the strength of his market. Cushmore wore nothing to identify him with the Dukes or the league, just his usual chinos, a collarless chambray shirt, and thick-soled deck shoes. On the field Cushmore shook hands perfunctorily with Bedell and said good-bye to a few players. No tears flowed. The owner wore his sadness like a mask. He had been beaten.

In the middle of the ninth inning of a 9–2 Dukes loss, their sixtieth defeat of the year against nineteen wins, Ted Cushmore quietly left Wade Stadium out a side gate, crossed the gravel parking lot, and stepped inside his car for the drive home. His season had ended. He already had decided not to attend the Dukes' final game on Sunday. It was rained out anyway.

Doug Kimbler *(left)* and Greg D'Alexander

FIFTEEN

*Once it's over, it's going to be over, and you can't
play anymore.*

—St. Paul Saints third baseman Vince Castaldo

For all the player shuffling and attempted deal making, all the pregame conferences and late-night telephone calls, for all of Van Schley's scouting trips and Marv Goldklang's methodical deliberation, the 1994 St. Paul Saints just weren't a very good baseball team.

The other clubs considered the Saints the bullyboys of the independent league. St. Paul had the deepest pockets, the biggest and liveliest crowds, the most inspired promotions, and league officials in their hip pocket. Partly out of envy, no one wanted to help St. Paul. Ricky May in Thunder Bay had refused a three-for-one deal because he didn't want to help the Saints win another championship (forgetting that his goal should have been to improve his own team). Doug Simunic had talked Howie Bedell out of trading pitcher Dominic Desantis to the Saints late in the season.

For all its efforts St. Paul didn't make the necessary moves to turn the club into a contender. Schley finally got his wish when the team released Ranbir Grewal and signed Julio Solano in the middle of August—but by then it was too late, pointless almost. The Saints were 12–12 and Winnipeg 18–5, and even though the

239

teams faced each other six more times, St. Paul knew it didn't have a prayer of winning.

It was to have been a summer of pure joy. The Saints players were supposed to capitalize on their second chance in baseball; instead, with the big-league players' strike, they worried whether organizations would spend the money to sign them. Younger players were expected to learn from their elders how to play the game seriously; most ignored the advice. St. Paul was supposed to coast to another championship; they were picked off first, struck out looking, and allowed late-inning leads to evaporate. Schley was to be reunited with his close friends for a fun summer building a baseball team; now he was contemplating leaving his partners to help Ted Cushmore turn around the Duluth franchise in 1995. "It's almost like I'm past frustrated," Schley said in August. "Let's get the season over."

The disgruntled players told the manager whom to release and got their way. They threatened to boycott a game because they resented how much money the club was making—through them. Goldklang, Schley, Blackwell, and Veeck never figured out a way to communicate. Instead of taking decisive action the vaunted Saints organization dissolved. Rookies were shuttled in and out. Late-season moves smacked of panic. With three or five or sometimes seven people involved in every decision—and a manager with a reputation as soft on players—the Saints couldn't find solutions. "That's why they have GMs in major league baseball," Mike Veeck said.

Like a barking dog that detects fear in a stranger, the players understood what had happened: The manager lacked complete authority, and the front office was indecisive. The Saints resembled the very thing that everyone involved detested. They had become like a major league organization.

"As bad," Vinny Castaldo said, "as any I've ever been in."

For the Saints star the second half was pure frustration. Where hard line drives had been singles and doubles earlier in the year, now they were speared for outs. Castaldo's average tumbled, from .340 to .310, in just a couple of weeks. His impatience mounted.

His tolerance for losing withered even more. "It'd just be nice to play with people who treat the game right," he said. "I took that for granted."

But Castaldo never left the lineup, and his work ethic never wavered. He was still the first player out for early batting practice. While his teammates played touch football with a baseball in the outfield, Castaldo worked on his swing. As the opposition finished their infield drills, Castaldo still was the first on the field.

In short, he continued to love playing baseball, a game he could play only hard. Around the league Castaldo was disliked. A Sioux Falls coach, delivering a locker-room lecture on public displays of anger, urged his players not to be like Vinny Castaldo, who threw helmets and bats and dropped "F-bombs" that the fans could hear.

That was fine with the Canaries, who had been feuding with St. Paul and Castaldo all season. The first incident came early, when Scott Centala plunked Sioux Falls's Rex De La Nuez twice in a game. De La Nuez thought it was intentional and glared at the pitcher. "Take your fucking base," Centala snapped. De La Nuez walked toward the mound and had to be restrained by the umpire. Later he dispatched a batboy to deliver a message to Centala: "Rex said when you're in Sioux Falls to watch your back."

The teams chattered at each other all season. Castaldo's bat-slamming theatrics struck the Sioux Falls players as provocative. On July 4, when Castaldo swaggered to the plate, he received a fastball near his earlobe. On the next pitch he homered. The next time up he flew out to the right-field fence. Both shots bore a message.

When the Canaries arrived at Municipal Stadium for the Saints' final home series of the lost season, neither team had changed. In the bottom of the seventh inning of the first game, Castaldo was on first base when a reliever named Cliff Jones entered with a count of one ball and no strikes on Matt Stark. Despite season-long bench jockeying, Jones hadn't pitched against St. Paul. He threw three straight balls to Stark, and Castaldo trotted to second.

"Nice fucking outing, you fucking pussy," Castaldo commented.

The twenty-three-year-old Jones was lean and lanky—no match for the muscular Castaldo. He threw his glove and the ball at Castaldo and then backpedaled hastily toward the Sioux Falls dugout. The benches emptied, and the pile followed Jones. The normally impassive Saints manager, Tim Blackwell, went in search of Jones and another talker, pitcher Jamie Ybarra. Canaries owner-manager Harry Stavrenos went out as a peacemaker and wound up in the middle of the fray. After a twelve-minute delay, five players were ejected.

But the clubs weren't through. With two outs in the bottom of the ninth and men on first and second, Sioux Falls' closer Rob Andrakin, protecting a 5–3 lead, hit the Saints' Benny Castillo with a pitch. It clearly wasn't intentional—the Canaries were still in the pennant race and Andrakin didn't want to load the bases— but the Saints didn't care. Castillo threw his bat at the mound and charged Andrakin.

In the Sioux Falls locker room, a nearly naked Pedro Guerrero glanced at the field. "Oh, shit, not another one!" he exclaimed. Guerrero grabbed his pants and jersey and ran onto the field wearing shower thongs.

On the other side of the field, Vinny Castaldo emerged from the Saints' dugout dressed in his street clothes in search of Cliff Jones.

Tim Blackwell and Marv Goldklang

Stephen Bishop had been released with just two and a half weeks to play in the season. It was a particularly cruel time to cut a player, especially one who was of marginal importance to a team fading from a pennant race. Players let go so late have trouble landing elsewhere, the blot of another release on their résumés.

Bishop lucked out. Thunder Bay immediately claimed him, but money-conscious Ricky May, his team sinking toward last place, vetoed any signings. Stavrenos, though, needed an outfielder to replace an injured starter, and when he heard Bishop was available grabbed him. Bishop flew to Duluth the next day to meet the Canaries.

Bishop didn't know that Marv Goldklang had had second thoughts about the release. Leon Durham had pulled a hamstring sliding into home on a curious delayed double steal, and with David Kennedy already finished for the year with a broken foot, the Saints' chairman realized the team lacked depth at first base. He asked a surprised Nick Belmonte about retrieving Bishop.

Van Schley had signed Bishop with great hope after seeing an angry and determined kid with talent at a Florida Marlins tryout one rainy day in February. But he'd lost interest in the project as Bishop's attitude appeared to deteriorate. That's how it is with players, Schley felt. You can't get too close or care too much because you'll end up disappointed. Schley didn't care one way or another about Stephen Bishop, but he felt the moody young player could have been handled more effectively: "It's not as if the guy's a child molester. He's just a baby. If he was told what his role was and treated better, he might have done better." And to try to reclaim the player after he'd been cut with such fanfare? Schley recalled that he wasn't consulted. "The guy gets released because he's a cancer on the club. What happened? In two days he had chemotherapy?" Goldklang dropped the case when he learned that Bishop already had played for Sioux Falls.

For Bishop it was a blessing to be out of St. Paul. The season was too far gone for him to improve his game, and under their owner-manager the Canaries weren't in the business of training ballplayers anyway. Bishop's batting average sank further, but he seemed relieved to be rid of the agony of being benched, disliked, ignored, and criticized.

When he returned to Municipal Stadium, he wore uniform number 25 instead of his beloved 24. His jersey was too tight, and his pants were shorter than he liked. He wasn't coming back a hero, with twenty stolen bases and a .300 average, waiting to accept player-of-the-year honors. He didn't homer against St. Paul. The fans didn't respond to the mention of his name. He was humbled but just as angry as in the spring. Stephen Bishop still had something to prove to the world. St. Paul was just a bad memory.

"Fuck this place," he said. "Fuck everyone here."

It was September eve, and in the Midwest that means the inhospitable winter is fast approaching. Minnesotans fought determinedly, wearing short pants despite the fall chill as if to delay or deny the inevitable. But with evening temperatures already dipping into the fifties, all one could do was wait.

The night after the brawls and before the home finale, there was little left for the faithful to cheer at Municipal Stadium. The Saints weren't going to win any championships. But while the St. Paul fans could recognize a botched lead—Frechtman played "Will You Love Me Tomorrow" by the Shirelles with alarming frequency in the second half—they rarely booed their players and never abandoned them. It wasn't that way everywhere in the Northern League. After Rod Steph threw a no-hitter against the Saints, the next Thunder Bay pitcher repeated the performance through four innings. When St. Paul recorded its first hit in fourteen innings, the Canadians booed their pitcher.

The word *fan* is derived from either *fanatic* or *fancier*. Saints supporters were both. In a season without a World Series, their club stood for baseball at its purest. The fans protected their players and their league like a family heirloom. In two short seasons the Saints, in fact, had become a city heirloom. For the fanatics of St. Paul, the baseball year that was ending had been another remarkable one, as they all could be.

There was the July day it had rained all afternoon and when the gates to Municipal Stadium opened at five o'clock, 3,000 people were waiting to enter. They sat through a torrential downpour while the Saints players launched oranges from a slingshot that splattered on the outfield walls. They waited while the Sioux Falls Canaries wrote "GO HOME" in the dirt by their dugout and "ENOUGH AL!" to the annoying announcer who always dubbed them (and every other team) "pesky." They waited while Mike Veeck rolled up his sweatpants and swept and shoveled muddy water beneath the left-field fence, while other Saints staffers squeegeed the outfield to remove as much water as possible. They waited until 9:07, when the umpires decided the game could be played, waited until it began at 9:40, and waited until it was suspended under Northern League rules shortly after 11:30. They understood that night that Mike Veeck and everyone else on the St. Paul Saints staff loved baseball, as did they.

They camped out at the ballpark on a muggy Saturday night in late July after the game to watch Arnold Schwarzenegger movies on a screen in center field. There were a few hundred viewers, and they dropped out like marathon dancers, until at five in the morning about fifteen people caught the last reel of *Predator*. They watched Saint Paula the pig, dressed in saddlebags and tutus, grow from 35 pounds to 150. They chanted "Lose the tie!" at passing fans who came to the stadium straight from work. They bought iced latte and ice cream sodas. They tossed their hats in the air à la Mary Tyler Moore on a night dedicated to the '70s sitcom set in Minneapolis.

They sang to Vinny Castaldo.

They had fun.

They enjoyed one last magical inning.

The last home game of the year is a show, Fan Appreciation Night, a free souvenir and the opportunity to glimpse the players one final time before the long Minnesota winter. But even in St. Paul, after a season to remember and a season to forget, the penultimate home game was a tough sell—emotionally, that is, because despite the team's record, 6,249 fans passed through the gates at Municipal Stadium on a cold and cloudy Wednesday evening.

But the usual excitement generated by a Saints game was missing. Fans politely applauded the first train of the evening, absent their normal lusty enthusiasm. This was the night to be let down gently, to accept that baseball was leaving town for the bad months. Tonight, we reach understanding with our baseball soul; tomorrow, we party.

On the Sioux Falls side the Canaries needed and wanted a victory. They still had a mathematical chance of winning or tying Winnipeg for the second-half crown: three games back in the loss column with five to play. In the St. Paul clubhouse, the players just wanted the season to end. Starter Mike Lewis wondered why he was pitching. The lefty had a 9–3 record and 2.51 ERA and already had been signed by the Marlins. When he woke up that morning, Lewis told his roommate, infielder Doug Kimbler, that he didn't want to pitch. He had already told his manager that he'd rather not start again because he had nothing left to prove. Blackwell told him to pitch. Lewis tossed meatballs.

He surrendered a leadoff homer to Darren Glenn. Pedro Guerrero doubled. Mike Burton walked. Carl Nichols doubled to drive in two runs. Stephen Bishop singled home Nichols. Lewis registered one out and trailed 4–0. He was lifted after the inning. During the ensuing break, the Saints' radio announcer and public relations director, Dave Wright, removed his headset. "Gutless," he said. Kimbler, who had had arthroscopic surgery to repair torn cartilage in his left knee the previous day, watched the game from beneath the grandstands. "That's the whole problem with this team," he said. "A bunch of guys with bad attitudes."

But the fans were oblivious to the performance. They watched the Saints tie the game at 4–4, relinquish the lead, regain it at 6–5, and—holding to season-long form—retake it again at 7–6.

When the Sioux Falls dugout learned that Duluth had beaten Winnipeg that night, players began calculating how many games they needed to win over the weekend to force a tie and then a one-game playoff. They wanted another crack at Doug Simunic, who after taking two of three in Sioux Falls had taunted the team. "We'll send you some playoff tickets," he'd said.

The Canaries pushed across an insurance run in the top of the ninth, making the score 8–6. The players pounded on the chain-link fence as Carl Nichols scored. With closer Rob Andrakin suspended for two games following the fights, Stavrenos stuck with a righty named Glenn Meyers, who had four saves to his credit. Meyers ran out of the locker room to pats on his back, grabbed his glove, and jogged to the mound.

Greg D'Alexander led off with a double.

"Damn," said Pedro Guerrero, who already had taken off his spikes and was drinking a Pig's Eye light beer in the clubhouse. Guerrero set the can on top of a locker and returned to the end of the dugout to watch.

Vinny Castaldo beat out a dribbling ground ball to first base.

Stavrenos walked into the clubhouse. "I can't watch this shit," he said.

Matt Stark lofted a sacrifice fly to right field, scoring D'Alexander. Sammy Davis, Jr., sang.

"Son of a fucking bitch," Meyers said after he was lifted from the game. He regretted giving D'Alexander something good to hit. "Throw a slider, not a fastball."

"I'm nervous," Cliff Jones said.

Left-hander Ken Grundt, with a 1.64 ERA, entered to pitch to the left-handed-hitting Luis Alvarez, who had a .365 batting average. Lefty versus lefty was the best matchup Stavrenos could hope for. When the Cuban defector hit a ground ball up the middle, it looked as if the move had paid off. It was an easy, game-ending double-play ball. But it rolled under the glove of shortstop Matt Davis for an error. "There it was," Stavrenos said. "Shit. There it was."

Catcher Mason Rudolph lofted the next pitch to right center field. Sure-handed Chris Powell raced over, leaned for the ball, and it plunked off the edge of his glove and dropped to the ground like a live hand grenade.

Castaldo scored. 8–8.

Someone kicked the clubhouse door. Sammy kept on singing. The outcome was inevitable.

Grundt walked Brett Feauto to load the bases with one out and set up a double play. But rookie Brad Dandridge, the nephew of Negro Leagues great Ray Dandridge, recently called up by the Saints from Ogden, singled cleanly to center. The Saints won 9–8, dooming Sioux Falls. Al Frechtman played the *Shaft* theme again. The stunned fans received one more gift from their memorable, if not altogether successful, season of baseball.

When his father owned the St. Louis Browns in the early 1950s, Mike Veeck's family lived in a converted apartment on the second floor of Sportsman's Park and the toddler played in an ivy-covered space just beyond the left-field fence. Watching Veeck work the Municipal Stadium office and grandstands, it was obvious his up-bringing had paid off. He looked as if he could live at the ballpark.

The baseball year is a grind, no matter how much one loves the sport. "The season starts too early and finishes too late and there are too many games in between," Bill Veeck once said. For his son the second year of the Northern League was especially long. In the spring Veeck had attended about fifteen Minnesota Twins spring training games (the Fort Myers Miracle was a Twins affiliate). He took in another thirty Miracle games before the Saints' forty home games. By the first of September he was tired.

During the season, and in the winter, Mike Veeck promoted his team, and the game of baseball. He talked to groups large and small, just like his father, who had typically delivered at least two and, once, as many as seven speeches in a day. Mike Veeck ripped tickets at the turnstiles and greeted customers. He leaned on the wall where the ramp ended and the grandstand seats took over, the spot where the field of green and brown suddenly becomes visible, smoking a cigar and talking to whoever happened by. He whirled around the front office, cheerfully barking commands, tossing Ping-Pong balls, and trading sarcastic quips with staffers. When suppliers or advertisers had a question, Veeck talked to them. When fans complained, Veeck took every call and answered every letter personally. In short, he was his father.

Not only had the 1994 season been long for Veeck but it had been frustrating. The city failed to complete construction of critical new concession stands and bathrooms that had been promised by July 15. (Every night Frechtman announced, to applause, that the men's room in the main concourse was a women's room.) That hurt the Saints' ability to serve their fans. The city also never built eighty seats called for in the grandstand expansion blueprints. The Saints had sold tickets the previous winter based on the plans, so at least that many fans had to be relocated every evening, some to a bench atop the home dugout. By season's end Veeck's negotiations with the city had become acrimonious.

The Saints would set an attendance record for a short-season minor league team with 241,069, an average of 6,181 per game. They sold out the stadium twenty-seven times, and beat back Winnipeg, which averaged 5,314 in a 30,000-seat football stadium. St. Paul's game-day operation was better organized (despite appearances to the contrary) and the fans better serviced (despite the bathroom and concessions shortage) than in 1993. But per capita fan spending was down by about twenty-five cents a game from the inaugural year. Souvenir and food and beverage sales at the park had also dropped.

And the team itself was fragmented, divisive, rebellious, and ultimately disappointing. For the first—and he hoped the last—time in his career, Veeck had to spar with players in an angry clubhouse before heading to the outfield for a conversation with his daddy. "I never, ever felt so empty," he recalled a few hours before the season finale, sitting in the stands wearing a Saints sweatshirt, smoking a cigar, and savoring another view of a field quiet but for a couple of groundskeepers raking the pitcher's mound.

Veeck had known 1994 would be different, "the terrible twos of baseball." Fairy tales don't repeat. He took the championship season and placed it in a box on a shelf with other fine baseball memories. That season had marked the first exciting, sweaty, palpitating throes of love. Nineteen ninety-four was about moving in together.

It was difficult, and therefore challenging, and therefore fun. "Saints," Mike Veeck observed, "are never that interesting."

He tried to do it every night, but Veeck insisted that Fan Appreciation Night, the traditional season ender in baseball, live up to its name. Like his father, Veeck loves fireworks, so there would be plenty of them. Fans would receive a gift, or four or five; the Saints would clear out their inventory of team posters and baseball cards, various stockpiled CDs, even an old Roadrunner cassette that PR director Dave Wright had found lying around, returning something to the fans who had made it possible. Unlike the majors, where stone-faced employees grumpily hand out freebies to arriving fans, who are then frisked by security guards for bottles, cans, and weapons, Veeck emphasized the word *appreciation*.

This night the Saints and the city would rename the ballpark Midway Stadium, where St. Paul's old Triple-A club had played before the minors were pushed out by the Twins. The club would contribute $500 to memorial funds for two St. Paul police officers shot and killed that week, violence so unusual that it shocked the entire state. Also that night Veeck would receive an award from the Minnesota Wheelchair Athletic Association.

For all their complaints about the team and the season, and their sudden eagerness to return home to family and girlfriends, the players knew they would miss the baseball, the split second of their lives when they were paid to play. The bus rides were long, the club was fractured, the season lost. On that final night in St. Paul, the most bitter among them would have done well to listen to the song by 10,000 Maniacs that played while they swatted batting practice fastballs:

> These are days you'll remember.
> Never before and never since, I promise,
> will the whole world be warm as this.
> And as you feel it, you'll know it's true
> that you are blessed and lucky.

The front-office staff understood the meaning. They approached the end with relief after the season's exhausting, fourteen-hour-plus days. But somehow there remained a supply of earnestness and dedication to the fans—to the cause—that the players with their postadolescent emotions often failed to grasp. On the daily timing sheet outlining pregame duties and ceremonies, the Saints detailed the finale: 3:00 Parking list to Bob; logistics notched off. 5:00 Ticket window opens for will-call and walk-up sales. 6:50 Saint Paula strolls around. Weigh the pig. 6:57 Umps and managers meet. 7:01 National anthem performed by Jerry Jeff Walker. 7:05 Play Ball . . . The Official First Pitch!

Tacked on was a special objective: "Have a wonderful final night and do our best to make sure everyone else does. Give tons of stuff away!"

Vince Castaldo had struggled as the season neared an end. He wasn't troubled by his swing—he knew his bad stretch had lasted but a week and a half—but the hits just weren't falling. The strain of hanging around players whom he didn't respect was the worst part. The mistakes and the immaturity. That was what Castaldo kept returning to in his mind. It wasn't the kind of baseball to which he was accustomed. "When I leave I don't feel real good," he said. "I don't feel real satisfied."

He had sacrificed money to play in the Northern League, probably an additional $3,000 or $4,000 a month he could have earned in Mexico. He had ripped up the league's pitching in the first half and hoped for a call from an organization; the Orioles had needed a Triple-A third baseman but signed someone else. The phone didn't ring again. Castaldo focused on improving, on continuing to meet his high standards.

When the season ended he planned to return to St. Louis, keep lifting weights and exercising, and look for another opportunity. He hoped that the Saints would help him find an organization. But Castaldo wasn't interested in another year of Double-A ball or a fill-in job in Triple-A, and certainly not interested in returning to the Northern League. He wanted a chance to start in Triple-A, where he could move to the majors. If no club offered him a legitimate shot, for the first time in his career Castaldo would consider playing for money. Five months in Mexico would pay $25,000. He was coming to terms with disappointment, perhaps prematurely. He knew that the game was screwed up, that it wasn't run by people who knew baseball, that the best players often didn't make it.

As the year disappeared like a setting sun, Castaldo sat in the Saints' dugout, elbows on his knees, and fiddled with his glove, a Rawlings Pro 1000-H with a narrow pocket that was molded perfectly, its border shaped like a parabola. He squinted, looking like Stallone, at the outfield. His teammates were playing touch football. He shook his head. It was so frustrating.

Baseball is known for singular, heroic moments that can define a game or a year, a player or a career, a team or a franchise. Willie Mays's over-the-head basket catch in the 1954 World Series. Bobby Thomson's bottom-of-the-ninth shot heard round the world in 1951. Bucky Dent's 1978 playoff home run. Bill Buckner's 1986 error.

Metaphor plays out on smaller baseball stages as well. The Saints had gone quietly through seven innings in their final home appearance against Sioux Falls, which mathematically, but not realistically, still could tie for first place. Canaries rookie Jamie Ybarra, one of the league's top pitchers, was coasting with a 4–0 lead. In the bottom of the eighth, however, the Saints loaded the bases with two outs and a run already in.

It was a *Shaft* moment. Fireworks exploded in the distance at the Minnesota State Fair (Veeck had planned his own postgame show nonetheless), and the Saints fans were staring at one last possible comeback. The scene resembled Opening Night, when the Ferris wheel had blinked at the fairgrounds and Castaldo had introduced himself to the home crowd with a dramatic home run. Not much different at all.

Greg D'Alexander kept hope alive with a single to left field that narrowed the score to 4–2. Castaldo was due up next.

With head bowed, the player wearing uniform number 17 finished his methodical on-deck practice swings and strolled to home plate. He wore two blue-and-red batting gloves that he tugged for snugness after arriving at the batter's box. The packed stadium— 6,305, natch—knew that this was likely to be Vince Castaldo's last at bat for the Saints. They sang louder than ever: "*Vin-ny Ca-stal-do. Woe woe woe woe. Vin-ny Ca-stal-do. Woe woe woe woe.*"

Castaldo took a ball. Then another. Then another. He hated Ybarra, one of the Canaries who Castaldo said had been "mouthing off" all season. ("They've got to learn that they're going to suffer the consequences if they're not going to back it up, because I am not going to take it," Castaldo had said after the fight.) With the count three and oh, the bases loaded, the go-ahead run on first, and the crowd cheering him, this was a Vinny Castaldo moment. He loved the pressure.

Castaldo took strike one. It was a smart move by an unselfish veteran. Matt Stark was up next, and a base on balls would help the team, if not Castaldo's statistics. And the three-and-one pitch that would follow was a hitter's delight. Castaldo knew Ybarra had to bring the ball around home plate or move the tiebreaking run to second base with the Stark up. Castaldo looked for a fastball. And got it.

He kept his shoulder tucked properly, just as his father had suggested, and timed his swing perfectly. From his slightly hunched-over stance, Castaldo leaned into the baseball, his bent legs and twisting torso a unified, powerful force. His wrists and forearms were taut and extended, and his eyes followed the leather to the wood.

Castaldo crushed the baseball, and everyone in the ballpark knew it.

It was, perhaps, the hardest ball he had hit all season—not a towering fly that soared toward the fence but almost more satisfying: a line drive that screamed with deadly authority toward the right-field line. It would surely clear the bases and give the Saints the lead.

At first base stood six-foot two-inch Mike Burton, who fielded his position better than anyone in the league. As the ball ricocheted off Castaldo's bat, Burton leaped straight into the air, his left arm reaching for the sky, suspended for a moment like a kid straining to nick the bottom of a basketball net.

The irresistible force of the baseball, traveling at such great speed as it left first the pitcher's hand and then Castaldo's bat, met the immovable object of Burton's perfectly placed glove.

Time froze.

Castaldo, barely two steps out of the batter's box, spun around angrily to face the Saints dugout. The stadium anticipated what was coming. Castaldo wound up, drawing his bat parallel to his back, and released the stick at full force, like a boomerang that wouldn't loop back.

If the line drive was his hardest hit ball of the year, this was his hardest thrown bat. It helicoptered through the air, low to the ground, then whirled along the grass like a stone skipping across the surface of a still lake. Standing in harm's way in the on-deck circle, Matt Stark quickly danced out of the bat's path. It reached the dirt track along the fence—not at the dugout but at the wide entryway to the grounds crew equipment room, where the Saints staff and families and friends sat on metal folding chairs and watched the game. Even though the fence should have been protection enough, as they saw Castaldo's bat coming, the spectators jumped out of the way. The bat, still traveling fast enough to hurt, slid under the space between the fence and the dirt, rattled into the protected area, just missing a toddler, and came to a stop.

Castaldo bowed his head and walked to his position at third base.

The Saints lost the game by a score of 4–2, and as Al Frechtman once again asked the musical question "Will You Love Me Tomorrow" the crowd at newly named Midway Stadium let the Saints know how they felt about the team that had never seriously contended for the Northern League title in either half of the season.

They rose to their feet and applauded. They cheered and whistled and demanded a curtain call from their fourth-place club. They clambered atop both dugouts and shouted "thank you" over and over again. They blew kisses onto the field.

In Section J, they sang "Volare" to Vinny Castaldo, who removed his cap, wandered over to his fan club, and thanked *them*. Thrown bat? All was forgiven. The fans respected Castaldo's hard work, his demand of himself that he always do well, his pure, adrenaline-powered drive—and his overdrive.

The other Saints wandered about the infield, turning in circles and waving at the crowd before heading for the locker room. They too acknowledged, even if they didn't always understand, St. Paul's love affair with its baseball team, the independent one that played outside in the summer sun or the early-fall chill, sometimes after hours and hours of rain. Even if the players always didn't, they knew the fans had fun.

The crowd kept clapping. The stadium lights dimmed. In the press box Al Frechtman cued up a medley of Looney Tunes music, and an endless stream of fireworks began exploding high above center field, a truly American spectacle at this most American game. Mike Veeck stood alone in the dirt track beneath the grandstands, smoking a cigar, staring overhead, and smiling, dots of multicolored light reflecting off his aviator glasses. Players from both teams emerged from the locker rooms to take in the show.

No one wanted to leave.

The 1994 Northern League champion Winnipeg Goldeyes (© Rusty Barton/Winnipeg Goldeyes)

EPILOGUE

As their names were announced before the opening game of the best-of-five championship series, the Sioux City Explorers emerged from a thicket of cornstalks erected on the center-field warning track at Lewis and Clark Park, just like in the movie *Field of Dreams*. In town a billboard congratulated Ed Nottle, the Northern League's manager of the year.

Sioux City had won its last eleven games but met a confident second-half champion, the Winnipeg Goldeyes. Doug Simunic's team took the first game 5–3 behind stellar pitching from Jeff Bittiger, the ex–Minnesota Twin. In Game Two the Goldeyes unleashed twenty hits, including a grand slam by former big-leaguer Jim Wilson, in a 16–1 thumping. "Maybe it just wasn't meant to be," said Sioux City owner Bill Pereira, perched in a skybox. In the eighth inning Simunic waved home the final run around third base. "What a jerk!" shouted Sioux City radio announcer Jim Frevola. It was that sort of night.

Minor league playoffs are a tough sell because of the short notice before the games and, with school starting, reduced fan interest. But Sioux City's loyalists nearly filled the stadium for both home playoff games. In Winnipeg the gate was even stronger. More than

8,400 fans attended Game Three, pleasantly surprising league officials, and Sioux City stayed alive with a 6–3 win.

Another 7,000-plus turned out the following night, and the home crowd was rewarded. Former big-league catcher Dann Bilardello whacked a grand slam over the short left-field fence to lead Winnipeg to an 8–1 victory and the Northern League championship. The Goldeyes and their rookie owner, Sam Katz, rushed the infield to celebrate with champagne and beer showers. For the thirty-five-year-old Bilardello, the Northern League had made a dream come true: The championship ring was his first in what was likely to be the final season of a seventeen-year career.

In the losing clubhouse Ed Nottle walked from locker to locker thanking his players for their efforts. He lifted the athletes' slumped heads and shook their hands. "Appreciate it," he said, over and over.

Despite the turmoil in Duluth and the on-field struggles in St. Paul, the Northern League's second season was another success at the box office, thanks to its fans.

Leaguewide attendance totaled 910,931, an average of 3,860 per game. The addition of Winnipeg to replace Rochester helped boost the average gate by 20 percent, or 650 fans a night. Per game attendance rose 25 percent in St. Paul and 12 percent in Sioux City (3,506), and was virtually unchanged in Sioux Falls (2,558). Duluth's woes caused a 29 percent plunge (2,217), while in Thunder Bay the excitement of baseball indeed waned somewhat, with attendance off 19 percent, but the average was still more than respectable (3,327).

Every franchise but Duluth turned a profit, and none planned to move. After the season the league voted to add two teams in 1996. The strongest candidates were the twin cities of Fargo, North Dakota, and Moorhead, Minnesota; Lincoln, Nebraska; Madison, Wisconsin; and St. Cloud, Minnesota.

The six club owners each paid Miles Wolff the $50,000 start-up fee he had deferred for two years, and they assumed control of leaguewide decisions. They wasted no time hiring Wolff as the

Northern League's first commissioner, through 1996. The league empowered Wolff to act "in the best interests of baseball"—as the majors did when they had an independent commissioner. But the owners added a clause reflecting the spirit and goals of the independent league: "Best interests" included "the interests of communities and fans of Northern League teams."

The two issues that halted major league baseball in 1994 were revenue sharing and a salary cap. The Northern League already had a cap, which the owners increased only marginally (from $72,000 per team per season to $76,000) to accommodate four extra games added to the 1995 schedule. More interesting, they agreed that, based on attendance, St. Paul, Winnipeg, and Sioux City would pay a larger portion of league operating expenses than Sioux Falls, Duluth, and Thunder Bay. It was a fair and sensible move designed to help the smaller-market owners.

The salary cap and revenue sharing worked in the Northern League for one reason: Minor league players are unorganized and disenfranchised. In St. Paul and Duluth they had demonstrated that if they believed they weren't treated well they would revolt. To avoid future uprisings Wolff urged his owners to let managers control roster moves and playing decisions. Too many players had passed through the league in 1994, Wolff felt. The instability sent a message to players and fans that the league wasn't much different from major league organizations, as the Saints had painfully discovered.

While the owners agreed in principle, the nature of independent ball makes it impossible to ban owner involvement. It was why some of them were in the league to begin with.

None of the copycat independent leagues posed a threat to the Northern League. The Texas-Louisiana circuit, with two more teams and a schedule eight games longer than the Northern League's, drew nearly 300,000 fewer customers. The rookies-only Frontier League in Ohio and Pennsylvania drew under a thousand fans per game but showed some stability.

Two circuits formed by rejected Northern League owners placed franchises in Minneapolis, in hopes of stealing some of St. Paul's magic. They didn't. The Minneapolis Loons, in a league formed by pharmacist George Vedder, who had lured Miles Wolff to Duluth with a photo of Wade Stadium, drew about 700 fans a night to a college field that prohibited the sale of beer and fence signs—minor league revenue staples. The Minneapolis Millers, in a league set up by Dick Jacobson, the strip-joint owner who had wanted the Rochester franchise, played before a few dozen fans in a city park with a chain-link outfield fence, and no concessions, locker rooms, or rest rooms. The team quickly stopped releasing attendance figures.

Nonetheless, independent league plans were sprouting like dandelions—in Pennsylvania, California, and suburban New York, the Mid-Atlantic, Southeast, Deep South, and Northwest. The Northern League's success encouraged imitators who thought they could toss two teams on a field, call it minor league baseball, and rake in profits. Most had no prior baseball experience and charged hefty up-front fees. "We have created a monster," said Marv Goldklang, who was offered franchises in two leagues but declined.

The newcomers would learn that the product isn't just baseball. It is an ineffable, intangible feeling that in the right place, at the right time, with the right nurturing, sometimes evolves. Baseball is hard work. The success of the Northern League owes much to the fierce pride and commitment to public life that characterize the six frontier towns that have embraced the game. It isn't automatically transferable.

The Northern League owners had earned their rewards. For them the question was, What next? Would independent baseball, Northern League style, reorder the majors' player development philosophy? Was it an incubator for an alternative to major league baseball?

As the major league strike dragged on, organizations laid off scouts and farm directors. It wasn't a great leap to conclude that the low minors could face cutbacks. The eighty-two Class-A clubs eventually could shrink to twenty-eight, one per organization. Rookie ball could be eliminated.

The Northern League took baby steps toward an expanded role. Its owners agreed to explore ties with the Frontier League on a farm-club basis. More important, the National Association initiated talks on honoring Northern League player contracts, creating a mechanism to make its players available for the Rule 5 draft, and respecting each other's territorial rights. Predictably, many affiliated clubs opposed the overture, fearful that recognizing independent leagues would weaken the value of their franchises, still a scarce commodity, and threaten their cherished working agreements with big-league organizations.

But if the majors did start chopping, the minors would need a model for independent baseball that, in the long run, could benefit the owners of low-level clubs that lose their affiliations. The Northern League could serve as the top flight of an independent system.

During the strike the Northern League helped satisfy a baseball-starved media. Both a CBS Sunday morning program and National Public Radio taped segments on Mike Veeck, whose stock in trade was to bash the majors. A crew from "Dateline NBC" flew into Sioux City. *Sports Illustrated* positioned a crane beyond center field to photograph Sioux Falls Stadium for a feature on the league.

The Canaries quietly noted the walkout, posting a sign outside the ballpark reading: WE HONOR ALL MAJOR LEAGUE BASEBALL TICKETS DURING THE STRIKE. Fans could swap big-league tickets for free entry; the club received two apiece from Toronto and Colorado and four from Minnesota. Inside, the public address announcer read scores from around the major leagues. Pause. Silence. Laughter.

Sioux Falls's general manager, Gary Weckwerth, tried to persuade ESPN to televise a game between the Canaries and the Saints. "There's no other minor league team in the country that has former major leaguers with the backgrounds of [Pedro] Guerrero and [Leon] Durham," Weckwerth wrote in a letter to the network. "I'm confident your viewers won't be let down." But ESPN never contacted the club. Sioux City's Bill Pereira, who was friendly with a top executive and a broadcaster at CBS Sports, wanted to package a series of all-star games after the season—a time normally reserved for the major league playoffs and World Series. The network didn't bite.

To Miles Wolff it was the ideal outcome: The death of the majors didn't help or hurt the Northern League. The league stood on its own. To ensure more name players joining the league, the six clubs voted to permit one "marquee" player on every roster who could be paid up to $5,000 a month, only $2,000 of which would count against the salary cap. The owners also left open the possibility of modifying roster rules to allow clubs to sign major league free agents if they became available.

While the Northern League didn't want to become a bargaining chip in the labor negotiations—it hadn't set out to compete with the majors, unlike the United Baseball League, which planned to begin play in 1996—landing bona fide big leaguers certainly would drive home its antiestablishment message, and wouldn't hurt attendance either.

The strike did, however, affect Northern League player prospects. Signings by major league organizations fell victim to strike-related cost cutting and uncertainty. In addition to the five players whose contracts were sold during the season, only eleven more Northern Leaguers had been signed by the first week of 1995. Pedro Guerrero surprisingly received a Triple-A contract from the California Angels. After leading Hawaii Winter Baseball in home runs and runs batted in, St. Paul slugger David Kennedy was acquired by the Colorado Rockies organization. Four other Northern League players who excelled in Hawaii, which was stocked with Japanese and Koreans as well as some American prospects, were also picked up. A few more players were expected to win invitations to spring training camps, but the total still paled beside the thirty-five signed after the 1993 season.

Then the floodgates opened. Soon after the major league owners unilaterally implemented their salary cap and pledged to play the 1995 season with replacement players, organizations began scrambling. As the top independent, the Northern League controlled the best available players not already under contract to organizations, and its six clubs were inundated with calls. It posed a dilemma. On the one hand, the league's goal was to help players return to organizations. On the other, it didn't want to facilitate the big leagues' union-busting efforts. After acting commissioner Bud Selig's office inquired about the availability of Northern Leaguers, Miles Wolff did what he considered reasonable: He offered to set a standard up-front price of $3,000 per man—his long-sought target—or allow an organization to pay $1,500 if the player won a Single-A job, $3,000 for Double-A, and $4,000 for Triple-A. That way the Northern League couldn't be accused of trying to take advantage of the desperate major leagues, which could only jeopardize future relations.

As for the stigma of supplying scab ballplayers, the decision on whether to cross a picket line was left to the players themselves. Most were willing. They had almost no realistic chance of making the big leagues on merit, so they didn't have to fear bumping into union members someday in a clubhouse or a dark alley. After receiving paychecks of $1,000 a month for years, here was an opportunity for a quick score. The majors were offering $115,000 salaries for most big-league replacement players, plus a $110 spring training per diem, $5,000 for playing in spring training games, $5,000 for making an Opening Day roster, and a $20,000 termination bonus if the strike ended—far more money than they could ever dream of making in the minors.

Wolff didn't expect the majors to balk at his offer, but they did. The commissioner's office countered with $1,000 for Single-A, $2,000 for Double-A, $2,500 for Triple-A, and $3,000 if a player made a big-league replacement roster. "They're trying to squeeze us at every turn," Wolff said before sending a fax to all twenty-eight major league general managers reiterating the league's terms. Cleveland refused to wait for a go-ahead from the commissioner and quickly met the $3,000 asking price for eighteen of the league's best players. (It later cut back to four.) The feeding frenzy had begun. The Blue Jays, Marlins, Athletics, Angels, White Sox, Mariners, Cubs, Yankees, Giants, and Royals all called Wolff or began negotiating with Northern League clubs. Some didn't play by the rules; the Red Sox announced that they had signed Thunder Bay catcher Pete Kuld but didn't compensate or even contact the Whiskey Jacks, who still owned the player's contract. Carl Nichols decided to cut his own deal with the Cubs, even though he was still the property of Sioux Falls. (Both signings were invalidated. All

Northern League contracts contained an option year to be exercised by the club. Until a player was formally released, the team controlled his future.) "The guys in the independent leagues suddenly are homecoming queens," said Marlins farm director John Boles.

By the third week of January chaos reigned. Oil Can Boyd announced that he had signed with the White Sox and would eagerly cross the picket line set by his former union. Leon Durham contemplated scabbing—he needed just sixteen days in the big leagues to attain ten years of service and a full pension—but decided not to partly out of conscience but also because the Major League Baseball Players Association would help decide how much he received from an unresolved collusion damages case from the 1980s. Pedro Guerrero refused to cross a picket line. In the end, almost ninety Northern League players went to spring training camps, including nineteen Saint Paul Saints and even twelve members of the hapless Duluth-Superior Dukes. Most of the Northern League players were used to replace striking major leaguers. They were among the best scab ballplayers.

But league officials weren't happy. Bill Pereira worried not only that the majors were exploiting the league but that clubs would be left shorthanded in 1995. "Our league's best talent is being taken away for this rather cynical purpose," he said. "Ninety-nine percent of our fans have renewed their season tickets. I don't think they're expecting to see baseball that's not as good as it was." Pereira feared that, once the strike ended, organizations would release all Northern Leaguers, replacement players as well as those signed to farm clubs. To protect the league's integrity—and to tweak the absurdly frugal majors—Harry Stavrenos decided to ask for something resembling market value for his top talent, despite Miles Wolff's wishes. The asking price for former major leaguer Carl Nichols: $10,000.

"Why not?" the consummate rebel said. "He's worth more. You're talking about a guy who's going to be the big-league catcher for the team he signs with. You're talking about the Cubs' or the Yankees' or the Marlins' catcher. What's ten thousand bucks in this business? Nothing. That's fifteenth-round draft money for a rookie.

I think asking forty or fifty thousand would be sticking it to them. I don't think ten thousand bucks is at all."

Stavrenos decided to back off—but only because the Cubs had thought they were getting Nichols for free when the player earlier had misrepresented his contractual status; even the fearless Sioux Falls owner didn't want to damage the Northern League's relationship with an organization. He dropped the price to $5,000. The Cubs paid it.

But to Stavrenos the replacement player fiasco wasn't about money. It was just another example of the stupidity of the major leagues, of their abusive, careless, and arrogant treatment of the minors. "It's sickening," Stavrenos said. "They're just using these guys. They're ruining our league." Not that he was surprised. "They've been taking advantage of us," he said, "since the beginning of time."

Miles Wolff tended to focus on the problems at hand, and the postseason was no exception. In addition to the major league strike, the new Northern League commissioner worried about the player uprisings in St. Paul and Duluth, about the state of the Duluth and Thunder Bay franchises, and about securing the two expansion cities. But his concerns simply reflected how the league had thrived—"beyond my wildest expectations," he said modestly—and was maturing.

Two years earlier the goal had been to survive in the face of what Wolff and others thought would be a hostile reception from the big, bad baseball establishment. But the league's success—among cities, fans, and players—had made the establishment take notice. In spite of the occasional tampering and the strike-related turmoil, relations with the big leagues remained decent because it was in the Northern League's interest to sell its best players and in the majors' interest to acquire them. At the same time the league had attained the ability to demand and receive fair value. (Although the majors, it now could be argued, stood to make the most money. Former St. Paul pitcher Mike Mimbs, for whom Montreal had paid $375 after the 1993 season, was selected by Philadelphia in the Rule 5 draft.

The Phillies had to pay $50,000 to the Expos, leaving Montreal with a $49,625 profit for a player rediscovered by the Saints. Mimbs also became the first Northern League player to make a forty-man major league roster.)

Wolff's new goal was to make sure baseball was a permanent part of the communities that had made the Northern League possible. The league demonstrated how baseball was changing in the 1990s, proving that the majors' monopoly wasn't as strong as believed, that in the end political interests were overshadowed by the bond between the game and the people.

"The mission initially was to show baseball what could be done. That independent baseball could make it, that we know what we're doing," Wolff said. "Maybe our thinking was more global to start with. Maybe it's more local now. Cities have invested in ball clubs, fans have invested in ball clubs, owners have invested. It's not money. It's this psychic energy. Everyone's got a stake in it. We need to make sure it stays strong."

Van Schley was so frustrated by the Saints' disappointing performance that he contemplated leaving his friends in the St. Paul ownership to help Ted Cushmore revive the Duluth-Superior Dukes in 1995.

At season's end Schley lashed out in a newspaper article in St. Paul, implicitly criticizing Tim Blackwell and Marv Goldklang for the team's handling. He believed his strengths were scouting young players and making in-season roster moves—and he hadn't been allowed to do the latter. There were too many cooks in St. Paul, he decided. The year hadn't been fun.

Miles Wolff encouraged Schley to move to Duluth to stabilize a shaky franchise. But Veeck and Goldklang insisted that Schley sell his one-quarter ownership of the Saints, which he was reluctant to do. So he stayed. In the off-season Goldklang, Schley, and Veeck discussed how to improve the club's decision-making process. Schley simply wanted to hire a manager with whom he could work comfortably, as he had in Salt Lake. He didn't believe Tim Blackwell was the man for the job. Blackwell was an excellent field manager, but Schley felt he had lost control of the Saints.

The situation resolved itself. In the fall Blackwell interviewed for minor league positions with the Orioles, Twins, and Expos, and accepted an offer from Baltimore to manage at High Desert of the Class-A California League. Blackwell was the first Northern League manager to make it back to a big-league organization.

As the new year began, Schley resumed his player hunt in Australia, where he scouted two pitchers and a shortstop. To coach first base in 1995, the Saints hired Wayne Terwilliger, a veteran major league instructor who was let go by the Twins. Goldklang offered the managerial job to former Twins outfielder Dan Gladden, who had played in Japan in 1994. But when Gladden decided that he still wanted to play, the Saints turned to Marty Scott, the Texas Rangers' farm director for the past decade who was let go during a front-office shakeup in the fall. Scott hadn't managed in the minors since the early 1980s, but after so many years with an organization he decided that it was time to have some fun in baseball again.

Goldklang also talked to a couple of celebrated players about playing in St. Paul. One of those players was Dwight Gooden, the Cy Young Award winner who was banned from major league baseball for one year for failing to abide by the conditions of his drug rehabilitation program. The former New York Mets star received overtures from several independent clubs, including Winnipeg and Sioux Falls. Goldklang met with Gooden and his agent in January but no deal was made. The pitcher's main concerns were his aftercare program and the question of whether playing in 1995 would aid his reinstatement to the majors. Still, the disagreements went on in St. Paul: Schley thought signing Gooden wasn't worth the trouble.

The other name player was Jason Varitek, a two-time first-round draft pick who was holding out on the Seattle Mariners. In January, Varitek stunned the baseball world by signing with St. Paul for $1,200 a month—a far cry from the $850,000 bonus he had demanded of the Mariners. The catcher's agent, Scott Boras, clearly was using the Northern League to test major league rules. Boras maintained that Varitek, by signing with a professional team, wouldn't be subject to the amateur draft for a third time, making him a free agent. The case was expected to wind up before a judge or an arbitrator. Under his contract with the Saints, Varitek was free to continue negotiating with the Mariners, but Goldklang expected him to play in St. Paul. Once again, the Northern League was butting heads with the establishment.

Despite his constant worries about job security—even after reaching the playoffs in 1993 and winning the championship in 1994—Doug Simunic was rehired to manage Winnipeg. In the other Canadian city, Ricky May fired Dan Shwam and hired Doug Ault, an experienced minor league manager in the Toronto Blue Jays system. It was a smart public relations move: As one of the first members of the expansion Blue Jays in the late 1970s, Ault was a familiar name to Canadian fans. Shwam landed a job managing a team in one of the fledgling independents, the Northeast League. Howie Bedell joined the same league as director of player personnel, the position he so despised in the Northern League.

The Whiskey Jacks had nearly matched Duluth in futility in the second half of the season, winning just thirteen times and avoiding last place by a mere game and a half. Near the end May had released several players, including the bullpen catcher, a cost-saving move that disgusted his team and the rest of the league. The one bright spot was catcher Pete Kuld, who belted an all-time short-season record of twenty-seven home runs.

Thunder Bay's hardworking first baseman Todd Rosenthal injured his left knee rounding third base during a midseason game in St. Paul. Although he kept playing, Rosenthal never recovered. He batted just .262 in forty-four games before returning home to Scarsdale, New York, in the middle of August, his baseball career in doubt. "Personally, for me, it was really disappointing," Rosenthal said of his aborted year. "But you deal with it and move forward."

Rosenthal underwent reconstructive surgery to repair torn ligaments. But he still wanted to find a major league organization that finally would give him an opportunity to prove that, despite his lack of power and speed, he was a clutch .300 hitter and stellar fielder.

When he heard about the rush for replacement players, he quickly called Nick Belmonte. Rosenthal would happily scab. "What the hell do I care?" he said. "[The majors] never liked me anyway. I'll take the money." As a last resort, the three-year independent player would return for another season in the Northern League, possibly his last as a professional baseball player.

Carl Nichols quietly had a terrific season. He led the league in runs batted in with seventy, slugged fourteen homers, and batted .287, while catching seventy-eight games and terrorizing opposing base runners.

Nichols had decided to call it quits after a fourteen-year career. He turned thirty-two in October and wanted to take his major league memories and move on. But after returning to Milwaukee, working twelve-hour shifts stacking and sorting magazine bundles as they rolled off a print-shop line, Nichols changed his mind. The planned United Baseball League, promising major league–caliber play and average salaries of half a million dollars, tantalized him. Nichols figured he was just the sort of player the fledgling league would need.

The veteran catcher began searching for an organization interested in a proven defensive talent who still could hit with authority. In the replacement player market, Nichols was a hot commodity: a former big-league catcher willing to cross the picket line for a payday that he needed. He had ruined his relationship with Harry Stavrenos by telling the Cubs that his owner had declared him a free agent. (In fact, Stavrenos had sent Nichols a letter stating that Sioux Falls had renewed its option on him for 1995.) But Stavrenos agreed to sell the catcher to his preferred team anyway, in an effort to preserve goodwill for the league. If the strike lasted into the season, Nichols would likely be a starting catcher in the major leagues—the job he believed he had been unfairly denied—however tainted the achievement.

Stephen Bishop returned to Atlanta to ponder his first real failure as a baseball player.

In his brief tenure at Sioux Falls, Bishop had been accepted by his teammates but batted just .222 in sixteen games. He finished the year with a .251 average in sixty-two games, with one home run, nineteen runs batted in, and ten stolen bases. "I grant I didn't have a good year," he said. "I rubbed some people the wrong way. People didn't understand me."

Bishop was angry about how he had been handled in St. Paul. He felt that the coaches didn't like him, that his teammates had misrepresented him as lazy, which he wasn't. He was still stung by his benching. "I was never used to that. So it was just difficult to accept and understand, especially when I wasn't getting a reason. I honestly do feel I was not treated fairly. If a guy wins a job, he wins a job. They just were fucking around, just trying to put anybody and everybody in the lineup."

But he wasn't disillusioned. Bishop immediately began looking for a job in an organization. He still was relatively young and talented and believed he deserved a shot. He thought a contact with the Orioles might pay off—until learning that Tim Blackwell had been hired by the organization. "I knew fucking up with the Saints would haunt me," Bishop said. Still, his attitude had improved. In between shifts as a parking valet, Bishop took batting lessons from a former minor leaguer, understanding finally how to use his strong build to hit for power. When his Northern League colleagues began attracting offers, he chased clubs even harder, hoping at least for a tryout invitation. He got one—from the Orioles—and he called Tim Blackwell to apologize for his behavior during the season. "Regardless of what happens," Bishop said, "I'm supposed to act in a professional manner and I didn't." If he didn't make the cut in spring training, Bishop promised to return to the Northern League—Harry Stavrenos wanted him back—for one final season of baseball. He would switch-hit, have fun on the field, build on the adversity of 1994.

"I got better from it," Bishop said. "It was a brutal season and everything, but I learned something from it and got some experience."

Vince Castaldo was voted the Northern League Player of the Year.

Castaldo's numbers were the class of the league: .316 batting average, fifteen home runs, sixty-six runs batted in, and twelve stolen bases. He finished among the top five in eleven offensive categories. Managers also named him the league's best overall hitter and All-Star third baseman. Defensively, his throwing arm was rated tops among infielders.

The personal recognition was satisfying, and Castaldo hoped it would carry some clout with major league organizations, because he didn't believe his career was anywhere near over.

While Castaldo was frustrated in St. Paul, he was proud of his performance and savored what probably would be the only moments in his minor league career when he had stood up for what he believed—in this case forcing management to release unwanted teammates and listen to player grievances. But that wasn't why Castaldo had come to the Northern League. He wanted exposure, to prove to himself and to baseball at large that he deserved a second chance. He believed he had achieved his goals.

After the season Castaldo went home to St. Louis. He worked a shift on a United Parcel Service loading dock and, after losing ten pounds over the summer, lifted weights to regain his strength. In November the Angels asked the Saints about the third baseman. The Red Sox and Padres showed some interest. Marv Goldklang contacted five more organizations but none bit. The Saints chairman blamed the strike and asked Castaldo to be patient. But the player worried that he wouldn't have a place to play come spring, so when he was offered $3,500 a month and a free apartment to play for Campeche of the Mexican League, Castaldo grabbed it. The next day the Florida Marlins called. Mexico could wait.

When the replacement player search intensified, Castaldo was valuable property. But he was also among the few Northern League players with the ability to make The Show on talent alone, not as a scab. Castaldo was concerned that a club would force him to join a replacement team, threatening his future relationship with striking players. But the Marlins—who had treated Northern Leaguers more fairly than any other organization—signed Castaldo to a contract targeting him for Triple-A. The words *replacement player* were never mentioned. Florida's farm director, John Boles, called Castaldo a prospect who, at age twenty-seven, had several major league seasons ahead of him. Castaldo, ever determined, planned to make it happen.

"This is why I went to St. Paul, to get this kind of opportunity," he said. "I'll take it from there."

The long, losing summer in Duluth devastated Ted Cushmore.

The joy he had anticipated was overwhelmed by the Dukes' abysmal performance and the acrimony with Howie Bedell and the players. The franchise posted a $120,000 operating loss that would have been worse if not for the dedicated fans who came to Wade Stadium to the bitter end.

Even during the worst moments, Cushmore said he didn't want 1994 to be his only season in baseball. At the league owners' meeting in late September, he appeared committed to turning around the Dukes. He was disappointed that neither Van Schley nor Harry Stavrenos would join him and began searching for a manager who understood independent baseball.

A few days later he called Miles Wolff in Durham and said he wanted to sell the team.

Away from Wade Stadium, away from his fellow owners, away from Bedell and the rebellious players, Cushmore realized he wasn't cut out to own a professional baseball franchise by himself—no matter how much he liked and respected people like Wolff, Stavrenos, and Schley, and no matter how often he heard that next year would be different.

"There don't seem to be a lot of psychic rewards in being an owner," Cushmore said. "I found myself being criticized a lot by the press, by fans. I really found that being close to the players was hard. I love the game, but I'm not sure I love the business of the game. When I was up there, I was very much into the game, but I needed to be walking around being an owner. It began to feel more like an obligation than the enjoyable thing it should. I was so much into the baseball part of it. Every loss took a piece out of me. In one year I just got burned out."

Wolff tried to talk Cushmore out of selling. He truly believed that Cushmore was good for the league, that his season of turmoil would make him an even better owner. Cushmore apologized to Wolff for Duluth's performance and thanked his fellow owners for their support but stuck by his decision. He still planned to retire early from General Mills. Only now he had to find a new avocation, maybe teaching business, maybe writing. It wouldn't be baseball.

"I was reaching for something," he said. "I was at the tail end of the corporate thing, and I was trying to go back and retrieve something. I learned you can't go back."

In November, however, Cushmore began to have a change of heart. He decided that he couldn't let his lingering anger over Howie Bedell kill his interest in baseball. Cushmore knew he couldn't run the Dukes on his own; he understood his limitations only too well now. So, as he began interviewing potential buyers, Cushmore decided to keep a piece of the Dukes. He sold 80 percent of the club for $400,000 to a San Diego clothing and frozen foods executive named Jim Wadley. (Cushmore ate the 1994 operating loss and sold enough General Mills stock options to pay back nearly three-quarters of his bank loan.) Wadley teamed up with Tom Romenesko—a former minor league general manager, San Diego Padres farm director, and consultant to the commissioner's office—who would run the baseball operation in Duluth. Cushmore's new titles were vice president and secretary. He would advise the majority owner, attend as many games as he wanted, and maybe even enjoy it. A happy compromise. Cushmore once again wanted to stay in baseball for a long time.

"I can't move away until that franchise is successful," he concluded. "I can't move away until I feel that the year I invested is worth something, has some lasting value. I really want, for those long-suffering fans up there, for this team to do well."

Even after the season ended, St. Paul kept its love affair with baseball alive.

On a crisp late-October evening, on the anniversary of Carlton Fisk's classic sixth-game homer in the 1975 World Series, Mike Veeck gave Midway Stadium over to the fans. He called it Field of Dreams Night.

The plan was beautiful. Parking and admission would be free. Inside the Saints would replay radio broadcasts of nine classic innings from 1942 to 1988—the final outs of Don Larsen's perfect game, Bobby Thomson's playoff home run, a gimpy Kirk Gibson's game-winning World Series shot for the Dodgers. Kids would frolic on the diamond, fans mingle in the stands. Concession prices would be rolled back to 1965, when the Twins played in the World Series for the first time. After the traditional Veeck fireworks display, the faithful would watch a baseball movie on a screen set up in the outfield.

It would be an appropriate coda to the season, another heartfelt thank-you to the people of St. Paul, and a final, symbolic message to the majors on a day when there would have been a World Series game but for the players' strike. And it worked nearly perfectly except for one thing: someone told the spoilsports at major league baseball.

When Field of Dreams Night was included in a things-to-do listing in the local paper, a fax arrived at the offices of Major League Baseball Properties, which held the rights to the radio broadcast tapes. The Saints conceded they hadn't requested a license to use the material in a promotional event. After a series of back-and-forth telephone calls, at five o'clock on the day of the event, with fans tailgating outside Midway Stadium, major league baseball refused to grant the Saints permission to play the tapes. Technically, it was within their rights to do so. Practically, it was petty.

But the Saints didn't let the bureaucrats ruin the fun. The parking lot opened at four, the stadium at six. At precisely seven the Queen of Snows of the St. Paul Winter Carnival sang the national anthem. Former Twins great Tony Oliva threw out the first pitch before a two-inning game on the neatly manicured field between two Little League teams. Beer and hot dogs sold for fifty cents apiece. While fans wandered around the stands, the Saints popped videotapes of a few great World Series games into a VCR, placed a

Mike Veeck (© Dale Gates)

microphone next to the television, and, voilà, classic broadcasts for all to hear, no permission necessary. One thousand eight hundred people attended, some of whom had never been to a Saints game.

After a twenty-minute fireworks display, everyone was invited onto the field to watch an hour-long highlight film of the 1965 Twins-Dodgers World Series, followed by *The Natural*. The evening went without a hitch until 11:45, when, with Robert Redford as the great Roy Hobbs stepping up for his climactic at bat, the heavens opened above Midway Stadium and washed the ending away.

It didn't matter. On behalf of the Northern League, the message was sent—to the thumb-twiddling big-league labor negotiators, to the pencil-pushing killjoys at major league baseball, to the Minnesota Twins and the people who ran the Metrodome and the proprietors of all the other silent baseball coliseums around the country in October 1994.

Mike Veeck had devised the perfect celebration of the spirit of baseball: a tribute to the game when there was no game on the field.

No one, after all, owns the game more than the fans.

ACKNOWLEDGMENTS

W hen I approached Miles Wolff about writing a book on the Northern League, he agreed, on one condition: He didn't want to be the focus of the story. Wolff was being more than humble. He attributed any success to the collective effort of the league's owners and, even more, the communities that had welcomed independent professional baseball.

Wolff proved an entirely gracious subject. He ensured me complete access throughout the league, patiently sat for lengthy interviews at his office and home in Durham, and answered innumerable questions over the course of the year. If there were more people in baseball like Miles Wolff, the game wouldn't be in its current troubled state.

Van Schley was unfailingly generous with his time and insight—and was a terrific travel companion in Florida and around the Midwest. Marv Goldklang spent countless hours talking baseball with me. Ted Cushmore was patient and candid during the most stressful times. Nick Belmonte insisted that I accompany him to Duluth. Harry Stavrenos, who can't stand publicity, did a fellow Greek a favor. Ed Nottle's friendliness, humor, and style will stay with me forever.

I am also indebted to the league's other principal actors: Bill Pereira, Mike Veeck, Tim Blackwell, Howie Bedell, Dave Wright, Tom Leip, Doug Simunic, Dan Shwam, Sam Katz, Ricky May, Bill Fanning, and Gary Weckwerth. Thanks also to Tom Whaley, Annie Huidekoper, Brad Ruiter, Pete Orme, John Spolyar, Bill Fisher, Jack Carnefix, Jim Frevola, Dave Popkin, Dave Kemp, Frank Gahl, Howie Hanson, and Dan Weidner.

The Northern League runs on the dreams of its players. I'm especially grateful to Vince Castaldo and Stephen Bishop for tolerating my tape recorder and notebook. Todd Rosenthal, Carl Nichols, Rex De La Nuez, Darius Gash, Tom Paskievitch, Greg D'Alexander, Doug Kimbler, Benny Castillo, Rob Swain, Joe Brownholtz, Jason Bullard, Scott Centala, David Kennedy, Matt Connolly, Andy Skeels, Mark Skeels, Leon Durham, and Oil Can Boyd all sat for interviews or helped in other ways.

Stan Brand of the National Association of Professional Baseball Leagues guided me through the thicket of baseball politics. Gary Hughes and Dave Dombrowski of the Florida Marlins generously let me roam around spring training. Thanks also to Bill Miller of the Durham Bulls.

Mike Wilson of the *St. Petersburg Times* and Michael Bamberger of *The Philadelphia Inquirer* supplied the advice, contacts, and encouragement that allowed me to begin this project. Thanks also to Jon Scher and Stefanie Krasnow of *Sports Illustrated*, Steve Berkowitz of *The Washington Post*, Ken Rosenthal of *The Baltimore Sun*, Bill Bradley and Mike Augustin of the *St. Paul Pioneer Press*, and Bill Woodward of *The News & Observer* of Raleigh. Bill Menezes, William and Laura Rittenberg, and Kevin and Amelia Capalbo put me up during my travels. Jonathan Hock and David Lazarus read various incarnations of the manuscript and provided helpful suggestions. Michael Goldberg's technical support was indispensable. John Rae donated his time and talent. Thanks also to Jeff Salamon, Adam Sexton, and Sharon Z. Miller.

Jim Kennedy of the Associated Press, where I worked for more than eight years, was supportive beyond the call of duty from the moment I told him I wanted to write a book about minor league baseball. I'm also grateful to Darrell Christian and Patricia Lantis of the AP.

George Gibson is everything an author could ask for, and more. He took a chance on a rookie and provided skillful editing and boundless enthusiasm. Thanks also to Liza Miller, Judi Powers, Marlene Tungseth, Jo Ann Sabatino, Patty Moosbrugger, Duane Stapp, and Ramsey Walker at Walker and Company. My agent, Robert Shepard, who edited my first daily newspaper story years ago, single-handedly made this project happen. I can't thank him enough for his advice, support, and encouragement, and for the unexpected phone call that brought us back together.

Finally, I'd like to thank Mariann Caprino and Hannah Brennan for their love, support, and patience.